Human Relationships
A Skills Approach

Richard Nelson-Jones
Royal Melbourne Institute of Technology

Brooks/Cole Publishing Company
Pacific Grove, California
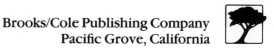

Brooks/Cole Publishing Company
A Division of Wadsworth, Inc.
© 1990 by Wadsworth, Inc., Belmont, California 94002.

Printed in the United States of America
10 9 8 7 6 5 4 3 2 1

Library of Congress Cataloging in Publication Data
Nelson-Jones, Richard.
    Human relationships : a skills approach / Richard Nelson-Jones.
        p.   cm.
    Includes bibliographical references and index.
    ISBN 0-534-12654-5
    1. Interpersonal relations.   2. Social skills.   3. Interpersonal communication.   I. Title.
HM132.N44   1989
158'.2--dc20
                                                                                89-35893
                                                                                    CIP

Sponsoring Editor: *Claire Verduin*
Editorial Assistant: *Gay C. Bond*
Production Editor: *Timothy A. Phillips*
Manuscript Editor: *Cathy Cambron*
Permissions Editor: *Carline Haga*
Interior and Cover Design: *Katherine Minerva*
Art Coordinator: *Suzi Howard*
Interior Illustration: *Ted Goff*
Typesetting: *Dharma Enterprises*
Cover Printing: *Phoenix Color Corporation*
Printing and Binding: *The Maple-Vail Book Manufacturing Group*

Preface

This book explores how to relate effectively. Though its primary focus is on personal relationships, the skills described have a broader application—for instance, to work and recreational settings. The book is intended for anyone who wishes to gain more fulfillment and joy from their relationships, as well as for people like me who have to be careful not to spoil them. In particular I hope that young people like the book.

Three main sets of values permeate the book. First, as a pragmatic existentialist, I view people as personally responsible for making their lives through the quality of their choices. Relationship skills are sequences of choices in various skills areas that you may make well or poorly. Life is a continuous experiment in which you evaluate the consequences of your choices and change your behavior if necessary. Second, I am heavily influenced by Christian ethics. Relationships involve not just asking what others can do for you, but what you can do for others. Third, I am a social scientist. Much of this book is based on research evidence as well as on my professional and personal experience.

The book has three main objectives. First, to help you acquire the attitude that you are personally responsible for your relationship skills choices. Second, to provide you with specific knowledge about what skills are. Third, to impart the how-to skills that I encourage you to develop and use on a daily basis.

The first chapter of the book defines and identifies the skills of relating. It also provides statistical evidence showing that, at some stage in their lives, most North Americans experience major difficulties in their personal relationships. The second chapter explores what you bring to relationships: for instance, your biological sex, sexuality, fears, and cultural background. Then follow a series of chapters on the skills of disclosing yourself, good listening, helpful responding, overcoming shyness and making initial contact, choosing people to relate with, developing relationships, preventing problems by perceiving yourself and others accurately, managing anger and hatred, and managing conflict. The final chapter focuses on the need for inner strength in maintaining and developing your relationship skills. Nowhere are you encouraged to think that relating well is always easy.

I have tried to make the tone of the book what President Bush might term "kinder and gentler" than some of the other writing in this area, which implicitly or explicitly promises too much. This book is essentially a how-to manual. The practical emphasis is highlighted by exercises and personal experiments. The experiments involve you in deciding to change your behavior in some specific way, testing it out in your daily life, and then evaluating whether it works for you. The book offers numerous illustrations of people who use good and poor relationship skills. I have tried to write in simple and clear English, using words that human beings (even psychologists!) use in their everyday lives.

This book is based on the work of numerous theorists, researchers, and writers. To maintain the book's flow, I have economized in providing references in the text. However, a full bibliography is provided at the end of the text, with references likely to be of special interest to the nonprofessional reader marked with an asterisk.

A brief word about myself: no stranger to North America, I arrived as a 3-year-old evacuee from London and spent the next five years in the San Francisco Bay Area. I returned to California in 1961 and obtained a master's and a doctorate from Stanford University. In the late 1960s I worked first for the New England Board of Higher Education and then for the Association of Canadian Medical Colleges. Many of my own personal and professional relationships are with North Americans.

I thank the following people: Claire Verduin, Gay Bond, Tim Phillips, Cathy Cambron, and the production team at Brooks/Cole for their work in preparing the book; Dawn Butcher of the Royal Melbourne Institute of Technology Wordprocessing Unit for typing the manuscript; and the undergraduates in my relationship skills classes, who constantly challenge me to try to make my material more easily accessible and directly appealing to laypersons.

A number of reviewers have given me invaluable comments, many of which have led to significant revisions. They include Dorothy Bushnell, Merced College, Merced, California; William J. Jacobs, Lake City Community College, Lake City, Florida; Carla Karmichael, SRS University, Alpine, Texas; Elizabeth Palmer, Alverno College, Milwaukee, Wisconsin; George P. Pilkey, Fulton Montgomery Community College, Johnstown, New York; Douglas Risberg, Saint Cloud State University, Saint Cloud, Minnesota; Bruce E. Shertzer, Purdue University, West Lafayette, Indiana; Velma Walker, Tarrant County Junior College, Hurst, Texas.

I hope you enjoy the book and take something from it that helps enrich your relationships now and in the future.

Richard Nelson-Jones

Contents

4
Being a Rewarding Listener
75

5
Responding Helpfully
95

6
Overcoming Shyness
and Making Initial Contact
119

7
Choosing Relationships
145

8
Deepening Relationships   159

9
Assertion in Relationships   179

10
Managing Anger   201

11
Preventing and Managing Conflict   227

12
Maintaining and Developing
Your Relationship Skills

251

Exercises

Experiments

Human Relationships
A Skills Approach

1
The Challenge of Relationships

I love mankind—it's people I can't stand.
Charles M. Schulz

This book is about the skills involved in human connectedness. People need people. Relationships are a central part of our everyday lives. They can be for good or ill, for pleasure or pain.

The following examples show people relating in *rewarding* ways.

Lupe and Julio, a recently married couple, enjoy coming home from work and having a nice dinner together where they share their thoughts, feelings, and experiences and take an interest in one another's news.

John works as a supervisor for a furniture manufacturer. The workers John supervises know that, when they take a work or personal problem to him, he will listen attentively and be helpful.

Tom finally got around to telling Beth he loved her. She glowed with pleasure and said she felt the same about him.

Betty and Maria, both committee members at a tennis club, were in conflict over plans to build some extra courts. After sitting down and talking through their differences in a cooperative way, they not only came up with a better solution but also liked one another more.

The following examples, on the other hand, show people relating in *unrewarding* ways.

Sue gets very jealous when her boyfriend spends time with his other friends. Her possessive complaints are driving him away from her.

Jeff wants his 12-year-old, Adam, to grow up "like a man." He refuses to respond to Adam's interest in ballet dancing, telling him it's "sissy."

Barbara, in her fifties, resents her husband's early retirement from his job at an insurance company. She keeps telling him that it was all his fault.

Carlos and Paco work as computer programmers in the same office. They are constantly complaining to third parties about each other. They have yet to sit down and discuss their problems face to face.

In each of these examples, people were using relationship skills with varying degrees of effectiveness. Those getting and giving rewards in their relationships effectively used their skills to achieve these ends. The people whose behavior was unrewarding, on the other hand, were deficient in the relevant relationship skills.

This book emphasizes skills for effective personal relationships. The skills involved in relationships have a very wide application. Relationship skills are important in all walks of life. Virtually everyone's work involves relating to others, in diverse settings—banks, factories, stores, schools, hospitals, and legislatures, for a few examples. Moreover, relationship skills are important in most recreational activities, from poker and pool games to more exalted endeavors.

What Are Relationship Skills?

Reasons For and Against the Skills Approach to Relating

Some of you may resist the notion that relating involves skills, for a number of reasons. You may focus on infatuation and falling in love, situations where feelings are paramount. This book, however, focuses on the skills of everyday relationships. You may consider a skills approach unnatural. Perhaps you believe you were born with a certain style of relating, and you don't want to interfere with it by acquiring artificial skills. You may also find it hard to accept how much of your behavior is learned habit. You may consider a skills approach superficial, thinking that it helps describe but not change behavior. You may consider it a mechanistic approach— maybe people can go through the motions of using skills without engaging in genuine contact. Also, you may think a skills approach is manipulative, teaching people to get what they want without necessarily caring about others.

These reservations touch on some dangers in viewing relating in terms of skills. But these dangers stem from the inappropriate application of skills rather than with the concept of relationship skills itself. Clumsy application of skills may interfere with spontaneity, for instance, whereas good use of skills should enhance it.

It may be dangerous *not* to view relating in terms of skills. Relationships are perhaps the major source of human pleasure and pain. Ample evidence, documented later in this chapter, shows problems in sustaining good relationships to be widespread in North America. Paradoxically, despite their importance, relationship skills are hardly ever systematically taught. Instead you are expected to pick them up informally, in the home, school, workplace, and community. What tends to happen is that you learn unhelpful habits along with helpful ones.

A systematic attempt to train people in relationship skills requires first that these skills be identified and clearly stated. A major advantage of viewing relating in terms of skills is that skills are specific. Advice and admonitions to relate better do not tell you how to do it—so you lack handles to work on your behavior. Clearly stating relationship skills, however, results in a number of important consequences. First, you can assess to what degree you possess these skills. Second, either by yourself or with a trainer, you can practice to improve skills you have identified as deficient. Finally, you are in a better position to maintain your changed behavior because you know what its component skills are. When relating is removed from the realm of magic and romance to a specific look at the skills involved, it becomes something you can strive to bring under your control.

What Are Skills?

The meanings of the word *skill* include "proficiency," "competence," and "expertise in some activity." The essential element of any skill, however, is the ability to make and implement an effective sequence of choices so as to achieve a desired objective. For instance, to be a good listener you have to make and implement the choices involved in good listening.

The concept of skill is best not viewed as an either/or matter. Instead of thinking that you either possess or do not possess a skill, it is better to think of yourself as possessing skills strengths and weaknesses, or a mixture of the two. If you make good choices in a skills area, say in listening or in talking about yourself, you have a skills strength. Poor choices in a skills area is a skills weakness. In all relationship skills areas, you are likely to possess both strengths and weaknesses in varying degrees. For instance, in listening, you may be good at understanding talkers but poor at showing them that you have understood them. The object of working on your skills is to help you shift the balance of your strengths and weaknesses in one or more areas in favor of strengths. Put another way, working on skills can help you affirm yourself and others more by becoming a better chooser.

A Definition of Relationship Skills

In your various relationships you need to use a repertoire of skills. Some of you may not have a particular skill in your repertoire—for instance, the ability to turn down an unreasonable request. Others of you may want to strengthen a skill in your repertoire, perhaps by learning how to say no less aggressively.

This book defines relationship skills as sequences of choices that enable you to affirm yourself and others in your relationships. These sequences of choices involve thoughts, feelings, and actions. Your repertoire of skills comprises your strengths and weaknesses in each skills area.

Identifying Relationship Skills

Relationship skills involve you in becoming an authentic person. In contacts other than casual ones, you are ordinarily encouraged to avoid being superficially "nice" rather than communicating what you really think and feel. One of the main themes of this book, however, is that relating to others requires self-awareness and self-discipline. You can be real with people without your genuineness being unnecessarily at their expense.

At this stage the skills of relating can only be identified in an introductory way. Further elaboration must be left to the remaining chapters. Exercise 1 encourages you to explore how you currently relate in a number of different skills areas. The meaning of some of the skills may not be altogether clear to you so early in the book; nevertheless, an exercise will encourage your active participation in assessing and working on your skills. Remember that you are viewed as having good skills if you make good choices and poor skills if you make poor choices.

Exercise 1
Assessing my relationship skills

Instructions: The questionnaire below lists a number of relationship skills in eleven broad areas. Rate how satisfied you are with your skills using the rating scale below:

3   Much need for improvement
2   Moderate need for improvement
1   Slight need for improvement
0   No need for improvement

Put a question mark rather than a rating beside any skill whose meaning is not clear to you at this stage of the book. Take as much time as you need.

Rating   Skills

Awareness of What I Bring to My Relationships

_____   Understanding the influence of my upbringing

_____   Assuming responsibility for my thoughts, feelings, and actions in
          relationships

_____   Ability to get in touch with my true feelings

_____   An adequate sense of my self-worth

_____   Absence of debilitating fears and anxieties

_____   Acknowledging and being comfortable with my sexuality

_____   Sensitivity to sex-role issues in relationships

_____   Sensitivity to cultural and social class issues

Disclosing Myself

_____   Communicating well with my body messages

_____   Using touch sensitively

_____   Communicating well with my voice messages

_____   Sending "I" messages that own what I say

Rating	*Skills*
____	Disclosing personal information
____	Expressing my feelings

Being a Rewarding Listener

____	Knowing the difference between my own and another's internal viewpoint
____	Not letting my emotions impede my listening
____	Showing interest and attention with my body messages
____	Showing warmth and interest with my voice messages

Responding Helpfully

____	Showing accurate understanding of another's words
____	Showing accurate understanding of another's feelings
____	Showing accurate understanding of another's feelings and why they feel that way
____	Being safe to talk to
____	Knowing when to confront
____	Confronting inconsistencies in what another says
____	Confronting distortions of reality in what another says

Overcoming Shyness and Making Initial Contact

____	Accurately understanding how I experience and show my shyness
____	Using coping self-talk to manage shyness
____	Possessing realistic personal rules regarding rejection
____	Not jumping to unwarranted conclusions about how others perceive me negatively
____	Predicting reward as well as risk from making initial contact with another
____	Breaking the ice skills
____	Conversational skills
____	Making a date skills

Choosing Relationships

| ____ | Avoiding impulsiveness |
| ____ | Choosing for myself rather than for others' approval |

Rating	Skills
_____	Assessing my compatibility with another
_____	Assessing another's relationship skills

Deepening Relationships

_____	Progressively revealing more intimate personal information
_____	Expressing my feelings about the relationship
_____	Showing caring and being considerate
_____	Being trustworthy
_____	Developing the sexual pleasure bond
_____	Being a good companion in sharing pleasant activities
_____	Making decisions democratically

Assertion

_____	Knowing the difference between nonassertion, aggression, and assertion
_____	Overcoming mental barriers to assertion
_____	Being assertive in taking the initiative in relationships
_____	Making assertive requests for changes in another's behavior
_____	Not letting others define me on their terms
_____	Ending relationships assertively
_____	Encouraging mutual assertion in a relationship

Managing Anger

_____	Acknowledging when I am angry
_____	Choosing realistic personal rules concerning my own and others' behavior
_____	Not jumping to conclusions by perceiving provocations unnecessarily
_____	Using coping self-talk to manage anger
_____	Handling aggressive criticism constructively
_____	Managing stress well
_____	Helping one another to manage anger in a relationship

Managing Conflict

_____	Owning personal responsibility for my choices when in conflict rather than just blaming and reacting

Rating	Skills
____	Developing an accurate model of the other person
____	Possessing a collaborative orientation toward managing conflict with another
____	Being prepared to increase the exchange of rewarding behaviors
____	Confronting conflicts constructively
____	Understanding another's position
____	Stating my position clearly
____	Defining problems constructively with another
____	Searching for and evaluating alternative solutions with another
____	Agreeing upon and making a clear "contract" to implement the best solution

Maintaining and Developing My Skills

____	Monitoring my relationship skills
____	Being committed to maintaining my relationship skills
____	Being committed to developing my relationship skills actively

Conclude the exercise by summarizing your relationship skills. Your statement should avoid generalities and specifically indicate (1) relationship skills strengths, (2) relationship skills weaknesses, and (3) goals for change.

Personal Responsibility for Relationship Skills

The basic assumption of this book is that ultimately you are personally responsible for your survival, happiness, and fulfillment (Nelson-Jones, 1984). To use President Truman's expression, "The buck stops here." Now what does this stark existential truth mean? Here are some considerations.

Defining Personal Responsibility

When you are being personally responsible you are in the process of making the choices that maximize your happiness and fulfillment. Personal responsibility is a positive concept—the idea that you are responsible for your well-being and making your own choices. This notion contrasts with a common meaning of responsibility, namely that of responsibility to others, including living up to their standards. Although the process of personal responsibility can be far from easy, adopting it as a basic attitude toward living liberates you to concentrate on how you can be most effective. It entails neither focusing on other people's faults nor feeling that you are at fault all the time.

Are you always responsible for your choices? The answer is yes, but with qualifications. First of all, there was a maturational lag between the development of your capacity for reasoning and your need to make some of the choices that would help you live most effectively. So you may have acquired skills weaknesses because you lacked the early reasoning power to make good choices. Your bad initial choices may then have developed into bad relationship skills habits. A second and related qualification is that the attitude of personal responsibility and the ability to make effective choices have to be learned. If your learning—from the consequences provided for your own behavior and from observing others' examples—has been deficient, that deficiency may well have diminished your effectiveness. And if your environment continues to be deficient, by failing to provide corrective learning opportunities, your relationship skills weaknesses may be maintained. Third, many social factors may work against your assuming personal responsibility. Adverse conditions like poor housing, urban overcrowding, unemployment, poverty, racial discrimination, and poor educational opportunities all can make it difficult for you to learn to make and to keep making the choices that serve you best.

Assuming Responsibility for Relationship Skills

Earlier, relationship skills were defined as sequences of choices that enable you to affirm yourself and others in your relationships. A number of considerations are relevant to your assuming responsibility for your relationship skills. It is fruitless to blame yourself or others if your skills are not as good as you would like. The important thing is to become aware of your present strengths and weaknesses and to work to shift the balance more in the direction of strengths. On the subject of blaming, the ancient philosopher Epictetus had this to say: "It is the act of an ill-instructed man to blame others for his own bad condition; it is the act of one who has begun to be instructed, to lay the blame on himself; and of one whose instruction has been completed, neither to blame another, nor himself."

All the skills mentioned in Exercise 1 involve choices for which you probably could assume more effective responsibility. If you want to change your skills weaknesses, you need to acknowledge responsibility for sustaining them. As this book progresses, you should gain a greater awareness of your present pattern of relating. If you do, you are also likely to become more aware of the range of relationship skills choices open to you. Then it may become a matter of whether you wish to make the choice to change or instead choose to stay "stuck in the mud." Relationship skills involve your feelings, thoughts, and actions. Assuming responsibility for these skills also involves this triple focus. For example, responsibility for feelings can involve both the capacity to be in touch with your feelings and to regulate them when appropriate. Responsibility for thinking emphasizes avoiding self-defeating thinking, which may contribute to anxiety, depression, anger, and blaming. Responsibility for acting entails communicating yourself to others in ways that affirm rather than disaffirm.

The following is a sample of self-talk—things you might say to yourself—that may help you understand this section.

> I am personally responsible for the way I think, feel, and act in my relationships. Adverse past and present circumstances may make it more difficult for me to be an effective chooser. Nevertheless, I am still responsible for making my life through the quality of my choices. For the sake of my future happiness and fulfillment I have much to gain from working hard to acquire, maintain, and develop my relationship skills.

Pain in Relationships

> The course of true love never did run smooth.
> *William Shakespeare*

Human relationships can be a celebration of life. On the other hand they can cause much psychological pain and despair. The world is full of beauty and hate. Not surprisingly, some data indicate that the course of relationships does not always run smoothly for North Americans.

Marital Breakdown and Distress

The rate of divorce in the United States is the highest in the Western world. In the early 1980s, the divorce rate for first marriages was 49% (Glick, 1984). In 1987, one out of every three marriages was a remarriage. Approximately 83% of divorced men and 78% of divorced women eventually remarry (Wilson & London, 1987). The number of second divorces is rising. It is projected that 61% of divorced men and 54% of divorced women who were in their 30s in 1980 and who marry a second time will experience a second divorce (Glick, 1984).

The divorce rate in Canada increased dramatically from 1960 to 1980. For 1960 the rate was 39.1 per 100,000 people. For 1970 and 1980, the corresponding rates were 139.8 and 259.1, respectively (Eichler, 1983). The change between 1960 and 1970 may largely have resulted from legislation passed in 1968 that made it much easier to obtain a divorce. Another indication of the rising divorce rate in Canada is that (assuming death and divorce are the only ways out of marriage) divorce increased from 13% of marriage endings in 1967 to 40% in 1976 (McKie, Prentice, & Reed, 1983). As in the United States, remarriage rates in Canada are high.

In both the United States and Canada the divorce figures underestimate the extent of marital breakdown. If figures for the separated population were added to those of the divorced population to form a "dissolution index," the statistics for marital breakdown would be considerably higher. Moreover, for numerous reasons—including concern for children, financial insecurity, fear of going it alone, and religious beliefs—many couples remain unhappily married. Add these people to the "dissolution index" and it could be argued that, definitely in the United States and very possibly in Canada, many more marriages end up being unhappy than happy.

Marital breakdown and distress involve children. Unhappy parents are likely to have less positive energy to direct toward their children. Also, the risk of children being used as unwitting soldiers in their parents' war games is ever present. Marital breakdown also leads to single-parent families and to remarriages. In the United States only 68% of children live with both biological parents (Bianchi & Seltzer, 1986). Of the remainder, 20% live with one biological parent and a stepparent, and 4% live with neither parent. There are ethnic differences among children living with both biological parents: the proportions for White, Hispanic, and Black children are 73%, 67%, and 38%, respectively. Of children in single-parent families, fewer than 10% live with their biological father. Of children in a single-parent household headed by their biological mother, 31% never see their father. Of children living with a remarried biological mother, 46% never see their father.

Rising to the Challenge of Relationships

Despite the disquieting statistics, undoubtedly families that break up experience good as well as bad times. Also, the situation relative to the past seems worse than it actually is because divorce is now both easier to get and less socially stigmatized. Nevertheless, the degree of family breakdown, separation, and distress suggested is staggering. Tens of millions of North Americans are hurting, hurting others, and getting hurt through difficulties in sustaining good relationships. The figures indicate how fragile human relationships can be, even when entered into with the best of intentions. They suggest all too many shattered dreams and broken promises.

Although these statistics focus on domestic relationships, serious relationship difficulties are frequently also found at work and in other settings outside the home. The challenge of relationships is that many of them are extremely difficult. You are constantly faced with your own and others' weaknesses and required to rise above them. Each of you has a huge capacity for effective relating. You are challenged by life to develop the skills and make the choices that allow you to express this capacity. You have many strengths already. I hope this book helps you build on these strengths.

Concluding Self-Talk

This and subsequent chapters end with a segment of self-talk that you can use to remind yourself of the chapter's main points.

To relate effectively I need to make choices that affirm both myself and others in my relationships. Ample evidence shows that many people have distressed rather than fulfilled relationships. I need to develop and use a repertoire of relationship skills. Each skill represents a sequence of choices made in an area. If I make good choices, I exhibit skills strengths. If I make poor choices, I exhibit skills weaknesses. Relationships are too important to be left to chance. I need to assess my skills strengths and weaknesses and to identify those skills requiring improvement. If I rise to the challenge of relationships by improving my skills I will benefit both myself and others. I can and will relate better!

Notes

2
What You Bring to Relationships

He who conquers others is strong;
he who conquers himself is mighty.
Lao-tzu

This chapter aims to raise your awareness of what you bring into your relationships and of the social and cultural factors involved. Each of you brings a personal history into your relationships. For instance, in the United States in 1984 the average age at first marriage was 24 for brides and 26 for grooms (Wilson & London, 1987). Consequently, the average female and male brought 24 and 26 years of prior living experience into their marriages. Respectively they would need to be 48 and 52 before having lived as much time within their marriage as outside it. If the trend toward later marriage continues, partners will bring even more years of previous living into their marriages. Just as people bring their personal histories into their marriages, they also carry their histories into all their other relationships, whatever the degree of intimacy. Moreover, relationships always take place in cultural and social contexts. These influence the previous personal histories of participants as well as how they behave together in the present and future.

How You Learned Your Relationship Skills

Unlike other animals whose behavior is programmed by instincts, most human behavior is learned. Humans tend to have instinct remnants rather than strong instincts (Maslow, 1970). The human animal is also distinguished from other animals by the capacity for self-awareness and conscious thought. Consequently, not only is human behavior learned in the first place but afterward humans keep regulating it by the way they think.

Acquiring and Maintaining Relationship Skills

A useful distinction may be made between acquiring skills and maintaining them. In a sense each one of you has at least two learning histories for every skill: acquiring the skill in the first place—the traditional definition of learning—and then improving, diminishing, or maintaining your initial level of skill. The distinction is important, because changing or improving a skill entails changing whatever is maintaining your skill at a lower level than you desire. It is impossible to go back and change how a skills weakness was first acquired.

For example, Mae, 17, initially learned to be shy because her parents had a rule that children should be seen and not heard. She maintained her shyness throughout her childhood and adolescence partly because her parents continued not to encourage her to talk about herself. Mae can't now change the way she became shy. She may well not be able to change her parent's behavior, which plays an important part in maintaining her shyness. However, Mae can work to acquire the self-help skills involved in being more outgoing. Also, she can if necessary seek professional help, perhaps from a school or college counselor, designed to provide her with learning experiences enabling her to become less shy. Thus she can create for herself a third learning history by making new choices to overcome previously acquired and maintained skills weaknesses. A further reason to stress the distinction between acquisition and maintenance is that even when you possess good relationship skills, you still have to struggle daily to maintain them.

Sources of Influence

From the moment of birth numerous people give you messages that influence the development of your relationship skills. Some of these messages help you to relate more effectively, whereas others weaken your effectiveness. Sometimes these messages are consistent; at other times they may be contradictory, involving different messages not only from different people but even from the same person. Children especially are influenced in acquiring good and bad relationship skills. They are physically and emotionally dependent on others, and they are also intellectually immature.

Let us now look at the kinds of people who may have influenced and may still influence the choices you make in relationships.

• *Parents.* Parents include stepparents and other substitute parents.

• *Brothers and sisters.* Siblings may be influential especially if older, but not too old to be out of frequent contact.

• *Grandparents.* Your grandparents brought up your parents and consequently their influence lives on through others as well as through themselves, if they are still alive.

• *Aunts and uncles.* Like grandparents, aunts and uncles may be important. However, greater geographic mobility than previously experienced within families may sometimes lessen their importance.

• *Older friends.* Friends of the family who visit fairly frequently may have an influence.

• *Community leaders.* These include people in church, medical, government, and other visible positions.

• *Peer groups.* A peer group consists of people of roughly your own age, outside your immediate family, with whom you play and study.

• *Teachers.* Contact with teachers may be either in class or in extracurricular activities like school plays or music.

• *Famous people.* Such people may be well-known sports, business, or entertainment personalities, or religious, political, or historical leaders.

• *Fictional people.* These are characters portrayed in books, on television, and in movies.

• *Advertising.* Advertising portrays people behaving in specific ways with the purpose of influencing purchasing decisions.

Learning from Example

"Monkey see, monkey do" is one way of viewing learning from example. However, frequently people do not just imitate behavior blindly but rather think about what they have seen. Albert Bandura is a psychologist who has done much research into learning from example. He considers that the observer is more likely to adopt another's example if the behavior demonstrated both is valued by the observer and also brings rewards to the person being observed (Bandura, 1977). The other main way of learning, learning from consequences, is discussed in the next section. In reality, learning from consequences overlaps with learning from example.

The behaviors you learn from example include feelings, thoughts, and actions. The following are some illustrations.

> Chuck's mother had a stroke when he was 17. As a result she was unable to dress herself and had much less energy than previously. He saw his father support her both physically, by helping her get dressed and do other things, and emotionally. His father never said "what a great guy I am"—he just quietly went about showing his care and concern.

Alice, 15, and Brett, 10, live in a family where both parents find it very hard to express their emotions. There is virtually no touching between parents and children apart from a brief goodnight kiss. When Alice and Brett please their parents, they seldom hear about it. However, the children's faults are painstakingly explained to them.

The style of managing conflict in the Wong family is one of competitive combat. Each parent has to be right, has "legitimate" reasons for anger, shouts, and points the finger. The parents don't listen to one another. Blame is the name of the game. The three children, aged 4, 7, and 9, get very upset when their parents fight.

A number of points are implicit in the illustrations just given. First, behavior that serves as an example may be unintentional as well as intentional. Second, demonstrating behavior often involves deficient rather than good relationship skills. Third, the observers may remain unaware that they are learning from example. In families, it is all too easy for children to adopt their parents' behavior without conscious choice. They learn relationship skills strengths and weaknesses while they are eating their breakfast cereal. As a consequence, you not only may have absorbed some deficient skills, but also may face the added barrier of not being aware that this has happened.

You are influenced to acquire and to maintain your relationship skills strengths and weaknesses through messages from many categories of people. The most important people in this respect are usually your parents. You were exposed to them first, in a very intense way, when you were dependent on them and at an age when your critical powers were still in the process of development. Exercise 2 is designed to help you explore the relationship skills behaviors (feelings, thoughts, and actions) that your parents demonstrated and may still demonstrate. These include both strengths and weaknesses.

Exercise 2
Learning relationship skills from the examples set by my parents

1. What were the examples set by your parents in each of the following relationship skills areas? (In most instances, "parents" refers to your biological parents; however, if a stepparent or surrogate parent has been more important to you, talk about him or her in your answer.)

Sender Skills	Your Mother	Your Father
Talking about their experiences		
Showing their feelings		
Standing up for themselves		

Exercise 2 (continued)

Receiver Skills	Your Mother	Your Father
Being a good listener		
Understanding what others say		
Responding helpfully to others		

Managing Anger and Conflict Skills	Your Mother	Your Father
Managing anger constructively		
Accepting responsibility for their behavior		
Working for rational solutions		

2. Summarize what you consider the effects of your parents' examples have been on your current relationship skills in (1) sending information; (2) receiving information; and (3) managing anger and conflict.

Learning from Consequences

As a child, when you were naughty, your parents may well have told you you were a "bad girl" or "bad boy." When you behaved well, your parents were more likely to say "good girl" or "good boy." In each instance, your parents were granting or withholding the reward of their approval. As a child you learned not only from the consequences of your behavior, provided by others, but also from the consequences or feedback given to you by your own feelings. For instance, if teasing one of your friends was pleasurable, the probability of your teasing that person in the future was likely increased. The main set of internal consequences provided by your feelings was whether your actions produced pleasure or pain for you.

Sometimes a conflict may have occurred, in that behaviors that were pleasurable for you were disapproved by your parents. If your parents' reaction was very strong you may have buried your true feelings and owned your parents' feelings as if they were your own. People tend to talk about themselves as though they have access to their own feelings without distortion. However, frequently their feelings are the result of their parents' examples and rewards rather than what they would truly feel given a more accepting upbringing. The following is an example.

> When José was a child he would cry easily both when he got into fights with other children and when he saw something sad on television. When José cried during a fight, other children were quick to put him down as a "sissy" and a "crybaby." His father, afraid his son might become a homosexual, told him what a wimp he was to cry watching television and that he was behaving more like a girl than a boy. After a time, José began to think of crying in boys and men as a sign of weakness.

Many people provided positive and negative consequences for your relationship skills behavior as you grew up. Both your strengths and your weaknesses may have been either rewarded, discouraged and possibly punished, or ignored. The basic idea is that behavior that has resulted in positive consequences for you has a higher probability of being repeated than behavior that resulted in negative consequences. Exercise 3 is designed to help you further understand how you came to learn your current relationship skills behavior. Although others also may have provided important consequences, the exercise focuses on the consequences provided by your parents.

Exercise 3
The consequences provided by my parents
for my relationship skills behavior

1. Indicate the extent to which you were rewarded by your parents for each of the following behaviors by putting an M in the box that best describes your mother's reaction and an F in the box that best describes your father's reaction. Try to give one or two specific examples of their behavior as well. If answering in terms of a biological parent is inappropriate, answer for a stepparent or surrogate parent.

Reward From Parents

Your Behavior	Much	Little	None	Punished	Example(s)
Expressing affection to him/her					
Expressing anger to him/her					
Expressing your opinions on current affairs					

Exercise 3 (continued)

Your Behavior	Much	Little	None	Punished	Example(s)
Expressing negative feelings about yourself (e.g., depression)					
Expressing positive feelings about yourself (e.g., happiness)					
Saying you wish to be left out of parental disagreements					
Being prepared to listen to him/her					
Responding helpfully to him/her					
Requesting participation in decisions involving you					
Wanting to discuss a conflict between you					
Stating your position in the conflict					
Trying to understand his/her position					
Placating and giving in to him/her					
Working for a rational solution to a conflict with him/her					

2. Summarize what you consider to be the effects of the consequences for your behavior provided by your parents on your current relationship skills strengths and weaknesses.

_____

_____

_____

This section has focused on how you initially acquired your relationship skills (what others did to you) rather than how you maintain them (what you do to yourself). You bring to your relationship your skills strengths and weaknesses. Though change can be difficult, you can choose to change skills that do not work for you.

Your Thinking Skills

> Since wars begin in the minds of men, it is in the minds of men
> that the defenses of peace must be constructed.
> *UNESCO Constitution*

Apart from casual contacts, when you relate to another you think about what happens before, during, and after you see them. Consequently, your relationship skills include your thinking skills. Your thinking skills are the choices you make in various skill areas. You can either support or oppress yourself and others by your thinking choices. In turn these choices lead to helpful or hurtful actions toward yourself and others.

You bring your thinking skills strengths and weaknesses into your relationships. A major theme of this book is that if you are to relate well, you must work hard to overcome the thinking skills weaknesses that are conducive to fear and hatred. Effective thinking involves dealing with yourself and others on the basis of reality. If you are open to all significant incoming information, you can appraise it rationally and then act appropriately. Ineffective thinking is characterized by rigidity, defensiveness, and insufficient attention to the available facts. Since you deny and distort significant information, you may not have an adequate data base for relating to others as both you and they are.

Thinking skills that are important in relating to others include the following (each skill is elaborated in later chapters).

• *Use of self-talk.* You can talk to yourself in ways that calm you down, keep you focused on what you want to achieve, and help you to emphasize positive rather than negative aspects of yourself and others. Alternatively, you can talk to yourself in ways that heighten negative feelings like hatred, depression, anxiety, and jealousy.

• *Choosing realistic personal rules.* Each person has an inner rule book of personal rules for living. Your personal rules are the standards by which you live. Your rules can either blight your relationships through their rigidity and irrationality or provide you with realistic and flexible guidelines for your own and others' behavior. The skill of choosing realistic personal rules includes becoming aware of when your rules may be oppressing rather than supporting you. In such instances, you need either to discard the unrealistic rules altogether or to reformulate them into more rational standards for your own and others' behavior.

The following are some examples of traditional personal rules in the areas of dating, sex, marriage, and family.

Dating. People should act politely on dates and not reveal too much of their inner thoughts and feelings.

Sex. Sex before marriage, even in a steady relationship, is wrong.

Marriage. In marriage, each partner must meet all the intellectual, emotional, social, and sexual needs of the other.

Family. The worst thing that can happen is for a family to break up, however unhappy everyone may be.

In a time when traditional rules and values are being challenged, you face more pressure to choose your own personal rules. You may have acquired many of your rules from others and be maintaining them without having thought them through for yourself. When these rules are life-enhancing, it may not matter that you have not acquired them through conscious choice. However, some rules may be destructive to your capacity to relate and consequently require attention.

• *Perceiving yourself and others accurately.* Two people in a relationship do not just relate to each other. Instead, they relate to their perceptions of themselves, one another, and their relationship. These perceptions may have varying degrees of accuracy. Another way of saying this is that in relationships, people develop *personifications* of themselves and of others. These personifications—the word literally means "making up or fabricating a person"—are the mental maps that guide people through their relationship journeys.

You bring into your relationships your skill of perceiving yourself and others accurately. Central to this skill is the ability to distinguish fact from inference. Your perceptions are subjective facts, but they are not necessarily objective facts. They may contain many inferences of varying degrees of realism in terms of the available information.

Other thinking skills are important in relationships. Fundamental is the skill of assuming responsibility for acquiring, maintaining, and developing your relationship skills. Also, you need a conceptual framework that allows you to think about relating in skills terms and to identify which skills are important. The challenge to work on your relationship skills requires specifying them. Additional important thinking skills include how you attribute causes, or offer explanations for your own and others' behavior; how you make decisions, including major decisions about marriage and parenthood; and how you manage your problems and conflicts.

To make an analogy to sports, relating entails an inner game, coming to grips with your thinking, as well as an outer game, how you act towards others. If you play a good inner game, you increase your probability of acting appropriately, preventing avoidable unhappiness, and working constructively to resolve conflicts.

Your Capacity to Feel

> Seeing's believing, but feeling's the truth.
> *Thomas Fuller*

You bring to your relationships your capacity to experience your feelings. Carl Rogers, in particular, stressed that a feature of modern life was that all people were to some extent out of touch with their inner valuing process (Rogers, 1961, 1980). Your capacity to experience your own feelings indicates both the degree to which you are able to accept yourself and also how open you are to others' feelings.

It is important to be responsive to the flow of your feelings when starting, maintaining, and if necessary ending your relationships for many reasons. Responsiveness to your feelings makes it possible to acknowledge liking and attraction, to be spontaneous, to be sensual, and to be rational. It may seem surprising to include rationality in this list. However, when you are truly in touch with what you feel about situations, you are less likely to react unthinkingly on the basis of your previous conditioning.

If you are out of touch with your feelings you are alienated from the core of your personhood. Relationships are most satisfactory when each person has a secure sense of his or her own identity as a separate individual as well as the identity he or she possesses in relation to another. People who think and feel that they don't really know who they are, or that they know who they are and don't want to change under any circumstances, exhibit underlying feelings of insecurity regarding their identity. Your capacity to feel and hence your sense of identity have almost certainly been inhibited and distorted by your conditioning as a female or a male.

What Are Your Feelings?

Dictionary definitions of feelings tend to use words like "physical sensation," "emotion," and "awareness." All three of these definitions illustrate a dimension of feelings. Feelings as physical sensations represent your underlying animal nature. People are animals first and persons second. As such they need to learn to value and live with their underlying animal nature, and to get it working for rather than against them. Emotion implies movement. Feelings are processes: you are subject to a continuous flow of biological experiencing. Awareness implies that you can be conscious of your feelings. However, you may also deny and distort them. Furthermore you may have learned some unexamined personal rules with their related feelings from your parents and others. Thus some of your feelings may be based more on others' standards than on your own valuing process.

Listening to Your Feelings

In your relationships you are constantly required to listen to your feelings. Paying attention to your feelings does not imply that you ignore others' feelings. Being sensitively attuned to your own feelings gives you an excellent basis for tuning into others' feelings. When you listen to your feelings, ideally these feelings are appropriate to the here and now rather than being residual feelings from your childhood or other relationships. Listening to past feelings in a present context lessens the relevant information available for you to meet your needs now.

As you read the last paragraph you may have thought, "Who, me? Surely only other people drag their past agendas and feelings inappropriately into the present without realizing what they're doing." The news is that this description probably also applies to you, to a greater or lesser degree. Most humans are subject to illusions of autonomy and rationality. They consider that they act independently and rationally most of the time without distracting interference from the residues of childhood and other learning experiences. Such illusions may block you from working to alter your thinking so that you can release your full capacity to feel.

Your Sense of Worth and Anxieties

> No one can make you feel inferior without your consent.
> *Eleanor Roosevelt*

You bring into your relationships your feelings of security or insecurity and your fears and anxieties. Vulnerability can be an attractive quality that helps others feel that you are part of the human race, too. Vulnerability makes it possible to care and be cared for. You can share your own and your partner's vulnerability in ways that enhance and deepen your relationship. Mutual sympathy and liking develop from sensitive understanding of one another's vulnerabilities as much as from appreciation of strengths. Moreover, if you are unable to acknowledge your own fears and anxieties, you are likely to lack responsiveness to other people's.

Your Sense of Worth

Insecurities and fears, if not confronted and managed, can be the breeding ground for hatred and distress in relationships. Nobody's upbringing is perfect. In varying degrees you have learned to feel "not OK" as well as "OK," even though these "not OK" feelings may be difficult for you to acknowledge. Robert Carkhuff categorizes families into two broad groupings, facilitative and retarding. The members of facilitative families help each other become persons. The members of retarding families are in the process of becoming nonpersons. In facilitative families, parents are likely to have a secure sense of their own worth, which is transmitted to their children. In retarding families, one or both parents feel insecure. Lacking a true sense of their own worth, they send messages that undermine their children's sense of worth (Carkhuff, 1983).

Intentionally or unintentionally, people send two broad categories of messages when they communicate. One set is specific, having to do with the ostensible purpose of the communication. The other set of messages may be more general and less intentional. These messages pertain to the receivers' worth as persons and also reveal how highly or poorly the senders value themselves. Children need the security of positive messages about their unique loveableness. Unfortunately many parents fail to realize that they often send messages that undermine the tender self-esteem of those they love. Sometimes these messages have devastating results, especially if parents compound their initial communication errors by not hearing and understanding the pain their children suffer. Life can be very unfair. Children whose parents mostly send retarding messages are less likely to be heard, even though their need for understanding may be much greater than that of children whose parents mostly send facilitative messages. Exercise 4 aims to help you explore how you learned to feel either worthwhile or worthless as a person and how this affects you now.

Exercise 4
Learning to feel worthwhile: helpful and harmful experiences

Instructions: Think back over what you saw and experienced when you were growing up that influences the degree of self-esteem you bring to your current relationships. Some of these experiences were helpful and constructive, whereas others were harmful and destructive.

1. Take a piece of paper and head it "Learning my sense of worth." Draw a line down the center underneath this heading. At the top of the left column write "Helpful experiences," and at the top of the right column write "Harmful experiences."

2. Under "Helpful experiences" list five experiences that you consider were helpful in developing your sense of worth and capacity to relate and that you would like to repeat with your children.

3. Under "Harmful experiences" list five experiences that you consider were harmful in developing your sense of worth and capacity to relate and that you would like to avoid with your children.

4. Summarize how secure and confident a person you feel now and how this affects your capacity to relate to others.

Your Fears and Anxieties

> Where fear is, happiness is not.
> *Seneca*

Definition of an adult: a child who looks grown-up but often has difficulty feeling that way.

The late American psychiatrist Harry Stack Sullivan reportedly said that 90% of human communication was specifically designed not to communicate. Anxiety on the part of both senders and receivers distorts much communication. Anxiety can be a powerful enemy of good relating. The fear of death and of nonbeing is the underlying fear from which all other anxieties are derived; the term *survival anxiety* describes this better than *death anxiety*. Anxiety can be both helpful and harmful. It has a survival value in that it alerts you to realistic dangers to your existence. Unfortunately all people suffer in varying degrees from anxiety that is greater than that required to cope specifically with life's challenges. Such anxiety is disproportionate and debilitating rather than facilitating.

The words *anxiety* and *fear* are often used interchangeably. Anxiety may be defined as your fears about your capacity to cope adequately with the future. This may either be a general trait of yours or a state that applies mainly to specific situations. Your sense of worth and feelings of anxiety are closely connected. Insecurity both manifests and engenders anxiety. People who feel worthwhile are relatively free from debilitating anxieties.

The following is an illustrative list of just a few anxieties people may bring into their relationships. These fears represent their subjective rather than objective reality. They are often exaggerated and result in self-defeating feelings and actions. Sometimes you may be more afraid of getting what you want than of not getting it. Consequently, I group fears into three categories: fear of failure, fear of success, and fear of change.

Fear of failure
Fear of rejection
Fears about the attractiveness of your body
Fears about sexual performance
Fears about making mistakes
Fears about being engulfed
Fear of loneliness
Fear of being unhappy
Fear of coping with the other sex
Fear of what others think

Fear of success
Fears about intimacy
Fear of not being able to maintain success
Fear of being happy
Fear of other's envy

Fear of change
Fear of the unknown
Fear of commitment and losing independence
Fear of practical changes—for example, buying a house

Along with your fears and anxieties, you bring into your relationships skills strengths and weaknesses in coping with them as well. Also, you possess strengths and weaknesses in coping with others' insecurities and anxieties. Exercise 5 encourages you to look at the fears and anxieties that you may bring into your relationships.

Exercise 5
Exploring my fears and anxieties

Instructions: Answer the following questions.
1. What fears and anxieties do you bring into your relationships in each of the following areas (if they apply to you): (1) fear of failure; (2) fear of success; and (3) fear of change?

_____

_____

_____

2. What fears and anxieties have you noticed other people bringing into their relationships with you?

_____

_____

_____

3. What do you consider the effects of your own and others' anxieties to have been on the quality of your relationships?

_____

_____

_____

Your Sexuality

> Passion, though a bad regulator, is a powerful spring.
> *Ralph Waldo Emerson*

All humans are sexual from birth. However, you have a choice concerning how much of your sexuality you bring into your relationships. Sexuality is at once both simple and complex. On the one hand, nothing seems simpler than being attracted to someone and wanting to hold him or her in your arms. On the other hand, your sexuality consists of a complex interplay of physiological, psychological, social, and cultural forces.

Sex and love are often confused. Your sexuality can be a powerful force for bridging your separation from others by making and maintaining contact with them. But you can love people—for instance, parents and friends—without being sexually attracted to them. Also, given the ambiguity of human nature and your capacity for choice, you can have affectionate relationships in which varying degrees of sexuality are implicit.

Your Sexual Feelings

Despite the strength of their sexual urges, people differ in their capacity to experience themselves as sexual beings, partly because humans need to learn how to express their sexuality. You bring into your relationships the fruits of your sexual learning, for good or ill. Your attitude toward your sexuality may be healthy and loving. However, ignorance and poor thinking skills may interfere with your effectiveness. People are probably generally less ignorant about sex now than they once were. Nevertheless, people enter into their relationships with skills weaknesses in respect to knowledge about their own bodies, being able to express tender feelings, and being able to give and receive pleasure. Despite the so-called sexual revolution, children's opportunities to learn about integrating their sexuality into loving relationships often leave much to be desired. How many parents are open in talking about their sexuality to their children without imposing their views on them?

Faulty thinking can lead people to either underemphasize or overemphasize their sexuality. Children can pick up their parents' inhibitions about being sexual. A major area for therapists working with sexually dysfunctional couples is that of helping one or both partners work through thoughts interfering with performance—for instance, that sex is dirty or that sharing sexual fantasies is wrong. Additionally, many people have counterproductive fears about their bodies: they may be concerned that their breasts or their penises are too small, for example. Especially for males, poor thinking skills may lead to an exaggerated emphasis on sexual performance. They may boast about their sexual conquests to their peers and treat women as objects rather than persons. Fears underlie both inhibited and exaggerated sexuality. They may include fears about acknowledging the strength of sexual feelings, performance fears, and fears about being seen as sufficiently "masculine" or "feminine."

Sexual Preference

You bring your sexual preference to your relationships. The world is not divided simply into heterosexuals and homosexuals. Alfred Kinsey and his colleagues conducted pioneering studies on sexual behavior in the late 1940s and early 1950s in the United States (Kinsey, Pomeroy, & Martin, 1948; Kinsey, Pomeroy, Martin, & Gebhard, 1953). In the large, predominantly white, middle-class population they surveyed, 4% of males and between 1% and 3% of females were exclusively homosexual. However, by age 45, half the males and about a quarter of the females had responded homosexually either by arousal or orgasm at some point during their lives. In short, although heterosexuality was very much the predominant sexual preference for both males and females and exclusive homosexuality very much the minority preference, the study showed a considerable amount of bisexuality.

The Kinsey studies are outdated; they were also based on an unrepresentative sample. Nevertheless they indicate that many females and males are confronted with choices about how to handle homosexual feelings, whether to engage in homosexual sex, and whether to admit their homosexual feelings openly. Kinsey and his colleagues considered that, if social constraints and taboos had not been so strong, they would have discovered a much higher incidence of homosexual response.

People not only bring their sexual preference to their relationships, but they also carry with them their fears about their sexual preference. Heterosexuality as well as homosexuality may be repressed. For example, a young man who experiences homosexual attraction to another man may wrongly label himself homosexual rather than, say, a bisexual who is predominantly heterosexual. Especially among males, people are often very anxious about being homosexual. For some, an exaggerated emphasis on heterosexual performance is an attempt to reassure themselves. It is preferable to acknowledge rather than to deny any homosexual feelings you may have, because you can then make a conscious choice about how to handle them. Exercise 6 enables you to explore your sexuality.

Exercise 6
Exploring my sexuality

Instructions: Answer the following questions.
1. To what extent are you satisfied or dissatisfied with your capacity to experience and express your sexuality?

   _____

   _____

2. Think of your body image. To what extent are you satisfied or dissatisfied with your body from the viewpoint of sexual relating?

   _____

   _____

   _____

3. What is your sexual preference and how do you know? If you are bisexual, identify the extent to which you are heterosexual or homosexual.

   _____

   _____

   _____

Exercise 6 (continued)

4. Do you bring any fears and anxieties about your sexuality into relationship(s) where sex may form a part? If so, be as specific as possible in identifying them.

_____

_____

5. Take a piece of paper and at the top write "how I learned about my sexuality." At the top of the left-hand column write "helpful experiences" and at the top of the right-hand column write "harmful experiences." List important experiences that have helped or harmed you in expressing your sexuality in a caring way.

Your Sex-Role Identity and Expectations

> There was, I think, never any reason to believe in any innate superiority of the male, except his superior muscle.
> *Bertrand Russell*

A fundamental value of this book is that of equality between females and males. Equality between the sexes means that both females and males should have the same opportunity to develop and express their humanity. Apart from the realistic constraints of their biological differences, they should have the same opportunity to exercise choice in their lives. Equality between the sexes is an ideal toward which progress is being made in Western societies. In the past both females and males have related both to their own sex and to the other sex in traditional ways that needlessly constricted choice. You are in a transitional period now, in which perhaps especially females but also many males are challenging conventional wisdoms about sex-related attitudes and behaviors. This transitional period poses threats and risks as well as exciting opportunities for both sexes. Gender is now on the agenda in all but the most unaware of male–female relationships.

Defining Terms

The following are some definitions of basic terms that help explore the sex-role expectations you bring to your relationships.

• *Sex.* In this context sex refers to biological differences between males and females—for instance, differences in genitals, reproductive functions, bone structure, and size.

• *Gender.* Gender refers to the social and cultural classification of attributes, attitudes, and behaviors as "feminine" or "masculine."

• *Sex-role identity.* Your sex-role identity is how you see yourself on the dimensions of "masculinity" and "femininity."

• *Sex-role expectations.* These are your thoughts and feelings about how you and others should think, feel, and behave on account of differences in your biological sex. They are your personal rules in this area.

• *Sexism.* Individual sexism describes any feelings, thoughts, and actions that assume the superiority of one sex over the other. Institutional sexism describes institutional structures that discriminate against and devalue a person on the ground of sex.

Masculinity, Femininity, and Androgyny

In Western societies, certain psychological characteristics have been traditionally viewed as either "feminine" or "masculine." Feminine characteristics have included being affectionate, gentle, sensitive to the needs of others, tender, and warm. Masculine characteristics have included being aggressive, ambitious, assertive, analytical, and dominant (Bem, 1974). The predominant traditional roles of women have been those of the nurturer and social harmonizer within the home. Men's traditional roles have focused on being the breadwinner outside the home and the enforcer of discipline within the home.

Because of differing views about their psychological characteristics and the different emphases of their lives, males and females have developed different relationship skills strengths and weaknesses. According to Argyle, the research evidence suggests that females may be more socially competent than males in a number of areas. Females may be more skilled at sending and receiving body language, being rewarding and polite, and disclosing and forming close friendships. However, he notes that being assertive is an area where women appear to have more problems than men (Argyle, 1984).

Underlying the "femininity–masculinity" dimension is the issue of nature versus nurture. The consensus among social scientists seems increasingly to be that humans have weak instinctual remnants toward either a male or a female sex-role identity and that such biological predispositions may be easily overwhelmed by the strength of their learning experience (Oakley, 1972). Related to the importance of nurture over nature has been the increasing popularity of the concept of psychological androgyny. The androgynous male or female "is flexibly masculine or feminine as circumstances warrant" (Bem, 1981, p. 362). Thus, females and males can be brought up with the capacity to express a range of characteristics independently of whether these characteristics have been traditionally viewed as "masculine" or "feminine." For example, men can be tender and women assertive.

So long as males and females increasingly adopt the strengths rather than the weaknesses of the other sex's gender characteristics, androgyny offers much promise for improving and enriching people's relationships, whether the relationship is between people of the same or opposite sexes. Already many people of both sexes are flexible in exhibiting masculine and feminine characteristics, to varying degrees. With any luck, the trend toward bringing up and encouraging more people to express and share the full range of their psychological characteristics will continue. This trend is likely to lessen the amount of loneliness and alienation in Western countries. In time, "masculinity" and "femininity" may become outmoded concepts.

The ways in which you learned your sex-role identity were many and varied. Rather than having you write about them, Exercise 7 is designed to tap your recollections of the influences on you to exhibit either "feminine" or "masculine" characteristics, or a mixture of the two.

Exercise 7
Learning my sex-role identity

Instructions: The way you think of yourself as "masculine" or "feminine" has been largely learned. Think back over your experiences as you were growing up and answer the following questions.

1. Did you get different toys on account of your sex? Illustrate with examples.

   _____

   _____

2. Did you get different clothes on account of your sex? Include differences in color, and illustrate with examples.

   _____

   _____

3. What roles did your mother and father play in caring for you as a child?

   _____

   _____

   _____

4. Who did the following household tasks in your family?

   Vacuum cleaning
   Dusting
   Shopping for food
   Cooking meals
   Washing dishes
   Making beds
   Polishing furniture
   Washing clothes
   Ironing
   Mending clothes
   Changing fuses

Interior decoration
Exterior decoration
Mowing the lawn
Looking after the car

5. Were you ever called a "sissy" or a "tomboy," either in your home or among your friends? If so, please give an example.

_____

_____

6. Which of the following psychological characteristics do you consider that your parents either encouraged you or discouraged you to show?

Being analytical
Gentleness
Ambition
Dominance
Showing feelings of vulnerability
Concern with your clothes
Competitiveness
Being nurturing
Career orientation
Home orientation

7. Did the books and magazines you read when growing up show males and females as having different psychological characteristics, interests, and activities? Please give examples.

_____

_____

8. Did the television programs you watched when growing up show males and females as having different psychological characteristics, interests, and activities? Please give examples.

_____

_____

_____

9. Did the advertising you saw when growing up show males and females as having different psychological characteristics, interests, and activities? Please give examples.

_____

_____

_____

Exercise 7 (continued)

10. Which of the following activities were you encouraged to participate in at elementary school?

   Football
   Baseball
   Cooking
   Needlework

11. Did your elementary school and high school teachers treat girls and boys differently? Please give examples.

   _____

   _____

   _____

12. In your high school do you think boys and girls were encouraged differently in relation to choosing the following subjects?

   Physics
   Home economics
   Computer studies
   Languages
   Mathematics

13. In your high school, assuming it was mixed, did boys and girls obtain (1) popularity and (2) high status from their peer group for the same or for different reasons? If for different reasons, please specify in what ways.

   _____

   _____

14. Do you consider that your choice of occupation either has been or is being influenced by your sex? If so, please specify how.

   _____

   _____

   _____

15. Summarize how you see your current sex-role identity. To what extent does it work either for or against you?

   _____

   _____

   _____

Changing Patterns of Sex-Role Expectations

Sex-role expectations are changing. The following are some possible emerging personal rules in the areas of dating, sex, marriage, and family life that treat the sexes more similarly than traditional rules do. Ultimately each individual and each couple has to choose the rules for themselves and for their relationship that work best for them.

> *Dating.* It's OK for either sex to initiate a relationship. The expenses of going out together are to be shared.
>
> *Sex.* Mutuality and sensitivity to each other's pleasure is important. It's OK for both females and males to want sex and to show enjoyment of it.
>
> *Marriage.* Marriage is a relationship between separate, equal, and interdependent partners. The roles that males and females play within marriage are to be decided by agreement rather than by tradition.
>
> *Family.* Child care is the responsibility of both parents.

One of the most important areas in which sex-role expectations are changing concerns the place of women in the world of work. In the United States, women's share of the labor force grew from 29% to 45% between 1948 and 1985. The participation rate of women grew from 33% to 55% (Bloom, 1986). In 1985, 42% of American families had two earners, with an additional 14% having three or more earners (Russell & Exter, 1986). Canada showed similar trends. During the 1970s the number of women in the Canadian labor force increased 61% compared to a 24% increase for men. The labor force participation rate for married women increased from 37% in 1971 to 52% in 1981. By 1981, 63% of women of childbearing age (15 to 44) were in the work force (Pryor & Norris, 1983).

The role of women in the work force is changing. In the United States, the proportion of managers who were women rose from 27% in 1972 to 36% in 1986. More women are also becoming entrepreneurs. In 1960, women started one in ten new businesses; in 1985, they started one in five. The figure for 1995 is projected at one in two (Bloom, 1986). Although in the early 1980s the average woman in the United States earned only about 60% of a man's earnings, 6 million wives earned more than their husbands (Bianchi, 1984).

As women increase their choices in relation to work, men will likely have more opportunities to make choices traditionally restricted to women. These choices include spending more time on homemaking and children. Furthermore, a second income allows some husbands to find more fulfilling work even though it may be lower paid or part-time. In the United States in 1981, more than half of all husbands who were secondary family earners worked either part-time or only part of the year, compared to fewer than one-fifth of all husbands who were primary earners in dual-earner couples (Bianchi, 1984).

The changing role of women in the work force may be associated with the increase in the number of divorces over the same period. The growing financial independence and willingness of women to seek fulfillment outside as well as inside the home may make many women less willing to stay in unhappy marriages. Furthermore, the fact that about half of all first marriages in the United States end

in divorce may reinforce women's desires to pursue their own careers as insurance against the possibility that they will be on their own. If people are increasingly
going to stay in marriages only because they want to be in them, not because they
have to be in them, both females and males have more incentive to develop
relationship skills for their own sakes and for their children's sakes as well.

Sex Differences in Communication

The area of sex differences in communication is a vast one. Differences, as well as
similarities, in the ways males and females communicate within their sex and with
the other sex are pervasive (Henley, 1977; Eakins & Eakins, 1978). The area of sex
differences in communication cannot be adequately covered in this book. However, subsequent chapters draw attention to some of the different relationship
skills strengths and weaknesses of males and females. All males and all females do
not possess the same strengths and weaknesses: individual differences are a fact
of life.

Exercise 8 concludes this section on how you bring your sex-role identity and
expectations to your relationship. Exercise 8 asks you to explore your views on
various aspects of male–female relationships.

Exercise 8
Exploring my sex-role expectations

Instructions: Answer the following questions.

Part A: Taking Initiatives
Below are a number of areas in female–male relationships where either or both
of you may take the initiative:

> Asking for a date
> Ordering a meal
> Paying the bill after eating out
> Arranging to go to a movie
> Arranging a vacation
> Driving
> Expressing affection
> Touching
> Making love
> Asking for support

1. To what extent are you prepared to take the initiative in each of the above areas?

   _____

   _____

_____

_____

_____

2. To what extent do you have a double standard—one for your own sex and one for the other sex—in regard to taking initiatives in each of these areas?

_____

_____

_____

_____

Part B: Female–Male Roles
1. What do you think about equality of the sexes in each of the following areas?

Being responsible for earning the family income _____

_____

Being able to have a career _____

_____

Nurturing children _____

_____

Disciplining children _____

_____

Doing housework _____

_____

Taking care of the garden _____

_____

Looking after the car(s) _____

_____

Sexual behavior _____

_____

Explaining the facts of life to girls and boys _____

_____

Showing feelings _____

_____

Exercise 8 (continued)

Offering emotional support _____

_____

Being able to dress in many colors _____

_____

Getting custody of children after divorce _____

_____

Engaging in professional and managerial work _____

_____

Engaging in manual work, for example repairing roads _____

_____

Being drafted into the armed forces in time of war _____

_____

Part C: Assessing My Sex-Role Expectations
1. Make a summary statement of the sex-role expectations that you bring to female–male relationships with people roughly your own age.

_____

_____

2. Do you think your current sex-role expectations help you or harm you in your relationships with the other sex?

_____

_____

_____

Your Culture, Race, and Social Class

> Human life is reduced to real suffering, to hell, only when two ages, two cultures and religions overlap.
> *Hermann Hesse*

You bring your cultural background, racial characteristics, and social class into your relationships. Furthermore, you bring your degree of sensitivity to these characteristics in yourself and others.

Culture

Both the United States and Canada are huge cultural melting pots. The 1980 U.S. census found that 83% of U.S. residents identified with at least one ancestral group. The four largest groups in descending order claimed some English, German, Irish, or African descent. Nearly 7 million people claimed some American Indian ancestry, though only 1 million identified themselves as Indian on the 1980 census race question. Hispanic and Asian ancestry are increasingly prominent. In the 1980 census, 31% of U.S. residents identified with two or more ancestral groups (Robey & Russell, 1984). This identification reflects the fact that much migration to the United States took place some years ago, and with intermarriage, cultures have intermingled.

Canada, like the United States, is largely a nation of immigrants. The 1981 Canadian census showed that almost 16% of Canadians were born outside Canada, whereas the corresponding figure in the United States was 6%. Among those reporting a single ethnic background, the largest group, comprising over 40% of the total population, reported a British background, followed by French (27%), German (5%), Italian (3%), and Ukrainian (2%). More than 80% of the residents of the Province of Quebec identified French as their single ethnic heritage. Only 8% of Canadians identified with more than one ethnic group. The pattern of Canadian migration appears to be changing. For instance, from 1978 to 1981, the proportion of immigrants from Asia was 44%, whereas immigrants from Europe made up about 30% of the total immigration (Pryor & Norris, 1983).

The message of these figures is simple. Although some national characteristics are undoubtedly common to most North Americans, sensitivity to cultural differences and the ability to transcend them can be very important relationship skills in both the United States and Canada. The figures disguise the amount of cultural variation: for example, immigrants from Vietnam and Indochina do not come from a single Asian culture. It is well beyond the scope of this book to pinpoint all the variations in the ways different cultures and subcultures conduct their relationships. In cross-cultural relationships, each of you can use your skills of giving and receiving information to learn about one another's culture. This learning can be a mutually enriching experience.

Race

You also bring your race to your relationships, whether you are White, Black, Asian, or of another racial grouping. With your race, you bring your attitudes toward race. In the United States, most intimate relationships are between people of the same race. Interracial marriages were prohibited in 20 states until the U.S. Supreme Court invalidated such legislation in 1967. Since then, in a sample of 31 states that kept marital records in both years, the proportion of interracial marriages rose from 0.7% of all marriages in 1968 to 1.6% in 1980. Hawaii is easily the state with both the highest number and proportion of interracial marriages (Wilson, 1984). While the United States is a great cultural melting pot, it has yet to become much of a racial melting pot. The same is true of Canada, although for different reasons. There the proportion of nonwhites has traditionally been small, a situation that is gradually changing.

Social Class

Many people migrated to the New World to get away from what they perceived as the stultifying social class systems of Europe. The United States and Canada do not have such obvious class systems based on very old money, large landed estates, and titles. However, North Americans still do come from different social classes. Income, educational attainment, and occupational status are three of the main ways social class is measured in North America. Every society throughout the globe has its pecking order or status system. These systems are open to varying degrees of vertical mobility. The U.S. myth is that everyone can become president, either of the United States or of General Motors. However, the reality is quite different. The social class in which you were born and raised influences your chances of surviving at birth, your educational and occupational opportunities, whom you are likely to meet and to marry, how much money you are likely to make, how well your health is looked after, and the quality of your funeral.

Social class can be an important consideration in starting and maintaining personal relationships. People from different social classes have different patterns of behavior. Those born on the "wrong" or the "right" side of the tracks can feel awkward about going out with or marrying someone from the opposite side. Moreover, families often exert pressure on children to relate to people only within their own social class or a higher one.

Each of you brings your social class to your relationships. You also bring your sensitivity to the effect of others' social class on you and your social class on them. If you allow them, social class considerations may lead to you putting up unnecessary barriers between yourself and others. Additionally, you may have to choose how to handle negative messages resulting from others' social class hang-ups. Exercise 9 enables you to explore the cultural, social class, and racial influences in your background and relationships.

Exercise 9
Exploring my culture, race, and social class

Instructions: Answer the following questions.

Part A: Culture
1. Other than your national culture as North Americans, from which ancestral culture are you?

---

2. What behaviors and expectations do you possess related to your ancestral culture(s)?

_____

_____

3. What are the main problems you experience in your relationships with North Americans from different cultures?

_____

_____

Part B: Race
1. From which race are you?

_____

2. What behaviors and expectations have you learned related to your race?

_____

_____

3. What are the main problems you experience in your relationships with North Americans from different races?

_____

_____

_____

Part C: Social Class
1. To what social class do you belong?

_____

2. What behaviors and expectations do you possess related to your social class?

_____

_____

_____

3. What are the main problems you experience in your relationships with North Americans from different social classes?

_____

_____

_____

Concluding Self-Talk

I bring many things, for good or ill, into my relationships. As I grew up I learned skills strengths and weaknesses from the examples and consequences provided by others. I now sustain my relationship skills weaknesses as well as my strengths. I bring the quality of my thinking into my relationships—for example my personal rules and how I perceive. I bring my capacity to be aware of my feelings, which in turn is related to how responsive I can be to others' feelings. I bring my sense of worth and my fears and anxieties. I can use my vulnerability to deepen or to destroy my relationships. I can choose how much of my sexuality I bring into my relationships. I also have many sex-role thoughts, feelings, and behaviors that reflect my upbringing more than my sex. These can interfere with equality in female–male relationships. Furthermore, I can help or damage my relationships through how I handle cultural, racial, and social class differences in them.

Notes

3
Disclosing Yourself

They do not love that do not show their love.
William Shakespeare

This chapter focuses on how you send messages to others—sometimes intentionally, sometimes unintentionally. In your relationships, being an effective sender of messages can serve at least four important functions. First, effectively sending messages is a means by which you create and define yourself. Second, as an effective sender you influence how others respond to you. Third, when you send messages effectively you may help others to be more themselves. Finally, you reduce the chances of misunderstanding and increase the chances of working through genuine differences.

All relationship messages are encoded by a sender and then decoded by a receiver (Argyle, 1983). Mistakes can be made at both ends. Senders may not send the messages they wish to send. Much human communication is either poorly carried out or unintentional. Senders sometimes also intentionally seek to deceive. At the receiving end even the clearest of messages may be decoded wrongly. However, the possibility of erroneous decoding is much greater when the message is unclear.

This chapter looks at five important ways to send messages.

- *Body messages.* Sometimes called body language, these are the messages you send with your face and other parts of your body.
- *Touch messages.* Touch is a special kind of body message involving physical contact with another.
- *Voice messages.* These messages relate to how you talk—for example, loudly or softly.
- *Verbal messages.* These are messages expressed in words—for example, what you say about yourself or how you express your feelings.
- *Action messages.* Action messages are what you do as contrasted with what you say or how you say it.

Since humans can send messages in so many different ways, the issue of genuineness becomes important. The question was asked concerning a prominent politician: "How can you tell when he's lying?" The response: "When his lips move." How do you know when someone is being real or phony, sincere or insincere? A simple answer is that you use your decoding abilities to look for congruence between whether how something is said matches what is said. The same will be true for decoding judgments made about your messages. If you send messages loud and clear, your voice and body messages match your words; if relevant, so do your touch and action messages.

The notion of social rules is important in both encoding and decoding messages.

Fearing the worst

Every group, however large or small, establishes rules for the expected behavior of its members. Thus all your relationship behavior—whether it involves friendship, dating, making love, marriage, raising a family, working, or pursuing leisure interests—is likely to be influenced by a network of social rules and expectations. In North America, some rules apply to everyone—for example, saying hello when you meet someone. Other rules differ according to your sex; for instance, it is more acceptable for women to wear skirts than men, and it may be more acceptable for men to interrupt than women. Still other rules vary according to your culture—for example, the greater emphasis in Asian cultures on saving face and on respect for elders. In your relationships you have a choice between sticking to the social rules or, if necessary, establishing rules that work better for you. For instance, Alan, 23, did not care for the rule that men should not show "feminine" feelings, like caring. Consequently, he decided to become very emotionally literate in expressing, where appropriate, the full range of his feelings.

Body Messages

> It ain't what you say, it's how you say it.
> *Anonymous*

> Man is the only animal that blushes. Or needs to.
> *Mark Twain*

When you talk about yourself, your communications consist of both verbal messages and voice and body framing messages, which may or may not match the literal content of your words. These framing messages are extremely important. The impact of your verbal messages can be heightened, lessened, or completely countermanded by your voice and body framing messages. For instance, Joanne may say, "Everything is all right in my relationship with Darren," while she is looking very unhappy, talking in a choked voice, and fighting back tears. It does not take an expert decoder to surmise that everything is not all right between Joanne and Darren. Before going into an examination, Ricardo says, "I'm feeling pretty confident," but he laughs and smiles nervously, paces up and down, and breathes shallowly and rapidly. Again, how Ricardo behaves speaks louder than what he says.

As you grew up you may have learned to mask many of your thoughts and feelings by choosing not to express them with your words, your body, or your voice. However, sometimes you deceive yourself more than others; although the meaning of your words points in one direction, your body and voice messages may point in another. Professional actresses and actors consciously try to control the body and voice messages of the characters they play to suspend your disbelief. People like Meryl Streep and Michael Douglas are experts in sending body and voice messages.

The following are some of the main forms of body messages.

• *Facial expression.* Facial expressions are perhaps the main vehicle for sending body messages. Ekman, Friesen, and Ellsworth identified seven main facial expressions of emotion: happiness, interest, surprise, fear, sadness, anger, and disgust or contempt (Ekman, Friesen, & Ellsworth, 1972). Much of the information in these facial expressions is carried through the mouth and the eyebrows; common phrases like "down in the mouth" and "raised eyebrows" reflect the importance of these parts of the face. Display rules prescribe what facial expressions may be shown when. For instance, at funerals downturned mouths are more appropriate than upturned ones—even for people at the funeral only to make sure the corpse is really dead!

• *Gaze and eye contact.* As Humphrey Bogart said, "Here's looking at you, kid." Gaze, or looking at other people in the area of their faces, is a way to both show interest and collect facial information. Women are more visually attentive than men in all measures of gaze (Henley, 1977; Argyle, 1983). Cultures also differ in terms of gaze. In the "contact cultures" of the Arab world, Latin America, and Southern Europe, the amount of gaze is high. Too little gaze is seen as impolite and insincere. However, in "noncontact" cultures such as North America, Northern Europe, and Asia, too much gaze is perceived as threatening (Watson, 1972). In fact, when conversing the Japanese gaze at the neck rather than at the face (Pease, 1981).

Eye contact is a more direct way of sending messages, whether of interest, anger, or sexual attraction. Seeing "eye to eye" is better than having "shifty eyes." Dilation of the pupils is another source of eye messages: dilated pupils can indicate "bedroom eyes" or sexual attraction, whereas constricted pupils may be decoded as "beady little eyes."

• *Gesture.* Gestures can take the place of words; for example, nodding your head up and down or side to side substitutes for saying yes or no, respectively. However, gestures have different meanings in different cultures. In Greece, people toss their heads back to say no. The OK sign in North America, with thumb and forefinger in a circle, in France and Belgium means "You're worth nothing" and in Southern Italy either means "You asshole" or signifies that you desire anal sex (Ekman, Friesen, & Bear, 1984).

Gestures can also frame or illustrate words. Gestures may be physical acts that help explain what is being said but have no meaning on their own. Argyle suggests four functions of gestures that accompany speech: displaying the structure of the utterance by enumerating elements or showing how they are grouped; pointing to people or objects; providing emphasis; and giving illustrations of shapes, sizes, or movements, particularly when these are difficult to describe in words (Argyle, 1983). An example of a gesture used to show an emotion, with or without words, is the clenched fist that displays aggression. Your gestures may also vary according to your sex. Eakins and Eakins suggest that men's gestures are larger and more sweeping and forceful, whereas women's gestures are smaller and more inhibited (Eakins & Eakins, 1978).

• *Body posture.* Various messages may be conveyed by your body posture. People who are confident and assertive "walk tall." Less confident people may not stand so erect, put their chests out, or square their shoulders. Height tends to be associated with status—for instance, you "talk down to" or "look up to" someone. This association may put children and women at a disadvantage unless the other's body posture is changed, say by crouching to talk to a child or by sitting down. Turning your body toward someone is more encouraging than turning away from them. Whether you lean forward or backward may indicate interest or disinterest. Your body posture may also communicate how anxious you are. For instance, sitting with your arms and legs tightly crossed suggests that you are emotionally as well as literally uptight. However, you may appear too relaxed, especially if you are female; for instance, uncrossed and open legs may be perceived as a sign of sexual availability, whether you are wearing a skirt, trousers, or jeans. This perception manifests the double standard at work in how people perceive body messages.

• *Physical distance.* The degree of physical proximity comfortable for North Americans, British, and Australians is generally the same (Hall, 1966; Pease, 1981). The zones vary according to the nature of the relationship.

1. *Intimate zone* (between 6 and 18 inches). Here it is easy to touch and be touched. This zone is reserved for spouses, lovers, close friends, and relatives.
2. *Personal zone* (between 18 and 48 inches). This zone is appropriate for less close friends and for parties and other social gatherings.
3. *Social zone* (between 4 and 12 feet). This zone is comfortable with shopkeepers, tradespeople, and for people not known at all well.
4. *Public zone* (over 12 feet). This is the distance for addressing public gatherings.

People stand or sit closer to those whom they like. Men may be readier to enter a woman's space than the reverse, and women more ready to move out of the way (Eakins & Eakins, 1978). Large cross-cultural differences also show up: for instance, Arabs and Latin Americans stand very close. Physical distance is often used as a way to start and end conversations; you may go up to someone to start and edge away as a signal to finish.

• *Clothing and grooming.* If clothes do not make the woman, man, or child, they certainly do send many messages about them. These messages concern social and occupational standing, sex-role identity, ethnicity, conformity to peer group norms, rebelliousness, how outgoing you are, and your sexuality. People dress for effect. They wish to influence others by engaging in impression management. A young man who goes to a party in a sober blue suit and tie projects a very different definition of himself than does someone who dresses in tight jeans that outline his genitals, a colorful open-neck shirt showing off his hairy chest, and a gold chain around his neck. Even children are quick to decode clothing cues. One study found that fourth and sixth grade children attributed different personalities to other children depending on whether the other children wore designer jeans, a medium-price traditional brand, or inexpensive Sears Roebuck jeans (Solomon, 1986). Your personal grooming also provides important information about how well you take care of yourself and how you wish to be seen by others. For instance, you may be clean or dirty, tidy or untidy, and smelly or fresh. In addition, the length, styling, and care of your hair sends messages about you.

Exercise 10 helps you explore how you send messages with your body.

Exercise 10
Sending messages with my body

1. Make out a worksheet for yourself based on the following.

My Body Messages

Area	Skills Strengths	Skills Weaknesses
Facial expression		
Gaze and eye contact		
Gesture		
Body posture		
Physical distance		
Clothing and grooming		

2. On your worksheet, analyze your strengths and weaknesses in each of the six broad body message areas.

3. To what extent do you think your body messages are affected by your cultural and sex-role conditioning?

_____

_____

_____

_____

4. Where appropriate, set yourself goals for changing your body messages to make you a better communicator.

_____

_____

_____

_____

5. Practice changing your body messages in real life to attain your goals.

Touch Messages

> Devils can be drawn out of the heart by the
> touch of the hand on a hand, or a mouth on a mouth.
> *Tennessee Williams*

When you touch another, you are in his or her close intimate zone. Touch connects humans in a most fundamental way. In parent–child relationships touch offers security, tenderness, and affection. Touch is a major way adults can demonstrate protection, support, and caring for each other.

Touch messages can be positive or negative. Positive touch messages are those recipients appreciate. Affection and tenderness may be expressed through a light touch on the hand, arm, or shoulder; holding hands; walking arm in arm; an arm over the shoulders; a caress on the side of the face; a half-embrace; a warm hug; or a kiss on the cheek or mouth—to mention just a few different ways.

Negative touch messages, with varying degrees of severity, violate another's physical and psychological well-being. Women, men, and children can be the victims of negative touch messages. Although occasionally males are raped by females (Timnick, 1983), the vast majority of rapes are committed by males on females. Sexual harassment is almost entirely a problem for females who are crudely and insensitively treated by males. Most child sexual abuse, whether of girls or boys, is done by males. Although wives sometimes may punch, scratch, and throw things at their husbands, acts of domestic physical violence are mainly committed by males. Within their own sex, males are more likely than females to send negative touch messages by pushing, shoving, and hitting. In short, blatant negative touch messages are mainly a skills weakness of males. However, other negative touch messages, such as the hurtful and aggressive pushing away of affection, are the preserve of both sexes. Moreover, touch messages sometimes may contain both positive and negative elements: to accentuate the positive and eliminate the negative can be good advice for both sexes.

A Touch Too Little?

An interesting question is whether most North Americans use too little positive touch. North America is a low contact culture. Numerous social rules and taboos regulate who may touch which parts of the body and when. Females may feel freer to touch other females than males do to touch other males (Jourard, 1971b). In relating to their own sex, males more than females may need to be more assertive in risking positive touch messages. Then males can find out which messages lessen their isolation without creating problems for them. In relating to the other sex, possibly females could assert their equality by initiating and risking more positive touching of males.

Voice Messages

The following examples illustrate how voice messages express emotion.

Tina, 17, feels scared when she goes on dates and speaks very softly.

Bernard, 26, is nervous when he meets new people and speaks very quickly.

Jeff, 42, feels very depressed and speaks in a slow and monotonous voice.

Angie, 22, is mad as hell with Nick, 22, and screams and shouts at him.

Steve, 19, is getting bored with his relationship with Barbara, 18; he says "I still love you" in a flat and mechanical way.

The way you use your voice can speak volumes about what you truly feel. Your voice can also give a skilled observer insight into your capacity to experience your feelings. For instance, some people who are out of touch with their feelings often speak in a flat and monotonous way, even though they use words that express strong feelings. Others show their anxiety by coming on far too loud and strong.

The following are some dimensions of voice messages.

• *Volume.* How loudly or softly do you speak? At the two extremes, do you whisper or scream?

• *Emphasis.* To what degree do you emphasize certain phrases, words, or syllables or speak monotonously?

• *Tone.* Is your voice pitched high or low? Is it shrill or deep?

• *Enunciation.* Do you speak clearly or is your speech mumbled or slurred?

• *Accent.* What national, regional, or social class variations appear in the way you speak?

• *Firmness.* When you need to, do you speak in a firm and confident voice rather than in a weak and diffident one?

• *Use of pauses and silences.* To what degree do you intersperse your speech with brief pauses and longer silences?

If you can control your voice messages, you have acquired a very useful skill in dealing with others. Experiment 1 is the first of the personal experiments in this book. The idea is that you first change your behavior in your daily life in some specific and desired way and then evaluate what happens. If the consequences of your changed behavior are positive for you—and possibly for others too—you may wish to retain the change.

Experiment 1
What happens when I change my voice messages?

Part A: Assessment
1. Assess your voice message strengths and weaknesses on the following dimensions. You may wish to record and play back your speech for evidence.

My Voice Messages

Area	Skills Strengths	Skills Weaknesses
Volume		
Pace		
Emphasis		
Tone		
Enunciation		
Accent		
Firmness		
Use of pauses and silences		

2. Ask at least two people who know you well to give you feedback on your voice and tell you whether they think it could be improved.

_____

_____

_____

3. Summarize your voice message strengths and weaknesses. Be specific about voice behaviors you wish to change.

_____

_____

_____

Part B: Make an "If . . . then . . ." Statement
An "If . . . then . . ." statement is in two parts:
1. In the "If" part, state as specifically as possible the change or changes you wish to make in your voice messages—for instance, "If I speak much more loudly. . .".

_____

_____

2. The "then" part of the statement indicates the specific consequences you predict will follow—for example, "If I speak much more loudly for 24 hours, then (a) during this period I will think of myself as less of a wimp and (b) others will take more notice of what I say." Now make your own "If . . . then . . ." statement.

_____

_____

Experiment 1 (continued)

Part C: Try Out and Evaluate Your Change of Behavior
Try out your changed behavior. Then assess whether you gave it an adequate tryout. Also assess whether it produced positive or negative consequences for yourself and others. Have your predictions been confirmed or disconfirmed? Is your changed behavior worth maintaining or modifying?

_____

_____

_____

_____

_____

Verbal Messages

The following illustrations show some of the implications for various people of their use of words.

Bernadette, 16, is very shy. She finds it hard to accept that anyone might be interested in her. She talks little about herself and has few friends since people find her too hard to get to know.

Mel, 24, has trouble getting on with people. He has a bad habit of putting other people down. His colleagues feel that underneath he is too angry with himself and the world.

Lorna, 63, found out that she has cancer of the uterus and that its spread has not been caught in time. She was able to talk about her situation and her fears to her family and close friends. She was warmed by their support.

Sharon, 18, has trouble making friends. She always seems to be promoting herself by stressing her accomplishments. Her acquaintances find this a turnoff.

Gerard, 19, feels much closer to Dominique, 20, after their last date. He was able to tell Dominique how hurt he had been by the displaced negative comments his mother made about him when she was really upset with his father. Dominique talked about growing up under the shadow of a handsome, successful, and spoiled older brother. Gerard thinks that his relationship with Dominique deepened as a result of their sharing.

Sending "I" Messages

Thomas Gordon, in his book *Parent Effectiveness Training,* makes a useful distinction between "you" messages and "I" messages (Gordon, 1970). "You" messages focus on the other person and are judgmental—for example, "You stop that now, do you hear me?" or "You're getting on my nerves." "I" messages are centered in you as the sender—for example: "I can't think when your stereo is so loud" or "I don't feel like playing when I've just gotten home." When sending an "I" message, you clearly own your message and talk for yourself.

You communicate more openly and honestly in relationships if you speak for yourself. A clear way of speaking for yourself is to send messages starting with the word "I" when you choose to disclose your feelings, thoughts, and actions. "I" messages can have a number of advantages. First, you can acknowledge that "I" and "you" are separate people; what I think or feel about you is my perception and not necessarily what you are. Second, you assume responsibility for your own thoughts, feelings, and actions. Third, "I" messages tend to cause less defensiveness than "you" messages, with their connotations of blame. Fourth, positive statements, such as "I love you," sound much more as though they come from your heart rather than your head.

Disclosing yourself entails talking for yourself. Ways in which you may avoid sending "I" messages include starting messages with words like "you," "people," "we," "that," and "it." The following are some possible examples of non-"I" messages.

> "Would you like the salt?"
> "My girlfriend somehow ended up pregnant."
> "Would you like us to buy that painting?"
> "You don't love me anymore."
> "Are you dumb?"
> "You are the pits."
> "A lot of people find you attractive."
> "You made me drive too fast."
> "We aren't too happy with you as a teacher."
> "They want me to run for public office."

You can either send or fail to send "I" messages in regard to your feelings, thoughts, and actions. Here are some examples.

• *Owning a feeling.* Rick and Karen are having a fight. Rick's non-"I" message is "You are the limit." Rick's "I" message is "I feel hurt and angry."

• *Owning a thought.* Betty and Steve go to a play that Betty enjoyed. Betty's non-"I" message is "What did you think about the play?" Betty's "I" message is "I thought the play was excellent."

• *Owning an action.* Julie has just dropped a plate when her mother arrives. Julie's non-"I" message is "It just broke." Julie's "I" message is "Mom, I've just broken a plate. I'm sorry."

Disclosing Personal Information

> It is in our faults and failings, not in our virtues,
> that we touch one another and find sympathy.
> *J. K. Jerome*

An important category of verbal messages is the personal information you reveal about yourself. All humans in varying degrees lead secret lives. For example, even in long-standing marriages partners sometimes know relatively little about each other. Humans are highly concealing as well as revealing. People often engage in deliberate lying, omissions, and telling half-truths.

Good self-disclosure skills are fundamental to relationships for many reasons. These reasons include the following.

• *Defining yourself.* Disclosing personal information lets you be known to others. If you do not define yourself, misunderstandings are more likely to occur. Another person may define you anyway, on their own terms rather than yours.

• *Knowing yourself.* As you talk about yourself, you can get deeper insights and understandings about the sort of person you are. You also give others the opportunity to provide feedback.

• *Making contact.* Talking about yourself and letting another talk about himself or herself gives each of you the chance to break out of your separateness and make contact. Each is given the opportunity to share and receive.

• *Developing intimacy.* A sharing of yourself is at the heart of intimacy. As you embark toward a deeper level of mutual disclosure, trust may be enhanced, misunderstandings cleared up, and each of you may become more comfortable about being open.

Appropriateness of Disclosure

Underdisclosing and overdisclosing each may be both a cause and a symptom of psychological maladjustment. Both extremes put others off. When you conceal yourself you are hard to get to know; but when you plunge in too quickly people know too much about you too soon.

Many considerations are relevant to the appropriateness of sending personal information messages. Among these are the following.

• *Your goals.* Is revealing the information likely to help you or harm you in attaining your goals?

• *Sensitivity to the receiver.* You need to show respect and caring for the recipient of your disclosures at the same time as asserting your right to define yourself.

• *Amount.* How much personal information do you reveal?

• *Topic area.* In what area or areas do you reveal personal information? Taylor and Altman have suggested 13 broad topic areas: religion; one's own marriage and family; love, dating, and sex; one's parental family; physical condition and appearance; money and property; government, politics, current events, and social issues; emotions and feelings; interests, hobbies, and habits; relationships; attitude values, ethics, and self-evaluation; school and work; and biographical characteristics (Taylor & Altman, 1966).

• *Breadth.* In what range of topic areas do you reveal personal information?

• *Depth.* How intimate are your revelations?

• *Timing.* When do you reveal personal information in a relationship?

• *Body and voice messages.* How do you frame your disclosures of personal information by body and voice messages?

• *Positiveness/negativeness.* What items of personal information do you like and dislike about yourself?

• *Target person(s).* To what person or persons do you reveal yourself?

• *Social context.* On what occasions or in what social contexts, with their accompanying rules, do you reveal information?

Fears About Disclosure

Revealing personal information involves both risks and rewards. Some rewards have already been suggested. The risks, sometimes more imagined than real, include being rejected, being misunderstood, having your confidences made public, and disclosing too much too soon and having your disclosures used against you. You may also be afraid of the positive consequences of your disclosures: people may start liking you; you may be in the position of having to choose among girlfriends or boyfriends; or you may be entering your first intimate relationship, thinking, "Help! How do I handle this?"

What items of personal information do people consider most negative? Stanley Strong and I asked 150 British undergraduates to rate 120 items on a positive–negative scale (Nelson-Jones & Strong, 1977). The instructions were that the students consider the statements as being true of themselves and then rate them. The 12 most negatively rated items were the following.

"I hate myself."
"I have attempted suicide."
"I am violent."
"I have suicidal thoughts."
"I am a homosexual or lesbian."
"I am dull."
"I often hurt people I care about."
"I am erotically attracted by some men (for males) or women (for females)."
"I pity myself."
"I am a hypocrite."
"I am generally uninteresting."
"I have a fear of the opposite sex."

In general males and females evaluated these characteristics in much the same way. Of course, people's responses showed individual differences. Furthermore, people may rate a characteristic of their own very negatively without necessarily being inclined to come down so hard on others who disclose that characteristic to them.

The difference between what you think of your personal characteristics and how others react to your disclosures may be even more pronounced if you reveal what you like about yourself. When you reveal positive characteristics, you risk being viewed as self-promoting or boastful, and you may also threaten others. You run less of a risk if you intermingle negative with positive disclosures rather than consistently extolling your virtues. Many people, with some justification, have fears about revealing positive personal information as well as fears about revealing negative information.

Cultural and Sex-Role Considerations

Many broader contextual considerations influence how much and in what ways people reveal themselves. With about 50% of first marriages in the United States ending in divorce, people feel less inhibited talking about their own or their parents' divorces than they once did. Differences between cultures also influence disclosure. For example, British female undergraduate students have been found to disclose less than their U.S. counterparts (Jourard, 1971b). Differences between the sexes are also apparent, with women tending to be more revealing than men (Cozby, 1973; Jourard, 1971b). This tendency may result partly from dissimilar expectations regarding the appropriateness of male disclosure as opposed to female disclosure. The "strong, silent type" may be perceived as a more likable role for males, whereas females may be more favorably evaluated when they are expressive and revealing (Chelune, 1976). Loneliness resulting from skills weaknesses in revealing personal information appears to be more of a problem for males than for females. However, females may also feel lonely if and when males fail to reciprocate the intimacy of their disclosures. Again, it should be stressed that individual differences among both males and females may be significant. Generalizations based on sex must be treated cautiously.

Experiment 2
What happens when I reveal more personal information?

Part A: Assessment
1. Assess your skills strengths and weaknesses in revealing personal information.

_____

_____

_____

2. Think of either a personal or a school or work relationship that you think could be improved by your deepening the level of your disclosure to the extent you feel you can handle.

_____

3. Using the scale below, assess how threatening it would be for you in this relationship to reveal personal information in the areas listed.

4　　　　Impossible, much too threatening
3　　　　Very threatening
2　　　　Moderately threatening
1　　　　Slightly threatening
0　　　　Not threatening at all
N/A　　　Not applicable

Rating　　*Personal Information Areas*

_____　　　Positive thoughts/feelings about my parents

_____　　　Negative thoughts/feelings about my parents

_____　　　Positive thoughts/feelings about the other person

_____　　　Negative thoughts/feelings about the other person

_____　　　Problem areas in our relationship

_____　　　Feelings of loneliness

_____　　　Feelings of inadequacy

_____　　　Feelings of depression

_____　　　Failures in my work

_____　　　Successes in my work

_____　　　Work habits

_____　　　Successes in my personal relationships

_____　　　Failures in my personal relationships

_____　　　Things I like about my body

_____　　　Things I dislike about my body

_____　　　Leisure interests

_____　　　Feelings about death

_____　　　Religious beliefs

_____　　　Political preferences

_____　　　Past sexual experiences

Experiment 2 (continued)

Rating	*Personal Information Areas*
____	Sexual fantasies
____	Masturbatory behaviors
____	Homosexual tendencies
____	Intellectual ability
____	Musical preferences
____	Financial position
____	Times I have lied/cheated
____	Things that make me happy
____	Things that make me miserable
____	Things that make me angry
____	Things that make me afraid
____	My goals in life
____	My central values
____	How worthwhile I feel
____	The people I love
____	The people I hate
____	My peak experiences in life

Part B: Make an "If . . . then . . ." Statement

1. The "If" part of your statement states as specifically as possible the change or changes you wish to make in how much you reveal in this relationship—for instance, "If I reveal (a), (b), and (c) to . . .".

_____

_____

_____

2. The "then" part of the statement indicates the specific consequences you predict will follow from the changes in your behavior stated in the "If" part of the statement.

_____

_____

Part C: Try Out and Evaluate Your Changed Behavior

Try out your changed behavior. Assess its positive and negative consequences for yourself and others. Have your predictions been confirmed or disconfirmed? Has the experiment taught you something about how you can strengthen your skills of sending personal information messages? If so, what?

_____

_____

_____

_____

Expressing Your Feelings

> The finest people marry the two sexes in their own persons.
> *Ralph Waldo Emerson*

In Chapter 2 I emphasized the importance of emotional self-awareness—tuning in to yourself. All your feelings are OK; they are a fundamental part of your humanness. However, your degree of skill at sending messages about your feelings can help or hinder others in tuning in to you. Here the focus is on appropriate ways of sending feelings messages. Although much of the emphasis is on verbal messages, voice and body messages are so important when you express your feelings that they are included as well. Later chapters will discuss how you can regulate your feelings—for instance, shyness and anger—by regulating your thinking.

Expressing your feelings involves releasing and revealing to the outside world what is going on inside you. Thus expressing feelings involves a translation of your inner sensations into outer expressions. Sometimes the translation process is immediate—for instance, your startle reaction to a loud noise. On other occasions, expressing your feelings is less reflexive. It can involve conscious choices regarding both how you label feelings and also whether and how you reveal them.

Identifying and Labeling Your Feelings

Labeling your feelings involves putting your physical sensations into words. Feelings as such have no words. You supply the words to describe them. The feelings you experience are related to your interpretation of situations. For instance, Bob asks Lois for a date, and she politely but firmly refuses. Bob might have a range of possible feelings, including hurt, anger, humiliation, inferiority, anxiety, tension, relief, resolution, confidence, cheerfulness, and optimism. Each of these feelings involves an interpretation of Lois's refusal. For instance, Bob could choose to think "It's the worst thing that has ever happened to me"; or "That's her problem—how dare the stupid bitch turn me down!"; or "She's perfectly entitled to her opinion—I'm an OK guy, and I'll try someone else." The first choice may contribute to feelings of anxiety and depression, the second to anger, and the third to confidence.

If Bob were to think about his feelings or to try to describe them to a friend he would need to put them into words. Some slippage may occur between Bob's feelings and their verbal description. For instance, he may find it difficult to admit that he is hurt, finding it more comfortable to label his feeling as anger. He may have conflicting feelings that he does not fully admit. He may think about his feelings in black-and-white terms. Bob may acknowledge neither ambivalence nor nuances in the intensity of his feelings. Also, he may lack the vocabulary to identify and express his feelings adequately.

To send good feelings messages, it may be useful to build up a repertoire of words to describe and to catch the nuances of your own and others' feelings. Learning to become a skilled counselor or psychotherapist involves building up a repertoire of feelings words to help clients feel accurately understood. You need to become a good counselor to yourself and accurately identify and label your feelings. Table 3-1 lists some feelings words you may use; Exercise 11 helps you identify and label your feelings.

Table 3-1 List of feelings words

accepted	dependent	involved	supported
adventurous	depressed	irresponsible	suspicious
affectionate	discontented	jealous	tense
aggressive	embarrassed	joyful	tired
ambitious	energetic	lonely	trusting
angry	envious	loved	unambitious
anxious	excitable	loving	unappreciated
apathetic	fit	optimistic	unassertive
appreciated	free	outgoing	unattractive
assertive	friendly	pessimistic	underconfident
attractive	frightened	powerful	uneasy
bored	grieving	powerless	unfit
carefree	guilt-free	rejected	unfree
cautious	guilty	relaxed	unfriendly
cheerful	happy	resentful	unloved
competitive	humiliated	responsible	unsupported
confident	hurt	sad	unwanted
confused	indecisive	secure	uptight
contented	independent	shy	vulnerable
cooperative	inferior	stressed	wanted
daring	insecure	strong	weak
decisive	interested	superior	worried

Exercise 11
Identifying and labeling my feelings

Instructions: Complete the following sentences regarding your feelings in rela-
tionships. Focus on how you actually feel rather than on your thoughts about the
other person. Indicate the strength of your feelings. If you have conflicting feelings,
state what these are.

When someone ignores me I feel ———————————————————— .

When someone cries I feel ———————————————————— .

When someone praises me I feel ———————————————————— .

When someone talks about themselves all the time I feel ———————— .

When someone gets mad at me I feel ———————————————— .

When someone acts superior to me I feel ———————————————— .

When someone attracts me I feel ———————————————————— .

When someone breaks a confidence I feel ———————————————— .

When someone is very late for an appointment I feel ———————————— .

When I am in a group of strangers I feel ———————————————— .

When someone deeply understands me I feel ———————————————— .

How good are you at identifying and labeling your feelings in your relationships?

Feelings Difficult to Express

In revealing your feelings you may put yourself very much on the line. This is the
real you that you share, not just your social mask. Opening up can be scary.
Sometimes you may not like your own feelings; you may also be afraid of the
consequences to yourself and others of expressing your feelings. However, it is
risky *not* to share your feelings, too. You lose vitality if you continually sit on your
feelings. Others do not get to know you and you do not get to know yourself. Your
relationships may be full of unfinished business, which can act as a triple negative.
First, the unfinished business or conflict itself is not dealt with. Second, your upset
feelings may show themselves in other ways, in unhelpful activities such as
nit-picking, sarcasm, and gossip. Third, the fact that you have not worked through
your negative feelings may interfere with your willingness to express positive
feelings.

Some feelings are difficult for most people to express, especially when they do not feel safe with the other person.

- *Feelings of being worthless.* "If you really got to know me you would realize how empty and unlovable I am."
- *Feelings of incompetence.* "I'm dumb. No matter how hard I try I still end up at the bottom of the class."
- *Feelings of being unattractive.* "I'm a dull person and I don't like my looks. I wish I had another body."

Some feelings may be more difficult for women to express, although some men may have difficulty expressing them too.

- *Feelings of ambition.* "I badly want to get to the top in my field and enjoy the status and money that goes with it."
- *Feelings of leadership.* "I like power and having people working under me."
- *Feelings of assertion.* "I'm determined not to let myself get pushed around against my will."

Some feelings may be more difficult for men to express, although some women may have difficulty expressing them too.

- *Feelings of vulnerability.* "I wear a suit of armor, yet underneath I feel frightened a lot of the time and want nurturing."
- *Feelings of sensitivity.* "The ballet last night was so beautiful that I wanted to cry."
- *Feelings of love toward children.* "I love my kids, though I don't know how to show it."

Often both men and women have difficulty expressing positive feelings in their relationships.

- *Acknowledging strengths.* "I'm always picking on her and yet I think she's a great person."
- *Expressing love.* "I never seemed to get around to saying what was in my heart and telling him I loved him. Now it's too late."
- *Accepting compliments.* "I really appreciate your saying that."

Exercise 12 helps you explore which feelings are easy or difficult for you to express.

Exercise 12
Feelings I find easy and difficult to express

1. Take a piece of paper. At the top write "feelings I find easy and difficult to express." At the top of the left column write "easy," and at the top of the right column write "difficult."

2. In each column list the feelings you find easy and difficult to express. Table 3-1 may give you some ideas about the different feelings.

3. Do you detect any pattern in the feelings you have listed as either easy or difficult to express? If so, please specify the pattern.

_____

_____

_____

4. Do you think the feelings you find either difficult or easy to express have been influenced by your sex-role or cultural conditioning? If so, please specify in what ways.

_____

_____

_____

Sending Feelings Messages

In sending feelings messages, you integrate verbal, body, and voice messages and sometimes touch and action messages as well. Most of the considerations about the appropriateness of revealing personal information also apply to expressing your feelings. These considerations include your goals, sensitivity to the receiver, amount, breadth, depth, timing, target person, and social context. You may think taking so many considerations into account is likely to make you wooden and boring. However, you probably consider most of them already. Moreover, not expressing your feelings well may make it more difficult for you to express your feelings later; others may be less willing to listen to you, for one thing.

Exercise 13 is designed to increase your awareness that, in sending feelings messages, you are a chooser not only in what you say but in how you say it. For example, Louise's mother died recently, and she wants to communicate to her boyfriend Rob how sad she feels. Her composite feeling of sadness message might include the following elements.

• *Verbal messages.* Louise might use such words as "sad, low, miserable, unhappy, or depressed." Phrases she might use include "I feel really low," "I feel under a cloud," or "I've got the blues." Louise might also state the reasons for her sadness in an "I feel . . . because . . ." statement.

• *Voice messages.* Louise's voice messages might include sighing, speaking slowly, a monotonous delivery, and speaking quietly.

• *Body messages.* Louise's body messages might include a downturned mouth, tears, sniffling, slouched body posture, and moving closer to Rob for a hug.

Practice is important in learning to express your feelings. The more you hold back unnecessarily, the harder it may be for you to break this habit. Nobody's perfect. In expressing feelings, often a good try is more than adequate. Feelings are processes. You can only state how you have felt in the past or how you feel at the moment. You may feel differently in the future, just as a result of being able to state your feelings if for no other reason.

Exercise 13
Sending feelings messages

1. For each of the following feelings write down (a) verbal messages; (b) voice messages; and (c) body messages that you could use to express the feeling appropriately in your relationships.

   Love _____   Anger _____

   _____   _____

   Fear _____   Anxiety _____

   _____   _____

   Happiness _____   Boredom _____

   _____   _____

   Shame _____   Depression _____

   _____   _____

2. Look at the feelings you listed in Exercise 12 as difficult for you to express. For each of these feelings write down (a) verbal messages; (b) voice messages; and (c) body messages that you could use to express the feeling appropriately in your relationships.

   _____

   _____

Action Messages

Suit the action to the word, the word to the action.
William Shakespeare

Action speaks louder than words.
Anonymous

Woody Allen was once asked whether he had ever taken a serious political stand on anything. He replied, "Yes; for 24 hours I refused to eat grapes." Had he been serious, his actions would have spoken louder than his words. In today's slang, the messages you send through your actions are the bottom line. Discrepancies between your words and actions can seriously erode the trust that is the foundation of any serious loving relationship.

If you love someone, you try to act in loving ways toward them. You are concerned for their happiness and development. Your loving is a gift of yourself displayed through your words and actions. Even small loving actions can have much meaning for the recipient. Such actions might include writing a letter, a card, or a poem; giving a surprise gift; going out to a favorite restaurant; or more mundane actions such as not leaving your stockings or socks around and doing your share of the household chores. Some couples initiate and worsen their conflicts because they have stopped doing positive things for each other. Partners may also be poor at signaling what they like and picking up such messages from each other.

The importance of genuineness in your words and actions is pervasive. The following are a few illustrations of people's actions not matching their words.

> Simon, 46, is always telling Simon Jr., 16, that he wants him to be his own man; but the only college where the father is prepared to enroll his son is the one he himself attended.

> Leroy, 24, has told his boss, Debbie, that he is no longer prepared to work late at short notice. Debbie comes up to Leroy one hour before he is due to go home with a three-hour job that *must* be done that night. Leroy stays behind and does it.

> Andy, 46, is a college lecturer who has written a book on the importance of family life. He is married with two young children. Gradually it emerges that he has been having an affair with his 22-year-old secretary, Roberta.

> Cindy, 19, says she believes in equality between the sexes. However, when she goes out on a date, her boyfriends always end up paying.

Each of these vignettes was built around a major theme where actions can contradict words.

- *Nonpossessiveness vs. possessiveness.* You may talk of respect for the individuality of your loved ones and yet act in controlling ways toward them.
- *Assertion vs. lack of assertion.* Assertion entails backing up your words with your actions when appropriate.
- *Trust vs. mistrust.* Trust entails keeping your formal and informal contracts or else openly attempting to renegotiate them.
- *Equality between the sexes.* Equality means that *both* sexes have to give up some of their traditional privileges.

Promises, promises. A good definition of a *phony* is "one whose action messages fall far short of his or her verbal, voice, and body messages." The importance of sending good action messages in initiating, developing, and maintaining stable relationships cannot be overemphasized.

This book is about the technology of relationships. I have tried to be a human engineer and show you the component parts of the process of sending information. You cannot *not* send messages. My hope is that by spelling out the body, touch, voice, verbal, and action components of sending information, this book as it proceeds will put you in a stronger position to gain more control over your relationship skills.

Concluding Self-Talk

I am always sending information about myself to others. These messages can be broken down into five main categories: body, touch, voice, verbal, and action messages. The messages I send are influenced by many considerations, including my goals, my skills strengths and weaknesses, social rules, and my upbringing, including my sex-role and cultural conditioning. I can choose to develop my relationship skills by disclosing myself more effectively. This means improving my skills within each of the five categories of messages. It also means improving my skills in matching my words with my actions and matching my body, touch, and voice messages with my words.

Notes

4
Being a Rewarding Listener

The reason we have two ears and only one mouth is
that we may listen the more and talk the less.
Zeno of Citium

A riot is at bottom of the language of the unheard.
Martin Luther King, Jr.

The next two chapters focus on the skills of being a rewarding listener. Listening is one of the most powerful psychological rewards you can give. But how many people do you have in your life with whom you feel you can be very open and share the secrets of your heart? The answer for some of you will be none. Probably most of you don't associate with as many highly rewarding listeners as you would like. Various unrewarding behaviors that masquerade as listening are widespread. Not being listened to can serve as a form of psychological punishment. Occasionally not being listened to may act as mild psychological punishment; often not being listened to, as moderate punishment; and mostly not being listened to, as severe punishment. Never being listened to is like a psychological death penalty.

How rewarding a listener are you? To what extent do you inflict varying degrees of psychological pain and punishment on others? A common illusion is that whereas others frequently listen poorly, one's own listening is good, a simple matter of "doing what comes naturally." For those not born deaf the capacity to hear sounds is natural; but the skills involved in listening—understanding and decoding the meanings of sounds—must be learned. Furthermore, rewarding listening also involves observation; thus the skills of decoding body messages should be learned as well.

Why Is Listening Such a Fundamental Skill?

Reasons that being a rewarding listener is a fundamental relationship skill include the following.

• *Affirming another.* Rewarding listening affirms; unrewarding listening disconfirms. When children grow up, the quality of listening they experience from the adults around them is almost as vital for their psychological development as food is for their physical development. Children who have been listened to sensitively are likely not only to be accepted by others but to accept themselves as well. Their sense of worth is intact. Furthermore, such children have had the safety to express and explore their feelings. Thus they have been helped to acquire the capacity for inner listening—listening to and trusting their own feelings and reactions—which is an essential part of outer listening—listening to others. In addition, having at least one parent who listens well provides children with a secure base from which to engage in exploratory behavior and make personal experiments. Children who have not been adequately listened to are likely to be more out of touch with their feelings, insecure, anxious, angry, and aggressive.

Getting the picture

Even if unintentional, unrewarding listening perpetrated on a regular basis constitutes a significant form of psychological violence. Disconfirmation of the core of one's being on a daily basis because of others' unrewarding listening is the stuff out of which severe mental illness is made. In adult life, listening can also affirm or disconfirm. Perhaps the most frequent complaint in distressed relationships is that partners no longer listen.

• *Knowing another.* Rewarding listening allows another to feel safe and to strip away the social masks he or she wears for protection. As a rewarding listener, you no longer need to make so many assumptions about what the other thinks and feels since he or she tells you. Loving other people involves knowing them in their separateness and prizing it. Your listening skills help you to know others on their terms. In doing so, you transcend your egocentricity. Listening allows for greater comparison: no one can know the weight of another's burden unless told by its bearer.

• *Knowing yourself.* Listening effectively to others provides you with valuable information about yourself. Although you may not always like what you hear, remaining open to others gives you the opportunity to use their feedback to grow. Defensiveness, or tuning out to information that does not fit your picture of yourself, is a major source of corrosion in relationships. Defensiveness is highly unrewarding to the sender; instead of facilitating an open communication system in which you and your partner feel free to share what you think and feel, defensiveness tends to develop a closed communication system. In a closed system, you and your partner tiptoe around one another's fragile egos at the expense of honesty. Each partner knows what triggers the others' unrewarding listening behaviors and may find it easier to avoid painful confrontations. As a further result, partners become progressively alienated from themselves because they lack the courage to be rewarding listeners in the face of difficult feedback.

• *Building trust and stability in a relationship.* Perhaps the major finding from research into self-disclosure is that intimacy levels of disclosures tend to be matched (Cozby, 1973). Your gradually telling me your secrets and my gradually telling you mine is a process that depends on both of us being willing to listen to the other as well as to disclose. Trust is built as much from acceptance of our disclosures as from our willingness to disclose.

Rewarding listening also builds trust and stability in relationships by helping partners prevent and manage problems. If partners are able to say what they think and feel, misunderstandings are less likely to occur based on misperceptions of the other's position. Additionally, if partners listen to one another when conflicts occur, they stand a much better chance of resolving their difficulties to their mutual satisfaction.

• *Bridging age, sex, and cultural differences.* Every person has a potential set of blinkers depending on their life circumstances. How can you know what it is like to be old; dying; female; male; White, Black, Asian, Indian, or Hispanic American; or English or French Canadian, if the description does not fit you? If you relate to people with different sets of life circumstances, they can greatly assist you in understanding them if you reward them by listening well. Similarly, if they are rewarding listeners for you, together you build bridges, not walls.

Rewarding Listening: A Nine-Skills Approach

The remainder of this chapter and most of the next describes nine key skills of being a rewarding listener. Some of the skills overlap; they are not presented in any particular order of importance.

Skills of Rewarding Listening

Skill 1.   Knowing the difference between me and you.
Skill 2.   Possessing an attitude of respect and acceptance.
Skill 3.   Sending good body messages.
Skill 4.   Sending good voice messages.
Skill 5.   Using openers, small rewards, and open-ended questions.
Skill 6.   Rewording.
Skill 7.   Reflecting feelings.
Skill 8.   Reflecting feelings and reasons.
Skill 9.   Avoiding unrewarding "don'ts."

Skill 1: Knowing the Difference Between Me and You

> Don't judge any person until you have walked
> two moons in their moccasins.
> *American Indian Proverb*

If you want the people to whom you relate to feel that you receive them loud and clear, you need to be able to "get inside their skins" and "see the world through their eyes." At the heart of rewarding listening is a basic distinction between "you" and "me," between "your view of you" and "my view of you," and between "your view of me" and "my view of me." Your view of you and my view of me are both inside or internal viewpoints, whereas your view of me and my view of you are both outside or external viewpoints. The skill of listening to and understanding another person is based on your choosing to acknowledge the separateness between "me" and "you" by getting into the other's internal viewpoint rather than remaining in your own external viewpoint.

If I respond to what you say in a way that shows an accurate understanding of your viewpoint, I am responding as if I am inside your internal viewpoint. If, however, I choose not to show an understanding of your viewpoint or lack the skills to understand it, I am responding from my external viewpoint. In short, if I respond to you as if I am inside your internal viewpoint, I respond to you from where you are. If I step outside your internal viewpoint, I respond in an external way that reflects more where I am or think you should be than where you are.

The following are some examples of responses by a listener from an external viewpoint.

"I'm interested in what's going right for you, not what's going wrong."
"You should always respect your parents."
"My advice to you is to drop him."
"*You* have troubles. Let me tell you *mine*."

Responding as if in the other's internal viewpoint involves you in understanding talkers on their terms. Such understanding requires careful listening and allowing talkers the psychological space to tell their own story. Furthermore, understanding entails decoding talkers' messages, especially if the messages aren't clearly sent. Decoding deals with voice and body as well as verbal messages. The following are examples of internal viewpoint responses by a listener.

"You feel that the last months have been terrible for you."
"You have mixed feelings about getting married."
"You found the thought of unemployment scary."
"You're thrilled that she finally told you she loved you."

Exercise 14 asks you to identify whether the listener has responded as if from the talker's internal viewpoint. Some of the responses may seem a little artificial: they were devised to make the point of the exercise clear. Answers for the exercise are provided at the end of the chapter.

Exercise 14
Understanding another's internal viewpoint

Instructions: This exercise consists of a number of statement–response excerpts from different relationships. Three responses have been provided for each statement. Write "IN" or "EX" by each response according to whether it seems as if it is inside the speaker's internal viewpoint or from an external viewpoint.

Example
Husband to wife.
Husband: "I'm worried about the kids. They always seem to be out late these days and I'm beginning to feel that I scarcely know them."
Wife:

EX   (a) "If you took a bit more interest you would know them better."

IN   (b) "You're concerned that you're becoming distant from the kids because you see so little of them."

EX   (c) "You're a good dad and deserve better than this."

1. *Girlfriend to boyfriend.*
   Girlfriend: "I think your mother's great. I hope I can be as energetic as she is when I'm her age."

Exercise 14 (continued)

Boyfriend:

_____ (a) "Mom likes you too."
_____ (b) "Wait until you get to know her better."
_____ (c) "You think my mother is terrific, and you admire her vitality."

2. *Student to teacher.*
   Student: "I'm finding the work load very heavy. I'm depressed at missing out on so much socially."

   Teacher:

   _____ (a) "You feel down because it's all work and no play."
   _____ (b) "All students have to work hard to pass these exams."
   _____ (c) "Life isn't much fun for the staff here either."

3. *Child to parent.*
   Child (crying): "Eric just beat me up. He's a big bully. I hate him."

   Parent:

   _____ (a) "You poor kid."
   _____ (b) "Big boys don't cry."
   _____ (c) "You hate that nasty Eric."

4. *Friend to friend.*
   Friend A: "Let's go to the beach this weekend and see if we can meet some neat guys."

   Friend B:

   _____ (a) "You would like me to go to the beach with you this weekend to try to meet some great guys."
   _____ (b) "I've got other plans for this weekend."
   _____ (c) "The beach is no place to meet guys."

Skill 2: Possessing an Attitude of Respect and Acceptance

It is one thing to know the difference between listening from the internal and external viewpoints intellectually and quite another thing to implement listening from the other's internal viewpoint in practice. Even professional counselors and psychotherapists, who are trained to respect their clients' right to make their own choices, can become external when they mean to be internal. Being internal is much more difficult in personal relationships where you are not protected by the rules and limited contact of psychotherapy. Your degree of self-love is integral to your capacity to accept another. Self-love entails respecting and accepting yourself as a worthwhile even though fallible human being. Having a basic attitude of acceptance of yourself as a person means that you can still endeavor to change those of your specific behaviors that do not work for you. Accepting yourself does not mean you have to accept those behaviors, too.

The extent to which you are able to respect and accept yourself is reflected in the level of acceptance and respect and hence the quality of listening you are able to offer another. Table 4-1 depicts the relationship between your level of self-acceptance and how much you can accept others on their terms. The table is a simplification because in close personal relationships, when you and your partner are angry or in conflict your own level of security and acceptance will be put to the test. Unless you discipline yourself, good listening can be the first casualty of a conflict. Consequently, self-acceptance should be extended to mean accepting yourself enough to control your temper and stay tuned in to your partner when the going gets rough.

Barriers to an Accepting Attitude

An accepting attitude involves respecting others as separate and unique human beings with rights to their own thoughts and feelings, independent of yours. You need not agree with everything they say; but when you have an accepting attitude you are secure enough in yourself to respect what others say as their versions of reality. You do not need to use barriers and filters to protect you from hearing the full range of their messages.

Barriers to an accepting attitude manifest themselves both internally and externally. They manifest themselves internally in that you operate on, distort, and filter out certain elements of the messages you receive. At worst you may deny or block

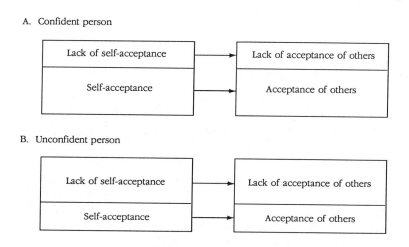

Table 4-1 Relationship between level of self-acceptance and ability to accept others

out the whole of an incoming message. Barriers manifest themselves externally in subtle and not so subtle voice and body cues to others, indicating to them that they should edit what they say. Barriers also manifest themselves in the more obvious verbal "don'ts" of being a rewarding listener, listed in Chapter 5.

The main barriers and filters that interfere with your receiving another loud and clear all are related to your sense of worth and to how much debilitating anxiety you possess. The stronger you are emotionally, the less need you have to use barriers and filters, so the more open you are to others. Barriers to an accepting attitude include the following.

• *Strong feelings.* Experiencing strong positive or negative feelings can interfere with your listening. Earlier we discussed how hard it can be to stay open to another when either of you is angry and in conflict. Strong positive feelings can also contribute to your not adequately hearing another.

> Anita, 18, thought that Marco, 19, was the most terrific boy she had ever met. Marco liked Anita, but still wanted to go out with other girls. He first tried hinting to her that he did not want to spend all his free time with her and she did not get the message. Marco now thinks he is going to have to be much more direct with her.

• *Trigger words and phrases.* Trigger words and phrases, which raise a "red flag" for you, are words that you find emotionally charged when used by others. Most trigger words and phrases derive their emotional impact from both their context and the tone of voice in which they are said, which are perceived as put-downs. Each individual has his or her own triggers. Many of these are "you" messages—for example, "You're weak," "You screwed it up," "You're a failure," and "Can't you do anything right?" Adjectives like "thoughtless," "clumsy," and "effeminate" can also act as trigger words. Being talked down to can trigger negative emotional reactions—for example, "You should really follow my advice" or "You do as you're told."

> Dan and his dad are not close on the surface, but they have a lot of feeling for each other underneath. Dan finds himself tuning out to his dad every time he uses phrases like "When I was your age" and "Be a man."

Positive words and phrases can also trigger feelings that interfere with your listening. For example, flattery ("Gee, you're wonderful Ms. Murgatroyd . . . I really admire you") may contribute to your not hearing other, less flattering feedback.

• *Unfinished business.* Unfinished business can interfere with your being open to another. For instance, if you have just had an argument with your auto mechanic you may be less ready to listen to your children who want to discuss their day at school. In addition, if you still have strong unresolved feelings about something that has occurred earlier in a relationship, you may listen less well to current information until the earlier issue has been processed.

• *Anxiety-evoking topics.* For reasons connected with your upbringing, certain topic areas may be anxiety-evoking. You may not like discussing them at all, or you may get defensive when others present positions that differ from yours.

A sensitive topic for Liz is her religion. She feels that her Roman Catholic faith gives her a good framework for living. She gets very upset when her faith is challenged and responds defensively.

Ken, 19, was brought up in a home where sex was not openly discussed. He gets very nervous at some of the locker room talk he hears where people tell dirty jokes and boast about their sexual conquests.

• *Prejudices.* Again for reasons connected with your upbringing, you may tune out to people different from you because of their age, sex, sexual preference, culture, race, social class, physical disability, or intelligence level, among other possible differences. Here are a couple of examples.

Homosexuality is a sensitive topic for Herb. He constantly draws attention to homosexual tendencies in others. However, it is impossible to hold a rational discussion with him about gay rights. He simply does not want to listen.

Trudy, 26, dislikes elderly people. She does not seem to realize that they were young once, too, and that they have thoughts and feelings that merit respect. She treats elderly people coldly and maintains her distance from them.

• *Anxiety-evoking people.* You may feel anxious with specific people or categories of people and hence not listen to them well. These people may include your parents, your relatives, friends of the same or the opposite sex, strangers, and authority figures.

Sally, a 35-year-old nurse, has a poor relationship with her boss Cassie. Sally says Cassie makes her nervous. As a consequence, Sally does not follow Cassie's instructions well. Sally then becomes even more nervous when Cassie criticizes her for not paying attention.

• *Anxiety-evoking situations.* Anxiety and threat are present to a greater or lesser degree in all situations. The following are some common situations where people may feel vulnerable, and so their own agendas may preclude their fully listening to others.

Going on your first date with a different person.
Going to a party where you do not know anyone.
Meeting for the first time your girlfriend's or boyfriend's parents.
Having to answer questions after giving a speech in public.
Going for a job interview.
Being teased on a sensitive topic.
Making love for the first time.

Many of these illustrations involve coping with new situations. However, even when you have been for a number of job interviews or fielded questions after a number of talks, you may still experience some debilitating anxiety that interferes with your listening.

• *Bringing the past into the present.* Sometimes you may inappropriately transfer reactions and feelings from your past into your present. These may be either positive or negative feelings. Here are two examples.

> Nancy and Brad are a couple in their early 30s. Nancy knows she reminds Brad of his mother. Sometimes she thinks he has difficulty acknowledging how different she is from his mother.

> Arthur, a single 42-year-old, moved into the house next to Helen, a widow in her early 60s. Helen had had a disastrous relationship with her previous neighbor, another bachelor. Her first remark to Arthur was: "People around here are going to take a long time getting used to you."

• *Information different from your self-picture.* You may find it hard to keep an accepting attitude when the information you receive differs from your picture of yourself. People vary in their thresholds of openness to such information. They may deny or distort positive as well as negative information.

> Rachel tells Bruce she finds him good-looking. Bruce looks shy and says "Oh, not really."

> Janet is a career-minded schoolteacher who prides herself on her professional approach. One day she gets feedback from her students that they find her approach dull and prefer another teacher. Janet gets angry and thinks that her students do not appreciate all the work she puts into her lessons.

• *Physical barriers.* Physical considerations may contribute to your being less accepting of others than you might be. For instance, fatigue, illness, the discomfort of being too hot or too cold, and external noise may all affect how well you listen. The stresses of your life may contribute to your being depressed, irritable, and tense. None of these feelings are conducive to your being open and accepting of another person.

So far, we have discussed ten barriers and filters to your adopting an attitude of respect and acceptance for the speaker when you listen. This list is far from exhaustive. Exercise 15 asks you to explore barriers and filters that may prevent you from being an accepting listener.

Exercise 15
Assessing my barriers to an accepting attitude when I listen

Instructions: Assess yourself in terms of how much each of the following internal barriers interferes with your possessing an accepting attitude when you listen.

Internal Barrier	*My Assessment*
Strong feelings	

Internal Barrier	*My Assessment*
Trigger words and phrases	
Unfinished business	
Anxiety-evoking topics	
Prejudices	
Anxiety-evoking people	
Anxiety-evoking situations	
Bringing the past into the present	
Information different from my self-picture	
Physical barriers	
Other(s)	

Summarize the extent to which you see yourself possessing an accepting attitude when you listen to (1) your spouse/partner/girlfriend/boyfriend; and (2) your friends.

_____

_____

_____

Skill 3: Sending Good Body Messages

To be a rewarding listener, you need to convey your attention and interest. Conveying attention and interest is sometimes referred to in the counseling literature as attending behavior (Ivey, 1971). Many aspects of training counselors in this skill are relevant to everyday interaction. However, especially once you get to know each other, you can be much more flexible in your relationships; too much formality is counterproductive. Some of the main messages by which you can show your attention and interest are as follows.

• *Physical availability.* People who are always off to the next event in their busy lives choose not to find time to listen adequately to the people they relate to. Close relationships require an investment of quality time. If this quality time is not forthcoming, sooner rather than later either or both parties are likely to feel they are not being adequately heard. If you are rarely or never available to listen, you have withdrawn much of your interest and attention from the other person.

• *Open and relaxed body posture.* Physical openness means facing the speaker not only with your face but with your body. You need to be sufficiently turned toward the other person so that you can receive all their significant facial and body messages. A relaxed body posture—provided you do not sprawl—conveys the message that you are emotionally accessible. If you do sit in a tense and uptight fashion, the listener may consciously or intuitively feel that you are too bound up with your personal agendas and unfinished business to be fully accessible to him or her.

• *Slight forward lean.* Whether you lean forward, backward, or sideways is another aspect of body posture. If you lean too far forward you look odd, and others may consider that you are invading their personal space. If you lean too far back, others may find this distancing. A slight forward lean to the torso can both encourage the talker and avoid threat, especially at the beginning of a relationship.

• *Positive use of gestures.* The head nod is perhaps the most common gesture in listening. Each head nod can be viewed as a reward to the talker, signifying your attention. Head nods need not mean that you agree with everything a talker says. On the negative side, selective head nodding can also be a powerful way of controlling a speaker and not showing an accepting attitude. Unconditional acceptance is thus turned into conditional acceptance. Arm and hand gestures can also be used to show your responsiveness to the speaker. However, listeners who gesture too little or too much with their hands and arms can be discouraging. Other negative gestures include tightly crossing the arms and legs as barriers, clenching your hands together, drumming fingers, fiddling with your hair, keeping your hand over your mouth, tugging an ear, and scratching yourself—to mention but some.

• *Good use of gaze and eye contact.* Good eye contact means looking in the other's direction so that you allow the possibility of your eyes meeting reasonably often. Any relationship has an equilibrium level for eye contact, depending on cultural and social rules, the degree of anxiety in each partner, the nature and state of development of the relationship, and the degree of attraction involved. Staring at another is threatening. Looking down or away too often may indicate that you are tense or uninterested. Good gaze behavior shows your interest and also enables you to see important facial messages. In addition, gaze can give you cues about when to stop listening and start responding. However, the main cues used in synchronizing conversations are verbal and voice messages rather than body messages (Argyle, 1983).

• *Appropriate facial expressions.* A friendly, relaxed facial expression, including a smile, initially demonstrates interest. However, as the other talks, your facial expressions need to show that you are tuned in to what the person speaking is saying. For instance, if another is serious, weeping, or angry, you need to adjust your facial expression to indicate that you observe and hear what he or she is communicating.

• *Sensitivity to physical distance and height.* Chapter 3 mentioned the various zones of intimacy for different kinds of conversations. Rewarding listening entails respecting these zones. If you move too quickly into others' personal space, they may feel uncomfortable and move away. On the other hand, if you are physically too far away, not only do others have to talk louder but they may perceive you as emotionally distant. Turning to height, the most comfortable height for conversations is with heads at the same level. Persisting in standing when a seated person talks to you is likely to make that person feel awkward. Listeners who sit in higher or lower chairs than speakers may also seem off-putting.

• *Appropriate use of touch.* When people are dating, they may use high levels of touch as they listen to and get to know one another. Their body contact as they listen and talk may include holding hands, a half-embrace, and sitting close so that their legs touch. In many relationships, touch can be an effective way of showing concern for someone who is hurting and in pain. Demonstrations of concern include touching another's hands, arms, shoulders, and upper back. The intensity and duration of touch should be sufficient to establish contact and yet avoid creating discomfort. Part of being a rewarding listener includes picking up messages about the limits and desirability of your use of touch.

Congruence, both *within* your body messages and also *between* your body messages and your voice and verbal messages, increases the chances of your being perceived as a rewarding listener. For instance, you may be smiling and at the same time fidgeting or tapping your foot. Your smile indicates interest and your foot tapping shows impatience; your overall message may thus be one of insincerity.

The damaging effects of poor listener body messages were highlighted in a study by Haase and Tepper (1972). They asked counselors to rate a number of ten-second videotaped interactions between a "counselor" and a "client." They found that even good verbal understanding messages could become poor messages when the counselor uttered the message without eye contact, in a backward trunk lean, rotated away from the client, and from a far distance. In short, sending good body messages is a crucial part of the skill of being a rewarding listener. Exercise 16 asks you to explore your behavior in this regard. Experiment 3 helps you discover the effects of varying your body messages when you listen.

Exercise 16
How rewarding are my body messages when I listen?

Instructions: Assess how rewarding you consider your body messages are when you listen by completing the following worksheet.

Body Message	My Assessment
Physical availability	
Open and relaxed body posture	
Slight forward lean	
Positive use of gestures	
Good use of gaze and eye contact	
Appropriate facial expressions	

Exercise 16 (continued)

Body Message	My Assessment
Sensitivity to physical distance and height	
Appropriate use of touch	
Congruence within my body messages	

1. Summarize how rewarding or unrewarding you consider your body messages when you listen.

    _____

    _____

2. Identify specific skills weaknesses in your body messages as you listen and set goals for change.

    _____

    _____

Experiment 3
What happens when I vary my body messages as a listener?

Part A: Assessment
Completed in Exercise 16.

Part B: Make an "If . . . then . . ." Statement
Design an experiment in which you systematically try to improve one or more of your body message skills weaknesses when you listen. Make an "If . . . then . . ." statement along the lines of "If I change (a), (b), and/or (c) when I listen in my relationship with John or Jane Doe, then these consequences (to be specified) are likely to follow."

_____

_____

_____

Part C: Try Out and Evaluate Your Changed Behavior
Try out your changed behavior. Assess its positive and negative consequences for yourself and others. Have your predictions been confirmed or disconfirmed? Has the experiment taught you something about how you can strengthen your skills of sending better body messages when you listen? If so, what?

_____

_____

Informal Experiment

Another option is to play a game with a friend in which you hold a conversation on a topic of mutual interest.

First two minutes: You converse normally.

Second two minutes: You try to send good body messages when listening as your friend talks.

Third two minutes: You try to send poor body messages when listening as your friend talks.

Evaluation period: Discuss what it felt like receiving and sending poor body messages. Your evaluation session may be more educational and fun if you play back a videotape of your six-minute conversation. Then reverse roles and repeat the second and third parts of the experiment.

Skill 4: Sending Good Voice Messages

Your voice messages can greatly enhance the emotional atmosphere you provide when you listen. Talkers need to feel you are responsive to their feelings. One of the main ways you can make talkers feel you are responsive is by sending voice messages that neither add nor subtract emotional meaning and emphasis.

The following discusses the voice messages mentioned in Chapter 2 in terms of being a listener who responds appropriately.

- *Volume.* You need to respond at a level that is comfortable and easy to hear.
- *Pace.* You can create a more relaxed atmosphere if you do not talk too fast when you respond and in general avoid interrupting.
- *Emphasis.* It is important that your voice is expressive in accurately picking up the major feelings and feeling nuances of speakers.
- *Tone.* High-pitched and shrill voices can disconcert. A harsh tone can threaten.
- *Enunciation.* Poor enunciation can interrupt the speaker's train of thought.
- *Accent.* Heavy accents can be very difficult to listen to, especially if accompanied by poor use of grammar and language. Thus accents also may interfere with the speaker's train of thought.
- *Firmness.* Speaking in a weak and diffident voice may indicate that you have problems and deter the speaker. Too much firmness overwhelms.
- *Use of pauses and silences.* Your use of pauses and silences can enhance your capacity to be a rewarding listener. If you want to make it easier for speakers to tell their stories, you can pause each time they cease speaking before saying anything, to see if they wish to continue. Good use of silences can also allow speakers more psychological space to think things through before speaking and to get in touch with their deeper feelings.

Exercise 17 helps you assess your voice messages when you are responding as a listener.

Exercise 17
How rewarding are my voice messages when I listen?

Instructions: Assess how rewarding you consider your voice messages are when you listen by completing the following worksheet.

Voice Message	My Assessment
Volume	
Pace	
Emphasis	
Tone	
Enunciation	
Accent	
Firmness	
Uses of pauses and silences	

1. Summarize how rewarding or unrewarding you consider your voice messages are when you listen.

_____

2. Identify specific skills weaknesses in your voice messages as you listen and set goals for change.

_____

Skill 5: Using Openers, Small Rewards, and Open-Ended Questions

Openers, small rewards, and open-ended questions all require the use of a few words as well as of good voice and body messages. They make it easier for the speaker to talk.

Openers

An opener, or permission to talk, is a brief statement indicating that you are prepared to listen. Openers can be used any time in a relationship. The message contained in all of them is "I'm interested and prepared to listen. I'm giving you the opportunity of sharing with me what you think and feel." A good time to use an opener can be when you sense something is bothering another and he or she needs a little encouragement to share it. Such an opener may be a response to another's body messages. Here are some examples of openers.

"How was your day?"
"You seem a bit down today."
"You look really happy."
"Is there something on your mind?"
"Would you like to talk about it?"
"I'd like to hear your viewpoint."

When using openers, you must be sensitive to others' reactions. They may not be ready to talk or may feel you're not the right person to talk to. They probably do not want information dragged out of them. However, sometimes you rightly sense that others want to talk but are having difficulty doing so. In such situations follow-up remarks—for instance, "It's pretty hard to get started," or "Take your time"—may further help the speaker open up. Poor body messages can totally destroy the impact of an opener. For example, if a father looks up, says "What's on your mind, son?" and then looks down and continues working on his car, his son is likely to feel discouraged rather than encouraged about opening up.

Small Rewards

Small rewards are brief verbal expressions of interest designed to encourage the speaker. The message they convey is "I'm with you. Please go on." Small rewards can be used for good or ill. On the one hand they can reward people for talking to you from their internal viewpoint. On the other hand, rewards may range from subtle to crude attempts to take others out of their internal viewpoint by shaping what they say. For instance, you may say "Tell me more" whenever someone says something you want to hear and remain silent when they do not. The following are some examples of verbal small rewards, though perhaps the most frequently used, "Um-hmm," is more vocal than verbal.

"Um-hmm."	"Sure."
"Please continue."	"Indeed."
"Tell me more."	"And . . ."
"Go on."	"So . . ."
"I see."	"Really?"
"Oh?"	"Right."
"Interesting."	"Ah . . ."
"Then . . ."	"Yes."
"I hear you."	"You're not kidding."

Open-Ended Questions

You may use questions in ways that either help speakers to elaborate their internal viewpoints or lead them out of their viewpoints, possibly into yours. Open questions allow speakers to share their internal viewpoints without curtailing their options. Closed questions restrict another's options for responding. Closed questions often give only two options, yes or no. An example of an open question is "How do you feel about Alison?" A closed question might be "Do you like Alison?"

Closed questions may have various negative outcomes. You may be perceived as leading and controlling the conversation. You may block another from getting in touch with and listening to themselves and thus responding from their internal viewpoint rather than to your external viewpoint. You may set the stage for an interrogation. Since closed questions can be disincentives to talking, they can create silences in which the stage is set for further closed questions. I do not mean to imply that you never use closed questions. It depends on the goals of your listening. Closed questions are useful if you wish to collect information. However, they may be dangerous if you wish to allow another to let you inside their internal viewpoint. Even open questions should be used sparingly.

Concluding Self-Talk

Rewarding listening is a fundamental relationship skill. If I listen well I affirm others, know them and myself better, build trust and stability in my relationships, and help bridge age, sex, and cultural differences. I can improve my skills of being a rewarding listener. I can become more conscious of when I am listening from my external viewpoint rather than from the speaker's internal viewpoint. I can work on my barriers and filters to possessing an attitude of respect and acceptance when I listen. I can discipline myself to send body and voice messages that encourage rather than discourage speakers. In addition, by using openers, I can make it easier for people to start opening up to me. Furthermore, by using small rewards and open questions, I can help them to keep sharing their internal viewpoint.

Answers to Exercise

Exercise 14

1. (a) EX   (b) EX   (c) IN
2. (a) IN   (b) EX   (c) EX
3. (a) EX   (b) EX   (c) IN
4. (a) IN   (b) EX   (c) EX

Notes

5
Responding Helpfully

No one would talk much in society if he
only knew how often he misunderstands others.
J. W. von Goethe

I only desire sincere relations with the worthiest of my
acquaintances, that they may give me the opportunity
once in a year to speak the truth.
Henry Thoreau

Rewarding listening requires you to be able to respond helpfully. You need to provide the gift of your listening so that another genuinely feels that you have understood them. Reaching out to others includes sensitively receiving and understanding their messages as well as sending your own messages. Furthermore, you have to communicate your understanding back to them so that they know you have received them loud and clear.

Lucy, 17, had a boyfriend Jesse, also 17. About a year ago Lucy's parents separated. This separation had numerous practical and emotional conse-quences for her. Whenever she tried to speak to Jesse about her pain she felt that he did not understand her. Furthermore, she wondered if Jesse even wanted to hear about it since his family life had been very happy.

Marge and Tom are a couple in their forties. Tom manages a small company of which Marge is the co-owner. Over the past months Tom has developed a relationship with Maria, the production manager of the company. This extramarital relationship has had a devastating effect on his relationship with Marge. Moreover, when Marge points out that such goings-on are not good for company morale, she feels Tom tunes her out and cannot face the negative consequences of his actions.

In each of these instances, separateness and alienation are encouraged by poor listening skills. Jesse remained unaware that he was not hearing Lucy loud and clear. Tom's own needs and defenses got in the way of his fully hearing Marge's feedback. Stories such as these are commonplace inside and outside family relationships. Getting on top of the inner enemy of your own anxiety and responding to another with accurate understanding and kindness can require considerable discipline. It is a form of love in which you may have to be tough with yourself.

The first part of this chapter continues the discussion of the skills of rewarding listening, which help you try to make it easier for another to share their internal viewpoint. The latter part of the chapter looks at confrontation, a responding skill that involves stepping out of the speaker's internal viewpoint.

Reflective Responding

In this book the term *reflective responding* is shorthand for "responding with understanding as if in the speaker's internal viewpoint." Reflective responding entails tuning in to and "mirroring," with your verbal, voice, and body messages,

Mending a broken heart

the crux of the meaning contained in the verbal, voice, and body messages of another. Before discussing the skill in more detail, here are a couple of examples.

Patient to friend

Patient: "When I first heard I had got terminal cancer, my world fell apart. I'm still pretty shaken and frightened at the thought of death."

Friend: "You feel scared about dying and are still reeling from the news of your cancer."

Wife to husband

Wife: "With the children nearing the end of their education I want to build more of a life for myself. I don't want to hang around the house all the time. I want to get out and be active."

Husband: "You're determined to carve something outside the home for yourself and not keep brooding over an empty nest."

When assessing how good a reflective response is, it is sometimes helpful to think of a three-link chain: first statement–reflective response–second statement. Good reflective responses allow the opportunity for another's second statement to be a continuation of the train of thought contained in his or her first statement; bad reflective responses do not.

Uses of Reflective Responding

When people are first introduced to the skill of reflective responding they frequently express reservations.

"It's so unnatural."
"People will just think I'm repeating everything they say."
"It gets in the way of my being spontaneous."
"It makes me too self-conscious."

When learning any new skill, from driving a car to driving a golf ball, for some period of time you are likely to have to concentrate extra hard on making the correct sequence of choices that constitute the skill. Reflective responding is no exception. If you work and practice at a skill, you ultimately are likely to own it, as a "natural" part of you. A skill is natural to the extent that it feels natural. One of the main reasons reflective responding seems so unnatural at first is that unhelpful ways of responding, such as judging, are firmly installed in many people's relationship skills. Thus you may need not only to learn a new skills strength but also to unlearn a current skills weakness.

Reflective responding should not be something you use all the time; instead it should be flexibly incorporated into your repertoire of responses. Reflective responding may help you on many occasions.

- When you need to show that you have understood.
- When you need to check out that you have understood.
- When others need to experience their feelings as valid.

- When others struggle to understand themselves.
- When others need help in expressing thoughts and feelings.
- When others are trying to manage personal problems or make decisions.
- When you need to be clear about another's position in a disagreement.
- When you wish to ensure that the responsibility for a decision or course of action in another's life rests with that person.
- When you wish to maintain and enhance your relationship by setting aside a regular time for listening to each other.

However, on other occasions you may benefit from not using reflective responding or using it only sparingly.

- When you think another person talks too much and it is time communication became more two-way.
- When it is important that you share your internal viewpoint.
- When you wish to match the level of intimacy of another's disclosures.
- When someone expresses praise or appreciation to you.
- When you are aware that you are listening as a means of avoiding defining and asserting yourself.
- When you feel too tired or hassled to listen properly.
- When you are unable to be accepting.
- When you consider another's solution might damage you, the other person, or both of you.

Skill 6: Rewording

There is an old and questionable joke about a counselor who firmly believed in reflective responding being seduced by a client.

Client: I quite like you.
Counselor: You quite like me.
Client: I think you're kind of cute.
Counselor: You think I'm kind of cute.
Client: I find you attractive.
Counselor: You find me attractive.
Client: I find you real attractive.
Counselor: You find me real attractive.
Client: I find you so attractive that I would like to go to bed with you.
Counselor: You find me so attractive that you would like to go to bed with me.
Client: Yes, why don't we go ahead and do it?
Counselor: I can't go to bed with you, I'm your counselor.
Client: Well, you're fired as my counselor. Let's go to bed!

In this sequence, the counselor has boringly and mechanically repeated what the client has just said. For most people, that would be sufficient to cool their ardor. As a frustrated spouse once put it, "If I had wanted someone to repeat everything I said after me, I would have married a parrot." If you are to avoid wooden reflective responses, you need to work on two subskills: rewording and reflecting feelings.

It is important to reword or paraphrase, because you drive speakers crazy if you repeat them all the time. When you reword, you may sometimes use the speaker's words, but sparingly. You do try to stay close to the kind of language the speaker used. Here are a few basic examples.

Wife to husband
Wife: "Go to hell."
Husband: "You're real mad at me."

Friend to friend
First friend: "I'm depressed."
Second friend: "You've got the blues."

Divorcée to friend
Divorcée: "It just hurts that all our mutual friends now see only Jim, my ex-husband."
Friend: "It's painful that friends you knew as a couple have stayed friends only with Jim."

A good rewording of verbal content can provide a mirror reflection that is clearer and more succinct than the original utterance. Speakers may show their appreciation with such comments as "That's it" or "You've got me." In other instances, rewordings may be insufficient. Rewording focuses on words; but voice and body messages need to be reflected as well.

Exercise 18 is designed to make you more aware of the degree to which you have choice in responding to verbal content. For each statement, many rewordings may be appropriate. Answers are provided at the end of the chapter.

Exercise 18
Reflecting words by rewording

Part A: Single Rewording
Instructions: Reword the content of each of the following statements into clear and simple language. Use "you" or "your" where the speaker uses "I," "me," or "my." Use "I" instead of "you." Remember, there is no single correct answer.

1. "It bothers me when you don't respond."

   _____

2. "I appreciate the help you've given me."

   _____

3. "I'll miss my girlfriend when she's away."

   _____

4. "I couldn't help laughing when he screwed up."

   _____

Exercise 18 (continued)

5. "You're putting me on."

_____

6. "Everybody here seems to pick on me."

_____

7. "I get so frustrated when I can't concentrate."

_____

8. "He's a handsome guy and doesn't know it."

_____

9. "Stop trying to manipulate me."

_____

10. "I find it difficult to show positive feelings."

_____

Part B: Multiple Rewording
Instructions: Think of at least three different ways to reword the content of the
following statements.
1. "I've always been shy in social situations."

_____

_____

_____

_____

2. "I'm very fearful of people getting psychologically close to me."

_____

_____

_____

_____

3. "I feel shut out by her and don't know why."

_____

_____

_____

_____

Skill 7: Reflecting Feelings

Most often it happens that one attributes to others
only the feelings of which one is capable oneself.
André Gide

The more faithfully you listen to the voice within you,
the better you will hear what is sounding outside.
Dag Hammarskjöld

A sure way of helping people to experience your understanding is to be sharp at
picking up their feelings. Reflecting feelings may be viewed as feeling along with
another's flow of emotions and being able to communicate this back to them.
Reflecting feelings entails offering an expressive emotional companionship. You
respond to another's music and not just to their words. When you reflect feelings,
you also give another the opportunity to listen more deeply to their own feelings.
    Reflecting feelings involves both receiver skills and sender skills.

Receiver Skills
Understanding another's face and body messages.
Understanding another's voice messages.
Understanding another's words.
Tuning in to the flow of your own emotional reactions.
Taking into account the context of another's messages.
Sensing the surface and underlying meanings of another's messages.

Sender Skills
Responding in ways that pick up the other's feelings words and phrases.
Rewording feelings appropriately, using expressive rather than wooden
    language.
Using voice and body messages that neither add to nor subtract from the
    emotions being conveyed.
Checking out the accuracy of your understanding.

Constant reflective responding focusing on feelings does run the risk of encouraging people to wallow in their feelings inappropriately. For instance, Neil may
persist in feeling sorry for himself when discussing his relationship with Christy,
which is not going well. People should exercise their judgment in deciding how
much and when to reflect feelings. For instance, you might use a reflective
response to allow Neil to express his feelings and then ask a question such as "Well,
is there anything you think you could do to improve the situation?"

Picking Up Feelings Words and Phrases

Let's start with the obvious. A good but not infallible way to discuss what others
feel is to listen to their feelings words and phrases. Sometimes people ask "Well,
what did you feel?" just after they have already been told. Sometimes feelings

words are not the central part of the message. For instance, Lavonne may say "it's just great" that her mother is getting married again, while her voice chokes and her face looks sad because the corners of her mouth are turned down. While the forthcoming marriage may be "great" for her mother, Lavonne's voice and body messages indicate she doubts it will be great for her.

The following is an example of someone using feelings words and phrases that communicate what he means. Mick says to Frances, "I really enjoyed our date last night. It was just great. Even after so little time I feel there may be something special between us. When can we meet again?" Mick's feelings words and phrases are "really enjoyed," "just great," "something special between us," and "can we meet again."

Exercise 19 attempts to help you become more disciplined at listening for verbal messages about feelings. It then builds on your rewording practice in Exercise 18 by asking you to reword the feelings words and phrases that you identify. Answers are suggested at the end of the chapter.

Exercise 19
Identifying and rewording feelings words and phrases

Instructions: For each of the following statements (1) identify the words and phrases the speaker has used to describe how he or she feels; and (2) provide rewordings of these words and phrases that accurately reflect how the speaker feels.

1. Tony to Wayne: "I find being without a job depressing. I'm young and want to get ahead. Right now my prospects look bleak."

Tony's feelings words and phrases: _____

_____

Rewordings of feelings words and phrases: _____

_____

_____

2. Eileen to Tricia: "I'm determined to be my own woman. It's exciting to think I could have a successful career."

Eileen's feelings words and phrases: _____

_____

Rewordings of feelings words and phrases: _____

_____

_____

3. Sophia to Mario: "I wish my folks got along better. I hate seeing them getting old and being so unhappy."

Sophia's feelings words and phrases: ————————————————

————————————————————————————————————

Rewordings of feelings words and phrases: ————————————————

————————————————————————————————————

————————————————————————————————————

4. Earl to Colleen: "Who the heck does he think he is telling me what to do? If I didn't need the job I would tell him to go to hell."

Earl's feelings words and phrases: ————————————————

————————————————————————————————————

Rewordings of feelings words and phrases: ————————————————

————————————————————————————————————

————————————————————————————————————

Picking Up Voice and Body Messages

Your job as a listener is to receive information in a way that shows emotional responsiveness to speakers. To do this you need to integrate mirroring voice and body messages into your overall responses. Much of this integration can be accomplished by varying your voice inflections and facial expressions. For instance, if a hypothetical suicide-prone friend said "I feel terrible," you could adjust your voice and facial expression to mirror, to some extent, a sense of desperation. This adjustment need not prevent your voice and face from also expressing warmth and sympathy.

Reflecting feelings entails expressive listening and responding. The reflection of feelings needs to be accurate in two ways. First, the feelings should be correctly identified. Second, the level of intensity of the feelings needs to be correctly expressed. At one extreme, the wooden responder continuously subtracts from the intensity of the speaker. At the other extreme, the melodramatic responder overemphasizes the speaker's intensity of feeling. North Americans may tend when responding to ignore or subtract from the speaker's level of intensity rather than to overemphasize feelings. Here is an example of a subtractive response:

Kurt: "I'm mad as hell that my boss has not let me take the day off to go to my cousin's wedding."
Cheryl: "You're rather annoyed with your boss."

Another consideration in reflecting feelings is whether and to what extent the speaker is prepared to acknowledge his or her feelings. For instance, as a listener you may infer that a parent is absolutely furious with a child. However, the parent may not be able to handle such an observation since it clashes with his or her self-image of being an ideal and loving parent. Thus you need to use your judgment in choosing how much feeling to reflect.

Children tend to express their emotions very openly. As you grew up you received and internalized numerous messages about which emotions were appropriate for people of your social characteristics, family background, and sex to express where and when. Consequently many emotional messages come out sideways rather than being expressed loud and clear. As such they are heavily encoded and need to be decoded. Even if the messages are decoded accurately, the further issue arises of whether the sender is sufficiently self-aware to acknowledge the messages if reflected back.

Exercise 20 is about observing feelings from voice and body messages. The first time you do the exercise focus on the more obvious manifestations of anger, friendship, sadness, and anxiety. Later you may wish to list some of the ways a negative emotion like anger may be expressed when it comes out sideways rather than gets expressed directly; for instance, the speaker may both smile and clench his or her fist, and you receive a mixed message that requires decoding. Some answers to Exercise 20 are suggested at the end of the chapter.

Exercise 20
Picking up feelings from voice and body messages

Instructions: By filling in the blank spaces, indicate what voice and body messages might serve as cues for you to pick up each of the following feelings.

Nonverbal Cue	*Anger*	*Friendship*	*Sadness*	*Anxiety*
Tone of voice				
Voice volume				
Eye contact and gaze				
Facial expression				
Posture				
Gestures				

Assess your effectiveness at picking up from their voice and body messages the feelings of your loved ones, friends, and colleagues at work or school.

Reflecting Feelings From Verbal, Voice, and Body Messages

You receive so many verbal, voice, and body messages from others; how do you know which ones really count? There is no simple answer. Some people communicate their feelings loud and clear, with a good matching of verbal, voice, and body messages. Others' styles of communicating feelings interfere with their effectiveness: for example, people may communicate less intensity of feeling than they are actually experiencing, or communicate some feelings loud and clear while expressing other feelings only with difficulty. A host of other factors may disrupt sending clear feelings messages, depending on the situational context, the person to whom the message is being sent, the sex of the sender, cultural rules, the attending skills of the listener, whether or not the sender had a good night's sleep and is in a reasonable temper today, and so on.

What you try to do is (1) decode the overall message accurately, and (2) formulate an emotionally expressive reflective response that communicates back the crux of the speaker's feelings. Put the speaker's feelings at the front of your response, even though the speaker may not have put them first. Picking up immediately on feelings helps convey your understanding. Here is an example. Gina has just failed an important math test. Gina's verbal message is "I flunked math and have to retake it. I'm so disappointed with myself." Gina's voice message comprises a quiet voice with an emphasis on "so disappointed," sighs, and her voice lowering and trailing away for "with myself." Gina's body messages include being down at mouth, pale, tearful, slouching, and moving slowly. A possible reflection of Gina's feeling is "You're bitterly upset with yourself."

The statement reflecting feeling is voiced somewhat tentatively, to check out whether Gina considers it accurate. When reflecting feelings you may risk putting feelings into another's mouth that are only partly accurate or even downright inaccurate. As you reflect Gina's feelings your voice messages convey kindness and concern and your body messages convey interest and attention. Because Gina feels bitter disappointment with herself, you emphasize the words "bitterly upset" in your reflective response.

If you are not confident that you have picked up the speaker's feelings accurately, you can make your response even more tentative. For example, you could say to Gina, "I think I hear you saying you now feel bitterly upset with yourself— have I got you right?" This response may not be as good as pinpointing the feeling accurately with less hesitation, but it is better than rushing in and getting it wrong.

Skill 8: Reflecting Feelings and Reasons

One kind of reflective responding that is often helpful entails reflecting back reasons as well as feelings (Egan, 1985). Reflecting back reasons does not mean that you make an interpretation or offer an explanation from your external viewpoint. Instead, where another has already provided reasons for a feeling, you reflect these reasons back in a "You feel . . . because . . ." statement that mirrors the other's internal viewpoint. Here is an example.

Chuck: "I have my law exams coming up, and it's vital for my career to get a good grade. My whole future depends on it. I'm so worried."

Mark: "You feel really anxious because you have these imminent make-or-break exams."

Chuck: "Yes. I can't sleep properly any more and I'm not eating well. I have a constant feeling of tension and wonder what I should do."

Here Mark correctly identified Chuck's worry and anxiety, rather than blocking discussion of Chuck's feelings. Mark's "You feel . . . because . . ." response showed more understanding than he would have had he stopped talking after saying "You feel really anxious." The "because" part of Mark's statement succinctly stated the crux of Chuck's thoughts on the cause of his worry. Chuck was able to use this reflective response not only to elaborate his feelings but also as a stepping-stone to wondering about how he should handle them. Reflective responding focusing on Chuck's feelings and their causes helped him move toward taking action to manage those feelings better.

Exercise 21 requires you to reflect feelings and reasons in a standard "You feel . . . because . . ." format. People who start listening training often have trouble identifying feelings and stating them accurately. The exercise tries to make sure you do this first before moving on to reflect the reasons for the feeling. Some possible responses to Exercise 21 are provided at the end of the chapter.

Exercise 21
Reflecting feelings and reasons

Instructions: For each of the following statements, formulate a "You feel . . . because . . ." response that rewords the speaker's main feeling and clearly states the crux of his or her explanation for it.

1. Maureen to Vince: "I hate being teased. I just hate it. I'm no different from the other girls, and yet they seem to enjoy ganging up on me. It makes me feel so angry and lonely."

    _____

    _____

2. Luis to Don: "I've got this neighbor who wants her little boy to play with mine. I would like to please her and yet my boy is very naughty. I feel confused and wonder how best to handle her."

    _____

    _____

3. Cindy to Monica: "Though it's not what we planned, I'm pregnant. I'm surprised how strongly I feel about having the baby. Fortunately, John wants it too."

_____

_____

4. Barry to Willie: "I get annoyed when people don't understand my relationship with David. Sure we are emotionally very close, but what's wrong with that? Some people can't understand intimate friendships between guys."

_____

_____

Skill 9: Avoiding Unrewarding "Don'ts"

> We're all of us sentenced to solitary confinement
> inside our own skins for life.
> *Tennessee Williams*

You cannot and should not listen to others all the time. However, if you like people, you try to help them out of their solitude. You endeavor to avoid making the kind of responses that close them up rather than help them to unfold and blossom. Many of the characteristic ways you respond to others in everyday conversation are not particularly helpful in encouraging others to share their internal viewpoints. A distinction is sometimes made between a counseling con-

versation, where the counselor listens carefully to the client, and a social conversation, cynically described as "two people taking turns to exercise their egos." Counselors are trained to make the listening choices that help clients feel safe and accepted. These choices avoid the kinds of threatening verbal responses prevalent in everyday conversations.

If people are going to give you the gift of revealing themselves, they need psychological safety and space. Such safety and space is both quantitative and qualitative. If you are not physically accessible, or if when you are physically present you monopolize the conversation or keep interrupting, you are scarcely giving others the quantity of safety and space they need. However, you can also deprive them of the quality of safety and space they need by choosing to respond in ways that show lack of respect for the importance of their internal viewpoints. Showing such lack of respect not only makes it more difficult for others to talk to you, but it also interferes with their listening to themselves. A sad difficulty in many close relationships is the way friends, partners, and lovers often put each other down unintentionally, through their skills weaknesses when they listen. You may wish to express your caring by helping your friends or partner; but instead you may communicate that they are not absolutely free to talk about and to be themselves.

Some of the "don'ts" to avoid if you wish to be a rewarding listener follow. Avoiding them does not mean you should never use these "don'ts" in your relationships at all. You simply need to be aware of their possible negative consequences before choosing to use them.

- *Directing and leading.* Taking control of what another can talk about: "I'm interested in what's going right for you, not what's going wrong"; "I would like you to talk about your relationship with your mother"; "Let's focus on how you get on at work."
- *Judging and evaluating.* Making judgmental statements, especially those indicating the speaker falls short of your standards: "I don't think you should be seeing her"; "You've made a real mess of your life"; "You are not very good at expressing yourself."
- *Blaming.* Assigning responsibility, in a finger-pointing way: "It's all your fault"; "You started it"; "I'm all upset now because of you."
- *Getting aggressive.* Making statements designed to cause pain and belittle another: "Can't you ever do anything right?"; "You fool!"; "Idiot!"
- *Moralizing and preaching.* Patronizingly telling another how he or she should live: "You should always respect your parents"; "Honesty is the best policy"; "Sex is not everything in life."
- *Advising and teaching.* Adopting a style of responding that says "I know what is best for you to do" and not giving another space to reach his or her own conclusions: "My advice to you is to drop him"; "No wonder you're lonely. You need to go out and meet people"; "You need to spend more time outdoors."
- *Not accepting another's feelings.* Telling people that their feelings should be different from what they are: "You shouldn't be feeling so sorry for yourself"; "Only sissies get nervous"; "I don't see why you're so happy."

• *Inappropriately talking about yourself.* Talking about yourself in ways that interfere with another's disclosures: "*You* have troubles. Let me tell you *mine*"; "I think I'm a good listener. A lot of people tell me that"; "I am going to tell you my experience so that you can learn from it."

• *Interrogating.* Using questions in such a way that another feels threatened by unwanted probing: "Do you masturbate? If so, what are your fantasies?"; "Tell me about your previous relationship"; "What are your weaknesses?"

• *Reassuring and humoring.* Trying to make others feel better, more for your sake than theirs, and not acknowledging their true feelings: "We all feel like that sometimes"; "You can get by. I know you can"; "Look, I've made you laugh. It can't be that bad."

• *Labeling and diagnosing.* Playing the amateur shrink and placing a label or diagnostic category on another: "You have a hysterical personality"; "You're paranoid"; "You're a real neurotic."

• *Overinterpreting.* Offering explanations that come from your external viewpoint that bear little similarity to what others themselves might have thought: "I think you are afraid of me, and that's why you don't go out with me more"; "Your indecision about getting a job is related to your fear of failing to live up to your father's standards"; "The fact that you were not loved as a child makes it hard for you to show your affection for me."

• *Distracting and being irrelevant.* Confusing the issue by going off in another direction or creating a smoke screen: "Let's go someplace else"; "Let's change the subject"; "Do we have to talk about this? Why don't we have some fun?"

• *Faking attention.* Insincerely pretending to be more interested and involved in what is being said than you are: "That's so interesting"; "I would never have believed it"; "Oh, really."

• *Setting up time pressures.* Letting the speaker know that your availability for listening is very limited: "I've got to go soon"; "You had better be brief"; "I'm very busy these days."

A major "don't" not listed above is breaking confidences. A leaky sieve is not very welcome as an associate. All these "don'ts" focus on verbal responses; but as we have seen, discouraging voice and body messages can be just as devastating. Exercise 22 aims at helping you explore which of your present ways of responding interfere with your being a rewarding and safe person to open up to.

Exercise 22
How safe am I to talk to?

Instructions: Using the scale below, rate each of the following "don'ts" according to how often you respond that way in relationships important to you.

Frequently	2
Sometimes	1
Never	0

Exercise 22 (continued)

Don'ts	*Your Rating*
1. Directing and leading	——
2. Judging and evaluating	——
3. Blaming	——
4. Getting aggressive	——
5. Moralizing and preaching	——
6. Advising and teaching	——
7. Not accepting the other's feelings	——
8. Inappropriately talking about myself	——
9. Interrogating	——
10. Reassuring and humoring	——
11. Labeling and diagnosing	——
12. Overinterpreting	——
13. Distracting and being irrelevant	——
14. Faking attention	——
15. Setting up time pressures	——

Look at the "don'ts" you rated 2 or 1, and assess the consequences in your relationships of these ways of responding.

_____

_____

_____

Using Rewarding Listening Skills in Your Daily Life

Let us now see whether changing some of your existing listening choices in your daily life will have positive consequences for you. Undoubtedly you already possess some listening skills strengths. Perhaps like most people you can build on these strengths if you use the rewarding listening skills just described in a more systematic fashion. The focus of Experiments 4 and 5 is on improving your skills of helping others to share their internal viewpoints. Remember to accompany your changed verbal behaviors with good voice and body messages.

Experiment 4
What happens when I use openers and small rewards?

Part A: Assessment
Review the section on openers and small rewards at the end of Chapter 4. Then for 24 hours behave as you normally do and monitor your use of openers and small rewards in your daily life. It may assist you to keep a log of your behaviors with the following column headings.

Time	*Other Person(s) Involved*	*My Use of Openers and Small Rewards*

Part B: Make an "If . . . then . . ." Statement
Design an experiment in which you systematically use openers and small rewards. Make an "If . . . then . . ." statement along these lines: "If I change (a) and/or (b) in my relationship(s) with one or more specific people, then these consequences (to be specified) are likely to follow."

_____

_____

_____

Part C: Try Out and Evaluate Your Changed Behavior
Try out your changed behavior. Assess its positive and negative consequences for yourself and others. Have your predictions been confirmed or disconfirmed? Has the experiment taught you something about how you can be a more rewarding listener by improving your use of openers and small rewards? If so, what?

_____

_____

_____

Experiment 5
What happens when I use reflective responding skills?

Part A: Assessment
Through completing the exercises so far in this chapter, you should already have some idea of how well you use reflective responding. For the next 24 hours, listen as you normally do and monitor your use of reflective responding in your daily life. It may assist you to keep a log of your behaviors with the following column headings.

Time	*Other Person(s) Involved*	*My Use of Reflective Responding*

Experiment 5 (continued)

Part B: Make an "If . . . then . . ." Statement
Design an experiment in which you systematically use reflective responding (but don't overdo it!). Make an "If . . . then . . ." statement along these lines: "If I use reflective responding more in my relationship(s) with one or more specific people, then these consequences (to be specified) are likely to follow."

_____

_____

_____

_____

Part C: Try Out and Evaluate Your Changed Behavior
Try out your changed behavior. How well did you use reflective responding? Assess its positive and negative consequences for yourself and others. Have your predictions been confirmed or disconfirmed? Has the experiment taught you something about how you can be a more rewarding listener by improving your use of reflective responding? If so, what?

_____

_____

_____

_____

Beyond the Internal Viewpoint: Confrontation

So far the discussion has focused on how to be a rewarding listener and make it easier for others to share their internal viewpoints. At times, however, you may help another with a different sort of response. Strange as it may seem, confrontation can be an important and helpful relationship skill.

What Is Confrontation?

Your fantasy of confrontation may have you sitting in the hot seat while others attack you psychologically, trying to strip you of your defenses. Admittedly that picture illustrates a form of confrontation—but not the sort advocated here. The skill dealt with here is that of challenging others' existing perceptions so that they can work with more and better information. Each of you lives in the world of your own perceptions. Sometimes a challenge or confrontation from outside can broaden your horizons and deepen your understanding. Egan views confrontation as an invitation to another to examine his or her style of relating and its conse-quences for self and others (Egan, 1977). Needless to say, how you confront is very important. Confronting inconsistencies and possible distortions of reality are two kinds of confrontation you can include in your repertoire of relationship skills.

Confronting Inconsistencies

When someone talks to you, you may experience inconsistencies in the messages the speaker sends you. Such inconsistencies may include the following.

• *Inconsistency between verbal, voice, and body messages.* "On the one hand you say that you are fine, but on the other I catch a note of pain in your voice and see you looking tearful."

• *Inconsistency between words and actions.* "You say you love your children from your former marriage, but you rarely try to see them and are behind on your support payments."

• *Inconsistency between past and present utterances.* "You now say you hate her, but a week ago you were saying how much you loved her."

• *Inconsistency between your view of you and my view of you.* "You say that you see yourself as unattractive, but I genuinely do not see you that way."

• *Inconsistency between your view of you and others' views of you.* "You see yourself as pulling your weight in doing the chores, but you seem to be getting a lot of messages that other members of the family see you differently."

Confronting Possible Distortions of Reality

When people talk to you they may make statements like the following.

"They're all out to get me."
"I have no friends."
"I'm a terrible mother."
"I'm no good with women (or men)."
"She (or he) doesn't love me any more."
"I'm no good at anything."
"I can't do anything about it."
"They made me do it."

All of these are examples of faulty thinking that may be harming rather than helping the speaker. One of your responding choices is to make a reflective response within the speaker's internal viewpoint. Another is to confront the speaker's version of reality. People often trip themselves up by jumping to conclusions on insufficient evidence ("I have no friends") and by thinking in black-and-white terms ("Either I'm perfect or I'm no good at all"). They also may fail to own responsibility for their thoughts, feelings, and actions adequately ("They made me do it"). You need to use your judgment to decide whether to go on listening within their internal viewpoint or to confront distortions of reality.

How to Confront

My emphasis here is on using confronting to help others expand and explore their perceptions. The starting point is their internal viewpoint rather than yours. On other occasions in your relationships—for instance, when you are confronting a conflict—the starting point may be your viewpoint. These occasions are covered in a later chapter.

How you confront involves verbal, voice, and body messages. The following are some possible verbal messages.

• *Confronting inconsistencies.* A common response here is "On the one hand you say . . . , but on the other hand . . ."—for example, "On the one hand you say that you are fine, but on the other hand I catch a note of pain in your voice." This statement is often shortened to "You say . . . , but . . ."—for example, "You say that you are fine, but I catch a note of pain in your voice."

• *Confronting possible distortions of reality.* A good form for confronting distortions is "You say . . . , but what's the evidence?" An example is "You say that you have no friends, but what's the evidence?" Such a response reflects the speaker's internal viewpoint and then invites him or her to produce evidence to support it. The speaker may then make a remark like "Well, Kathryn never phones me anymore." Then you may confront the speaker again, with a question such as "Is there any other way of looking at that?" With the questions "What's the evidence?" and "Is there any other way of looking at that?" you invite speakers to produce their own evidence or provide different perceptions to confirm or disconfirm their version of reality, rather than doing it for them. On other occasions you may suggest some evidence from your viewpoint for their consideration.

The following are some guidelines for how to confront.

1. *Start with reflective responding.* Always start your response by showing that you have heard and understood the speaker's message. Then build on this understanding with your confronting response. This way you are more likely to keep the speaker's ears open to what comes from your viewpoint.

2. *Where possible, help speakers to confront themselves.* By reflecting inconsistency, you allow speakers to choose their own conclusions about it. Similarly, by asking speakers to search for evidence to back their statements, you help them to confront themselves. Assisting others in self-confrontation often leads to less resistance than directly confronting them from your external viewpoint.

3. *Do not talk down.* Keep your confrontations at a democratic level. They are invitations for exploration rather than ex cathedra pronouncements. Avoid "you" messages. A major risk in confronting others is that they perceive what you say as a put-down rather than as helpful.

4. *Use a minimum of "muscle."* Only confront as strongly as your goal requires. Heavy confrontations can create resistances; although sometimes necessary, such confrontations are generally to be avoided.

5. *Avoid threatening voice and body messages.* Try to avoid threatening voice and body messages, like sighing and finger-pointing.

6. *Leave the ultimate responsibility with the speaker.* Allow speakers to decide whether your confrontations actually help them to move forward in their exploration. Many of your confrontations may involve slight challenges; if well timed and tactfully worded, such challenges are unlikely to elicit a high degree of defensiveness.

7. *Do not overdo it.* Nobody likes being challenged persistently. With constant challenges, you create an unsafe emotional climate for the speaker. You can help others move forward with skilled use of confronting responses; but you can block them and harm your relationship if you confront too often and too clumsily.

Experiment 6
What happens when I use confronting skills?

The approach to this experiment is more informal than that of the previous experiments since you do not control when another offers you the chance to use your skills.

Part A: Confronting Inconsistencies
For a 48-hour period use the skills of confronting inconsistencies described in the chapter whenever you consider it appropriate in your daily life. Extend the time period for the experiment if necessary. Keep a log with the following column headings.

Date and Time	Details of My Confronting Inconsistencies	Consequences of My Confronting Inconsistencies

Summarize what you have learned from the consequences that followed changing your behavior in confronting inconsistencies.

Part B: Confronting Possible Distortions of Reality
Whenever an appropriate occasion arises during the next three days, use the skills of confronting another's possible distortions of reality in your relationship. Extend the time period for the experiment if necessary. Keep a log with the following column headings.

Date and Time	Details of My Confronting Possible Distortions of Reality	Consequences of My Confronting Possible Distortions of Reality

Summarize what you have learned from the consequences that followed changing your behavior in confronting possible distortions of reality.

Concluding Self-Talk

Reflective listening is a rewarding listening skill that I can use in my relationships. It involves mirroring the crux of the speaker's verbal, voice, and body messages so that the speaker feels accurately understood. Component skills of reflective responding include rewording, decoding and reflecting back feelings, and reflecting back speakers' reasons for their feelings. I must try to avoid numerous pitfalls if I wish to be safe to talk to.

On some occasions I may help others more by responding to their messages from my viewpoint than theirs. Confronting is a skill I can use to challenge their existing perceptions and to try to expand those perceptions for others' benefit. Two major kinds of behavior I may choose to confront are inconsistencies and possible distortions of reality. How I confront is important since clumsy confrontations are threatening and lead to defensiveness.

Answers to Exercises

Exercise 18
The following are suggestions; other answers might also be appropriate.

Part A
1. "You feel upset when I don't reply."
2. "You're grateful for my assistance."
3. "You're going to be lonely when your girlfriend isn't around."
4. "You couldn't control your enjoyment of his mistake."
5. "You feel I'm making a fool out of you."
6. "You feel we all gang up on you."
7. "You become very irritated when you can't keep your mind on something."
8. "You feel he's a good-looking boy and isn't aware of it."
9. "Quit trying to take me places I don't want to go."
10. "You have trouble expressing affection."

Part B
1. "You've always been bashful in company."
   "You've always been timid when socializing."
   "You've always been anxious with people."
2. "I'm afraid of intimacy."
   "I find close relationships scary."
   "I get worried by emotional nearness."
3. "I feel excluded by her and can't find the reason."
   "I feel pushed away by her and can't understand it."
   "I feel rejected by her and have no explanation for it."

Exercise 19
Rewordings other than those suggested here may also be appropriate.

1. Tony's feelings words and phrases: "depressing," "want to get ahead," "bleak."
   Rewordings of feelings words and phrases: "a downer," "wish to be successful," "unpromising."
2. Eileen's feelings words and phrases: "determined," "exciting," "successful."
   Rewordings of feelings words and phrases: "resolved," "thrilling," "good."
3. Sophia's feelings words and phrases: "wish," "got along better," "hate," "being so unhappy."
   Rewordings of feelings words and phrases: "would like," "be on friendlier terms," "loathe," "being so miserable."
4. Earl's feelings words and phrases: "Who the heck," "need the job," "go to hell."
   Rewordings of feelings words and phrases: "Who on earth," "want the money," "get lost."

Exercise 20

The following are some illustrative voice and body messages; there are many others.

Nonverbal Cue	*Anger*	*Friendship*	*Sadness*	*Anxiety*
Tone of voice	Harsh	Warm	Soft	Timid Hesitant
Voice volume	Loud	Easy to hear	Quiet	Quiet
Eye contact and gaze	Direct	Good but unobtrusive	Averted	Averted Very intermittent
Facial expression	Clenched teeth	Smile	Tearful Mouth turned down	Strained
Posture	Rigid	Relaxed	Slouched	Tense
Gestures	Fist clenched Finger-pointing	Arm around shoulder	Holding head in hands	Drumming fingers

Exercise 21

1. "You feel mad and isolated because you loathe being treated and picked on as though you're different."
2. "You feel torn and uncertain how to act because you want to get on with your neighbor, but you don't want your son influenced by her boy's behavior."
3. "You feel amazed at the strength of your feelings because your pregnancy wasn't planned and yet you and John really want the baby."
4. "You feel upset because some people think that you and David being such close buddies means that you are gay."

6

Overcoming Shyness and Making Initial Contact

Venus favors the bold.
Ovid

Gather ye rosebuds while ye may
Old Time is still a-flying,
And this same flower that smiles today
To-morrow will be dying.
Robert Herrick

An essential relationship skill is the ability to step out of your solitude and make initial contact with others. It is an area that can cause much agonizing. Let us look at two young women who go to the same party, where neither knows anybody else well.

> Kay arrives at the party having made a big effort to overcome her nerves about going at all. Although she is attractive, she thinks people do not find her so. On arrival at the party she is given a drink and introduced to a group of people. She listens to them politely but never makes a contribution of her own. When later a young man, Craig, tries to engage her in conversation, she becomes very quiet and averts her gaze. She appears tense and lacking in warmth and vitality.

> Sara goes to a party excited and determined to do her best to have a good time. She is not afraid to go up to people she thinks look interesting and introduce herself. When conversing she appears interested in what others say and participates in a lively and unforced way. Since she wants

to meet new people she moves around. Even if she does not find someone with whom to develop a relationship, she will have enjoyed herself and helped others to do likewise.

Both Kay and Sara are attractive. Assuming it is a reasonably good party, both should be able to make an enjoyable time for themselves. However, Sara has better skills in making contact than Kay does. Consequently the chances of Sara finding people who wish to see her again are greater than Kay's chances are. Kay is far from alone in finding situations involving groups of new people difficult. This chapter focuses on some of the skills that Kay—and possibly you, too—might use to reach out and make contact with others. The chapter has three main sections, which discuss defining shyness, combating shy thinking, and making initial contact skills.

Defining Shyness

> I am afraid to tell you who I am,
> because, if I tell you who I am, you may
> not like who I am, and it's all that I have.
> *John Powell*

Dictionary definitions of *shy* use words like bashful, timid, wary, uneasy in company, and averse to contact. Shyness is a problem for children, adolescents, and adults alike. Based on a large-scale shyness survey conducted mainly among U.S.

college students, Zimbardo found that more than 80% reported that they were shy at some points in their lives. Of these, over 40% considered themselves presently shy (Zimbardo, 1977). Zimbardo's data focus on people who admit their shyness. My position is that anxiety is present in all social interactions to a greater or lesser degree, even though much of it goes unacknowledged. When meeting new people you wear a social mask to influence and control their reactions to you. You stage-manage their impressions of you. Your underlying anxieties can play a big part in blocking you from making good person to person contact. Instead of making good contact, you risk treating yourself and others as objects to be manipulated rather than as people to be liked or loved.

What is shyness? Although these lists are not exhaustive, the following are some considerations for defining shyness and for assessing how shy you are.

• *Feelings.* Feelings associated with shyness include anxiety, insecurity, bashfulness, loneliness, confusion, mistrust, embarrassment, shame, fear, tension, humiliation, and vulnerability.

• *Physical reactions.* Physical reactions associated with shyness include blushing, nausea, feeling faint, perspiring, knotted stomach, pounding heart, mind going blank, shaking, mouth going dry, and shallow breathing.

• *Thoughts.* Thoughts associated with shyness include the following.

Self-Talk About Myself
"It's OK to be shy."
"It's not OK to be shy."
"I am a solitary person."
"I am uninteresting."
"I am weak."
"I lack self-confidence."
"I am not as good as others."
"I might get hurt or rejected."
"I lack social skills."
"I need approval."
"I can't take embarrassment."

Self-Talk About What Others Think
"Others accept my shyness."
"Others notice my physical symptoms."
"Others may reject me."
"Others may think I'm incompetent."
"Others may consider me uninteresting."
"Others pay close attention to my behavior."
"Others are shy, too, and understand."
"Others get uncomfortable with me."

Thinking skills weaknesses
Shyness may be sustained by other thinking skills weaknesses, such as misattributing cause, negative self-talk, unrealistic personal rules, misperceiving, and predicting wrongly. Each of these skills weaknesses will be discussed shortly.

• *Verbal, voice, and body messages.* Illustrative verbal, voice, and body messages associated with shyness include the following.

Verbal messages
Keeping silent or talking as little as possible.
Low self-disclosure.
Being too ready to agree.

Voice messages
Speaking quietly.
Stammering.
Loudness masking insecurity.

Body messages
Avoiding or escaping from situations.
Averting gaze.
Smiling too much.
Tight body posture.

Conversational skills weaknesses
Shyness may also be sustained by poor conventional skills, including use of openers, listening, coordinating the switch from talking to listening and back, keeping the conversation flowing, and ending conversations.

Defensive roles
Many people handle their anxieties in social situations by wearing masks or acting out defensive roles (Powell, 1969). These roles include aggression; clowning; conforming; cynicism; inappropriate flirting; monopolizing; putting themselves down; and playing the strong, silent type.

• *People.* You may be more shy with some kinds of people than others. Zimbardo's shy students were shy with the following categories of people in descending order: strangers, the opposite sex, authorities by virtue of their knowledge, authorities by virtue of their role, relatives, elderly people, friends, children, and parents (Zimbardo, 1977).
• *Situations.* Situations associated with shyness include the following.

Meeting people for the first time.
Asking someone for a date.
Giving a talk in front of a group of people.
Participating in a discussion group.
Asking for help—for example, when ill.
Going to a party.
Situations requiring assertiveness—for example, returning something to a store.
Interviews.
Having a conversation with a person of the opposite sex.
Going to a dance or a nightclub.
Showing your body in a nonsexual context.
Situations involving sexual intimacy.

This section has provided a fuller definition of shyness than that set out in dictionary definitions like "bashful" or "timid." Additional dimensions are how severe you perceive your shyness to be, whether it is across the board or specific to certain situations, and whether you consider shyness to be a problem for you. Exercise 23 asks you to assess your current experience of shyness.

Exercise 23
My experience of shyness

Instructions: Fill in the worksheet below by assessing your current experience of shyness in each of the dimensions listed. Give specific illustrations where possible. Consult the text if in doubt about the meaning of a dimension.

Dimension	My Assessment
Feelings	
Physical reactions	
Thoughts	
Verbal messages	
Voice messages	
Body messages	
Conversational skills weaknesses	
Defensive roles	
People with whom I'm shy	
Situations in which I'm shy	

1. To what extent do you think that any shyness you possess is influenced by your biological sex and your culture? Please explain.

---

2. Summarize how shy you currently perceive yourself to be. What are the consequences for yourself and for others?

Combating Shy Thinking

If you are shy now, many early learnings contributed to it. These include the examples set by your parents. Zimbardo observes, "In general, then, about 70 percent of the time parents and children share the same shyness label; they tend to be shy together" (Zimbardo, 1977, pp. 62–63). The consequences provided by others for your reaching-out behavior undoubtedly contributed to your shyness as well. Your problem now is how to stop sustaining your shyness if it interferes with attaining your relationship goals. One of the main ways you sustain your shyness is by thinking shy. Your use of thinking skills can either support or oppress you (Nelson-Jones, 1990). The five thinking skills presented here can help you alter the balance in the direction of self-support, as opposed to self-oppression, to overcome your shyness.

Attributing Cause Accurately

Attributions are the explanations, interpretations, or reasons you give yourself for what happens. How you explain your shyness influences whether you work to overcome it or remain stuck with it. A number of misattributions or faulty explanations for shyness may weaken your motivation for change. These explanations are often partial truths; the error is to treat them as whole truths. The following are some possible misattributions concerning shyness.

• *"It's in my genes."* This is the position that you are shy by nature rather than by nurture. Although people may have different biological predispositions to anxiety and fears of rejection, a considerable part of shyness represents learned behavior sustained by your current thinking and action skills weaknesses.

• *"It's my unfortunate past."* Your unfortunate past, or what others did to you, may have contributed to your acquiring some skills weaknesses associated with shyness. However, you sustain your shyness by what you do to yourself. If you have had a very unfortunate past, you may require counseling to provide the nurturing and healing you never received from others. However many people, with or without professional help, have learned to overcome skills weaknesses caused by their unfortunate pasts.

• *"Others should make the first move."* Some of you may play a passive rather than an active role when meeting new people. You wait for events to happen to you rather than taking an active part in shaping events—letting others assume the responsibility for helping you out of your shell. But others may not help you escape your shell. Sometimes passivity is reinforced by social rules; for instance, females are expected to be less forward and to take fewer risks in making social contact than males. Such a social rule may have negative consequences for both shy females and males—for shy females because they have not been sufficiently helped to develop initiating skills, and for shy males because they feel the full pressure of the expectation that males take the initiative. A major theme of this book is that each person must assume responsibility for making the choices that work best for them. Sitting or standing around, waiting for something to happen, is frequently not the best choice.

- *"It's all my fault."* You may consider that everything that goes wrong in social situations is your fault. You may fail to take into account that when two people relate, each has a responsibility for the success of the contact—not just you. Your hypersensitivity to feelings of embarrassment and willingness to blame yourself may erode rather than help you gain the confidence to work on your shyness.

- *"I've tried before."* You may have tried to overcome your shyness before and been unsuccessful. However, the past need not be your guide to the future. This time you may try harder, understand your shyness better, possess better skills at managing it, and be better at enlisting the support of others. The fact that you have tried before does not mean you cannot now learn new and better skills to help you succeed.

- *"I can't stand setbacks."* Setbacks are part of learning any new skill. Moreover, problems like shyness are a part of living. Your unrealistic expectations about the learning process and smoothness of life make you vulnerable to setbacks. You can develop the skills of learning to handle shyness rather than to oppress yourself when faced with setbacks.

These attributions or explanations may describe not only how you became shy but also why you remain shy. Did any of them have the ring of truth for you? If so, work hard at challenging the faulty thinking that these misattributions represent. The following are some examples of more realistic attributions.

"Although like many people I'm naturally sensitive, my shyness has been largely learned."

"Others undoubtedly contributed to my becoming shy, but I currently sustain my shyness through skills weaknesses that I can work to overcome."

"It is not up to others to make the first move to help me out of my shyness since I am responsible for making the choices in life that work best for me."

"I am responsible only for my own behavior in social situations rather than accepting total responsibility for what happens."

"Even though I've tried before, circumstances are different now, and with more understanding of how I've sustained my shyness I can develop new and better skills to overcome it."

"Setbacks in my attempts to overcome my shyness may be both challenges and valuable learning experiences."

Coping Self-Talk

Coping self-talk is another thinking skill for managing feelings of shyness (Meichenbaum, 1983, 1985; Meichenbaum & Deffenbacher, 1988). The idea is that during your waking hours you continuously engage in an internal dialogue, or perform self-talk. The goals of coping self-talk are to calm your anxieties and to help you deal effectively with the task at hand. Thus coping self-talk contains two major elements: calming self-talk and coaching self-talk. Coping self-talk is about coping or "doing as well as I can" rather than about mastery or "being perfect" and "having no anxiety." Coping is a much more realistic goal than mastery. Altering your goal from mastery to coping is likely to increase your self-support and to decrease your self-oppression. You now possess an attainable standard toward which to strive.

Coping self-talk involves replacing negative self-talk statements with helpful ones. To return to the examples at the beginning of the chapter, about Kay and Sara going to the party, their self-talk was as follows. Note how Kay oppresses herself and Sara supports herself.

> Kay: "I know that I am going to find this party difficult. Everybody is looking at me. I feel unattractive. I don't want to make a mistake. I'm feeling tense and, when this happens, I know it will only get worse."

> Sara: "I enjoy parties and meeting new people. Although I get a little anxious with strangers, I know I can overcome it. I have developed some good party skills and these usually work. All I have to do is my best."

Calming and coaching statements tend to be interspersed in coping self-talk. Two important aspects of calming self-talk are as follows.

- *Telling yourself to stay calm.* Simple self-statements include "keep calm," "relax," and "just take it easy." In addition, you can instruct yourself to "take a deep breath" or "breathe slowly and regularly."
- *Telling yourself you can cope.* Sample self-statements include "I can handle this situation" or "My anxiety is a signal for me to use my coping skills."

Coaching self-talk can help you to cope with shyness in the following ways.

- *Specifying your goals.* An example could be "I will go up and talk to a minimum of three new people at the party."
- *Breaking tasks down.* Think through the steps needed to attain your goal.
- *Concentrating on the task at hand.* You instruct yourself, as pilots do when they talk themselves through difficult landings.

You may use coping self-talk before, during, and after stressful social situations— for example, going to a party full of strangers or out with a new date.

Possible coping self-talk statements before a stressful social situation include the following.

"This anxiety is a sign for me to use my coping skills."
"Calm down. Develop a plan to manage the situation."
"I know if I use my coping skills I can manage."

Possible coping self-talk statements during a stressful social situation include the following.

"Take my time. Breathe slowly and regularly."
"Relax. I can manage if I just take one step at a time."
"I don't have to be liked by everyone. All I can do is the best I can."

Possible coping self-talk statements after a stressful social situation include the following.

"Each time I cope it seems to get easier."
"I'm proud of the way I'm learning to manage my fears."
"I've shown myself I can do it now."

You can also use coping self-talk if, like me, you are prone to potentially destructive self-doubt when starting close relationships. For example, if you had a very successful date a couple of evenings ago, but have had no further contact with your date since then, you may handle your insecurity in negative ways like putting yourself down or later coming on too strong. Instead, tell yourself to calm down, realistically appraise the feedback you received on your date—much of which may have been very positive—and either initiate contact or wait and see what happens. If you cannot trust yourself to remember the positive feedback, write it down.

Exercise 24
Using coping self-talk to manage shyness

1. Identify any negative self-talk you may use that contributes to shyness and social incompetence.

   _____

   _____

2. Identify a specific social situation that you find stressful. Write out at least three coping self-talk statements, for before, during, and after the situation. It may help if you write each statement on an index card for practice and for use in an emergency.

   _____

   _____

Experiment 7
What happens when I use coping self-talk skills to manage shyness?

Part A: Assessment
Look back at your answers to Exercise 24.

Part B: Make an "If . . . then . . ." Statement
1. The "If . . ." part of your statement relates to rehearsing, practicing, and then using your self-talk statements before, during, and after the social situation you find stressful. Rehearsal and practice is important. Spend at least two separate

Experiment 7 (continued)

periods rehearsing and practicing your self-talk as you imagine yourself coping with anxiety before, during, and after the stressful social situation.

2. The "then" part of the statement indicates the specific consequences you predict will follow from the changes in your behavior.

Part C: Try Out and Evaluate Your Changed Behavior
Try out your changed behavior. How well did you use coping self-talk? Assess its positive and negative consequences for yourself and others. Have your predictions been confirmed or disconfirmed? Has the experiment taught you something about how you can support yourself with coping self-talk? If so, what?

Choosing Realistic Personal Rules

Your personal rules are the "dos" and "don'ts" by which you lead your life. Each of you has an inner rule book that guides your living. If your rules are self-supporting, they can motivate and help you to attain realistic goals. However, if your rules are self-oppressing, they leave you open to a triple dose of self-disparagement. For example, Marty has a rule that he must be successful on all his first dates. However, his first date with Ann does not go well, activating his first dose of self-disparagement. His second dose of self-disparagement is his resulting anxiety and depression about his dating ability. His third dose of self-disparagement comes when he starts devaluing not just his dating ability but his whole worth as a person.

Albert Ellis has coined the term "mustabation" to refer to rigid personal rules characterized by "musts," "oughts," and "shoulds" (Ellis, 1980). He has a simple ABC framework for showing how people's thinking affects their feelings and behavior.

A: the activating event.
B: your beliefs about the activating event.
C: emotional and behavioral consequences.

Ellis looks at the emotional and behavioral consequences determined by your beliefs in relation to the activating event rather than the activating event itself. I prefer the term *personal rules* to *beliefs*.

Let's look at a specific incident regarding Kay at the party.

A: Craig, after conversing with Kay, circulated.
B: Kay's personal rule is "I must be approved of by everyone."
C: Kay felt depressed because Craig moved away, and she then left the party early.

Kay's thinking at B represents an irrational or unrealistic personal rule. The rule "I must be approved of by everyone" involves a mustabatory overgeneralization in which Kay unnecessarily lays her sense of personal adequacy on the line. Craig may or may not have moved away because he was not interested in Kay. Even if Craig was not interested in Kay, Kay does not have to win Craig's approval; there are other males on the planet.

Three important unrealistic personal rules that contribute to people sustaining their shyness are the following.

1. I must be liked and approved of by everyone I meet.
2. ·I must never reveal anything about myself that might be viewed negatively.
3. I must never make a mistake in social situations.

Unrealistic rules such as these need to be identified and their consequences for your happiness and fulfillment rationally assessed. You then need to reformulate your unrealistic rules into realistic rules that work for rather than against you.

Reformulating involves substituting self-supporting for self-oppressing characteristics in specific personal rules. Some of the main characteristics of self-supporting personal rules include the following.

• *Expressing preferences rather than demands.* You distinguish clearly between your nonabsolutist preferences and your absolutist, mustabatory demands.

• *A coping emphasis.* You manage or cope with situations rather than being perfectionist about them.

• *Based on your own valuing process.* Your rules are not just rigid internalizations of parental, sex-role, and cultural directives.

• *Flexibility.* Where appropriate, you are amenable to change.

• *Absence of self-rating.* Your rules lead to a functional rating of specific characteristics according to whether they are useful for attaining your goals rather than leading to a global rating of your personhood.

The following are more realistic reformulations of the shyness-engendering personal rules cited earlier.

1. Although I might prefer to be universally liked, it is unreasonable and unnecessary to demand that this happen. I can meet my needs for friendship and affection if I just find some people who like me and whom I like.

2. Nobody's perfect. If I am to have honest and open relationships I need to reveal my vulnerabilities as well as my strengths.

3. To err is human. Though I would prefer not to make mistakes I can use them as learning experiences.

Exercise 25 focuses on managing shyness through identifying your unrealistic personal rules and reformulating them into realistic rules. As mentioned earlier, rules are frequently unrealistic when they contain words like "must," "ought," and "should." See if you can identify some of the rules that may be contributing to your being tense in social situations. Then attempt to arrive at confidence-engendering reformulations of these rules, or at the very least, reformulations that help you contain your anxiety.

Exercise 25
Identifying and reformulating personal rules to manage shyness

1. Make a list of any major unrealistic personal rules that contribute to your being shy in social situations. Put these rules into four categories: (a) rules learned from my parents; (b) rules on account of my biological sex; (c) rules specific to my culture; and (d) others. If a rule fits into more than one category, give priority to listing it in (b) or (c), if relevant.

   _____

   _____

   _____

2. Assess the consequences for yourself and others of your possessing these unrealistic personal rules.

   _____

   _____

   _____

3. Reformulate each unrealistic rule so that it offers a realistic standard for your future behavior.

   _____

   _____

4. Record your reformulated rules on a cassette tape recorder, and play them back at least once a day for the next week.

Choosing to Perceive Accurately

Perceiving and misperceiving is discussed briefly here in relation to shyness. The topic of misperceiving is revisited later in the book. If you are shy, the way you perceive many situations is likely to sustain your discomfort. Each person carries within them some pain and insecurity. Without necessarily knowing it, you can be so influenced by your self-doubts that you jump to unwarranted perceptual conclusions. These perceptual conclusions are often self-oppressing in four main ways. First, implicit in them is a low opinion of your worth. For instance, "That person doesn't like me" may be an accurate perception; however, it may be an inaccurate perception based on your underlying doubts about your worth. Second, perceptual conclusions distort the thoughts, feelings, and actions of others. Third, such conclusions engender avoidable negative feelings, such as depression and anxiety. Fourth, these conclusions may lead you to behave against your own best interests.

Often people are unaware that they may jump to the first perceptual conclusion rather than saying to themselves "Stop and think. What are my perceptual choices?" Psychiatrist Aaron Beck observes that frequently people have automatic thoughts and perceptions that influence their emotions (Beck, 1976). Either people are not fully conscious of these thoughts and images or it does not occur to them that these perceptions warrant special scrutiny. Beck collaborates with his patients in the scientific detective work of identifying these self-oppressing perceptions, or what you tell yourself. These perceptions are related to your mustabatory personal rules. For example, if you have a rule that you must be liked by everyone all the time, you are likely to be sensitized to cues of rejection.

When exploring upsetting perceptions, the ABC framework needs to be altered slightly, to look like the following.

A: The activating event.
B: Your perceptions.
C: Emotional and behavioral consequences.

The consequences of A for you are influenced by your perceptions of A at B. They do not automatically follow from A. You have a choice of how you perceive at B.

Here is an example within the ABC framework.

A: Craig talks to Kay at the party and then circulates.
B: Kay's perception is "Craig does not like me."
C: Kay feels depressed and leaves the party early.

However, Kay might have had many other perceptions at B, including the following.

"Craig is sensible in wanting to circulate at a party."
"Craig liked me enough to come and talk to me."
"I need to improve my conversational skills if I am going to hold the interest of guys like Craig."
"There are other guys at the party so why worry about Craig?"
"I quite liked Craig, but I didn't find him fascinating."

If you are like Kay and have a tendency to jump to negative perceptual conclusions, how can you combat this? First, become aware of your tendency. Second, identify the signals that you may be oppressing yourself. These include negative feelings about yourself and others without good cause and self-defeating behavior that distances you from others. Also, you can identify the kinds of people and situations associated with your self-disparagement. Third, monitor your thinking in specific situations and practice making the connections between upsetting feelings and upsetting perceptions. Fourth, question your perceptions by logical analysis, and search for better explanations. This process involves your engaging in the following kinds of self-talk.

"Stop and think. What are my perceptual choices?"

"Are my perceptions based on fact or inference?"

"If my perceptions are based on inference, can I perceive the situation in other ways that are more closely related to the factual evidence?"

"If necessary, what further information do I need to collect?"

"What is the perception I choose because it represents the best fit in relation to the factual evidence?"

Let's assume that Kay has some skills in choosing the most realistic perception. She went back in her mind over her contact with Craig and assessed the evidence for her perception that Craig did not like her. When she did this, she discovered that no facts supported this conclusion; it was an inference on her part. She generated alternative perceptions, such as the five perceptions listed above. She decided that these other perceptions taken together constituted an appropriate way to perceive what had happened at the party. None of them involved putting herself down. Exercise 26 will give you practice in treating any shyness you feel similarly.

Exercise 26
Choosing how I perceive in shyness situations

Part A: Generating Different Perceptions
Instructions: For each of the following scenarios, generate at least three different perceptions.

1. At a nightclub a stranger of the opposite sex winks in your direction.

_____

_____

_____

2. You go out on a first date and it goes well; five days later you have had no contact from your date.

_____

_____

_____

3. At a party a person you met 15 minutes ago pays you a compliment on how you dress.

_____

_____

_____

4. Somebody at a social gathering looks at you and then looks away.

_____

_____

_____

Part B: Perceiving Differently in a Specific Shyness Situation
1. Choose a situation in which you have felt shy or socially uncomfortable.

2. Make a worksheet in the following format.

Situation	Upsetting Perception(s)	Different Perceptions

3. Write down the situation and place any perceptions associated with your shyness in that situation in the "upsetting perception(s)" column. Assess the realism of your upsetting perception(s) using logical analysis.

_____

_____

4. In the "different perceptions" column, write down as many different perceptions of the situation as you can generate. Then evaluate which perception has the best fit—that is, which perception best explains the situation.

_____

_____

5. Assess the ways in which the emotional and behavioral consequences of your perception(s) of the best fit would have been different from those of your original perception(s).

_____

_____

Predicting Gain and Loss

A study of depressed and nondepressed students by psychologists Paula Pietromonaco and Karen Rook found differences in their decision making style (Pietromonaco & Rook, 1987). Depressed students were significantly less likely to assign weight to the potential benefits of acting in social situations and significantly more likely to assign weight to the potential risks. Furthermore, in decisions about initiating social contact and establishing intimacy depressed students expressed a greater reluctance to take the target actions than did the nondepressed students. If you are shy, you are not necessarily depressed; but many shy people do have a similar pattern of overestimating risk, underestimating reward, and hence being less prepared to act.

You lead your life into the future rather than into the past. Predictions are thoughts and images about the probability of future events. However, past circumstances in your life may adversely color your view of your future. You need to view the future realistically. For some of you, making a success in the future may be the risk that worries you. As one psychiatrist kidded, "There is only one thing worse than not getting what you want, and that is getting it!"

Shy people are prone to a number of thinking errors when predicting the future. These errors include the following.

• *Underestimating reward and overemphasizing risk.* Your balance sheet is based on erroneous accounting, so you conclude you do not have the funds to act.

• *Overgeneralizing.* You draw a broad conclusion from a specific observation—for instance, "Maria turned down my request for a date, so therefore all girls will in the future."

• *Black-and-white thinking.* You think in either/or terms—for instance, "If I go out with Kevin, he is either going to love me or hate me."

• *Catastrophizing.* You believe that the negative consequences of not achieving your goal will be much worse than you are justified in thinking.

• *Personalizing.* You predict that you will be more the center of attention than reality warrants.

• *Self-rating.* You predict that the outcomes of what you do are not only positive or negative in themselves but have global implications for your worth as a person.

• *Underestimating strengths and resources.* You misperceive your social strengths and resources and your capacity to cope with adverse feedback.

In my private practice I find that I can help shy people by building up their skills of generating and evaluating rewards.

> Sean, aged 30, had little experience with dating women; his longest relationship lasted three dates. In his church group, Sean was on a committee with Suzanne, who had been friendly to him and whom he wondered if he should ask out. Sean asked, "Why bother to take the risk of seeking the reward?" With his counselor, Sean generated the potential risks and rewards of taking this initiative. He was already expert at acknowledging risks and needed to learn that it was in his interest to

look at rewards as well as risks in his decisions. His list of potential rewards for asking Suzanne out included the following.

"I might have a chance of a strong relationship."
"I might gain more experience in developing relationships."
"This might contribute to helping me become happier."
"I might gain confidence and a more positive self-image."
"I might develop my ability to express my feelings more."
"I might give myself the opportunity to let Suzanne take some of the initiative, too."

Sean evaluated the rewards of asking Suzanne out as outweighing the risks. She later became his first steady girlfriend.

The most conclusive way of gauging the accuracy of your predictions is to put them to the test as Sean did. Testing the reality of your previous negative predictions may become easier if you carefully break tasks down, take small steps before larger steps, rehearse what you are going to do, and seek the support of other people when appropriate. Experiment 8 helps you test your predictions.

Experiment 8
What happens when I alter the way I predict reward and risk?

Part A: Assessment
1. Think of a particular person with whom you would like either to initiate or to deepen a relationship and yet have felt inhibited from doing so.

2. Make up a worksheet with the following format.

Rewards From Acting	*Risks From Acting*

Experiment 8 (continued)

3. On the worksheet first list your current predictions of reward and risk. These are the predictions that when balanced against each other may inhibit you from acting. Then draw a line under each list.

4. Now generate as many extra predictions of reward and risk as you can and list them in the appropriate columns beneath the lines you drew. Pay particular attention to generating rewards.

5. Assess your revised list of rewards and risks and, if appropriate, set yourself goals to alter your behavior.

_____

_____

Part B: Make an "If . . . then . . ." Statement
Make an "If . . . then . . ." statement along the lines of "If I implement my changed behavior (to be specified), then these predictions (to be specified) are likely to come true."

_____

_____

Part C: Try Out and Evaluate Your Changed Behavior
Try out your changed behavior. Assess its positive and negative consequences for yourself and the other person. Have your predictions been confirmed or disconfirmed? Has this experiment taught you something about how you can support yourself by predicting reward and risk more accurately? If so, what?

_____

_____

In the preceding pages I have taken what psychologists call a cognitive or thinking skills approach to shyness. If you are shy you may already possess the action skills of making contact in your repertoire. You just need the confidence to use your skills. Other shy people, along with many who would not consider themselves shy, need to develop their action skills of making contact. These action skills often closely interrelate with thinking skills.

Skills in Making Initial Contact

A group of you in a room together for the first time can be a collection of separate existences trapped within your own skins, or else you can start to make contact

with each other. Making contact involves different stages. Here the main focus is on helping you to make effective choices when you first meet people—the important time when you make and receive first impressions. During this period you may plant the seeds for relationships to grow later. Alternatively, you may curtail opportunities either by choice or by mistake. When meeting people for the first time you need to communicate (1) liking and interest in the other; (2) absence of threat; and (3) an initial definition of yourself. You communicate that you are a rewarding rather than a negative person.

Openers

Getting started and breaking the ice is easier if you have developed a repertoire of appropriate opening remarks. You can choose from those conversational openers and icebreakers the ones appropriate to the different situations in which you find yourself. Making initial contact is usually done by way of small talk, as you feel each other out psychologically to determine whether you want the contact to continue and on what level. "Safe talk" is another way of describing small talk. The level of disclosure is usually low in terms of intimacy, because trust and mutual acceptability have yet to be established. However, in situations where you are unlikely to meet again, the "strangers on a train" phenomenon can occur, and disclosures may be surprisingly intimate.

The following are some suggestions for conversational openers and icebreakers. The list is by no means exhaustive. Some of you may have your favorite opening gambits that have worked well for you in the past; if you do, why change? Others of you may wish to build up your repertoire.

- *Introduce yourself.* "Hello, I'm (my name is) _____."
- *Offer something.* "Can I get you a drink?"; "Would you like some peanuts?"
- *Exchange basic information.* "What brings you here?"; "Where do you live?"; What line of work are you in?"
- *Make comments relevant to the occasion,* perhaps following them up with a question. "I like this hot weather. Do you?"; "It's a great party. Do you agree?"; "I've just arrived. What's happening?"
- *Give compliments,* again perhaps following them up with a question. "I like your dress"; "You are really a great dancer"; "I like your dress. Where did you get it?"; "You are really a great dancer. Where did you learn?"; "I like your sense of humor."
- *Bring up current events.* "What do you think of the election?"; "What do you think of the new Arts Center?"; "Have you been watching the latest television series?"
- *Try self-disclosure.* "I feel nervous because this is the first time I've been here"; "I'm so relieved and happy. I've just heard that I passed my exams"; "I saw the latest film yesterday and really enjoyed it."
- *Encourage others' conversation.* "That's interesting"; "Uh-huh"; "Tell me more"; "Really?"; "Did you?"; "Oh?"

Body and Voice Messages

Two important body messages in starting typical interactions are eye contact ("catching someone's eye") and having your body openly oriented toward the other person (Duck, 1986). Your head and face play an important role in rewarding others. Smiling can indicate liking and absence of threat; however, smiling can be overdone and appear to be a phony mask. Others pick up whether your body messages match what you say. Lack of genuineness or incongruence is likely to distance you from others. A reasonable amount of gaze should be maintained. People gaze nearly twice as much when listening as when talking (Argyle, 1983). Too little eye contact may indicate bashfulness or lack of interest. A high degree of eye contact may be seen as domineering or possibly indicating sexual attraction. Of course, you may be choosing to convey the latter. Appropriately nodding your head when you listen is another way of being rewarding and reducing threat when you first meet.

Voice messages are very important. Good speech is easy to hear and relaxed. Shy people often need to work on speaking louder. Sometimes, without being fully aware of it, you may show your nervousness by speaking very quickly or by slurring your words. Even those without obvious impediments may need to work on the quality of their speech.

Keeping Conversations Flowing

A basic conversational sequence involves three steps: speaking, switching, and listening. You coordinate who has the floor by sending voice, body, and verbal cues. For instance, you may avert your gaze, stop saying "uh-huh," and not make a listening response if you think it is your turn to speak.

Three ways in which you can help keep a conversation flowing are using your rewarding listening skills, using questions to draw the other out, and having something to talk about yourself. You can keep yourself informed in a number of obvious ways: reading newspapers and magazines; watching the news on television; and keeping up to date on the latest developments in your specific areas of interest—for instance, by watching your local baseball team or the latest movies. You may also use jokes to loosen up the conversation. However, you may need to practice them in advance so you don't blow the punch line.

More often than not meeting new people involves searching for common ground, partly in order to find safe talk with which to fill or structure time. In general, people find silences awkward when they do not know each other well. This search for common ground also helps you explore whether you wish later to become friends, lovers, or marital partners with the other. The search for common ground can entail finding out specific factual information—for instance, a shared hobby or a mutual friend. It can also include discovering emotional information that may be more implicit than explicit—for example, mutual liking, compatibility, and closeness. In initial contacts a process of coordination takes place in at least two ways: you test out whether or not you wish to continue the contact, and you also coordinate the direction and intimacy of your disclosures.

You cannot *not* communicate. Your voice, words, and body always send out messages. However, you can choose what and how you reveal and define yourself to others. Furthermore, the way you reveal and define yourself will influence not only how intimate others' disclosures are, but also how others react to your disclosures. The way you present yourself and your activities to others guides and controls the impressions others form of you. An analogy may be made with the theater, where the actors are engaged in manipulating the audience's impressions. However, causing others to suspend their disbelief can interfere with starting and developing relationships. Others may perceive you as insincere. Consequently you are faced with a set of choices concerning how open and honest to be about yourself at each stage in the conversation.

Ending Conversations

Shy people, and even people who are not so shy, sometimes have trouble ending conversations. You may choose to end a conversation for numerous reasons, ranging from boredom to having to go do something else when you would really rather continue conversing with someone you find attractive. Breaking eye contact, starting to edge away, making your body orientation less open, and holding out your hand are all body messages that tell another you wish to go.

How you end the conversation can have positive or negative consequences for your subsequent relationship. If you wish to meet again, you can show appreciation—for example, "I very much enjoyed talking with you," said with a smile and with voice messages that indicate your sincerity. You could reinforce this message with a comment like "I hope we meet again." If your feelings are even more positive you might ask, "I wonder if we could get together again some time?" If your feelings are negative, your disengaging body messages can become more pronounced, even to the extent of holding out the palm of your hand as a stop signal. You can make closure comments such as "Well, that's about the sum of it" and "I must be off now," said in a firm voice. You can also avoid smiling too much.

Making a Date

Since the position in this book is that of equality between the sexes, both females and males are encouraged to take the initiative when they want to meet another person again. Receiving messages from another that they might be interested in dating involves using your decoding skills; even using those skills, you may get the message wrong. Males especially may be too ready to read sexual messages into the friendliness of someone of the opposite sex. Verbal messages that convey interest in dating include compliments, making it clear that you have noticed the other in the past, reflecting the other's feelings, being helpful, and asking the other questions about themselves. Body messages include eye contact, absence of arm and leg barriers, not looking elsewhere when conversing, and light touching with or without humor. Voice messages include animated speech involving variations in emphasis.

Asking for a date is often done on the telephone. Some of the thinking skills discussed earlier are highly relevant to asking someone out. Coping self-talk can help you calm your anxieties as well as stay focused on the task at hand. Possessing realistic personal rules can prevent you from oppressing yourself with exaggerated fears about rejection. Predicting rewards as well as risks can assist you in taking the risks that may bring you the rewards. Other telephone skills include the following.

• *Clearly identifying yourself.* "Hello, this is Jane/John Doe. We met at the Smiths' barbecue last week."

• *Sending an "I" message request.* "I was wondering whether you would like to come out for a movie (or a cup of coffee, or a drink) with me this weekend."

• *Offering specific alternatives.* If the answer is yes, be prepared to offer specific alternatives—for example, different movies or different places to get coffee. Be sure to make your suggestions in such a way that the other person feels safe discussing them.

• *Stating your agreement clearly*. At the end it can be useful to summarize your agreement: "Just to confirm, I'll pick you up at your apartment at 8 P.M. this Friday to go see the movie at the Roxie. I look forward to seeing you then." A misunderstanding over the first meeting is not the best way to start a relationship.

• *Taking refusals politely*. The other person has a perfect right to turn you down. With any luck, the other person will use tact. The other's courage in refusing you merits respect, and you should politely end the conversation.

Exercise 27 helps you assess your skills in making initial contact.

Exercise 27
Assessing my skills in making initial contact

Instructions: Using the following worksheet, assess your skills in making initial contact.

Skills Area	My Assessment
Openers	
Body messages	
Voice messages	
Keeping the conversation flowing	
Ending conversations	
Making a date	

1. Summarize how you see your skills strengths and weaknesses in making initial contact.

_____

_____

2. Are your skills in making initial contact influenced by sex-role and cultural considerations?

_____

3. Set yourself specific goals for improving your skills weaknesses in making initial contact.

_____

_____

Concluding Self-Talk

If I am shy, I am one of a large number of people who admit to shyness. However, everyone experiences some anxiety in social situations. One way I can combat my shyness is by developing self-supporting thinking skills and discarding self-oppressing ones. Such thinking skills include accurately attributing the cause for my shyness; using coping self-talk; choosing realistic personal rules, especially regarding approval and rejection; not jumping to unwarranted perceptual conclusions; and predicting rewards as well as risks. Whether I'm shy or not, I can gain from developing my skills at making initial contact. These skills include conversational skills such as using openers, coordinating who has the floor, keeping the conversation flowing, and ending conversations. In addition, I may need to work on my telephone dating skills.

Notes

7
Choosing Relationships

Charm: that quality in others of making us
more satisfied with ourselves.
H. F. Amiel

This chapter explores how you go about choosing an intimate relationship. Its contents also have relevance for choosing other relationships such as friends or business partners. The chapter should be taken in conjunction with the next chapter, on deepening relationships. Choosing a long-term partner is a process that starts with casual dating, in which the partners are not identified as a couple; progresses to serious dating, in which the partners are identified as a couple; and ends with marriage or de facto marriage (Hutson, Surra, Fitzgerald, & Cate, 1981). Hutson and colleagues distinguish four types of courtship.

1. Accelerated-arrested courtship, with a rapid initial move toward marriage slowing down just before final commitment.
2. Accelerated courtship, a smooth and rapid transition toward marriage.
3. Intermediate courtship, slower than the first two types, but more rapid than the fourth.
4. Prolonged courtship, where relationships "took a relatively retarded and rocky path toward marriage" (Hutson et al., 1981, p. 76).

The stark fact is that most intimate relationships start in hope and end in pain. The ultimate unhappiness of many relationships leads one to suspect that many partners could be making better choices about whom they relate to. If people were better initial choosers, they might increase their chances of achieving stability, happiness, and fulfillment in their relationships.

An important skill in maintaining a long-term relationship is that of selecting a partner. This chapter starts by exploring some potential sources of error in how people select their partners, then discusses some criteria for selection. These criteria go beyond vague statements like "We love each other" and "We get along really well." Chapter 8, on deepening relationships, discusses not only how relationships develop but also how the filtering or further selection process continues.

Making Unrealistic Choices

> Love is blind; friendship closes its eyes.
> *Anonymous*

How can you avoid unnecessarily landing yourself in an unhappy relationship? Relationships don't come with guarantees. All relationships go through cycles of alienation and affection and have their lows as well as highs. You have to steer a course between pollyannaism ("Everything will turn out for the best") and undue pessimism ("Everything will turn out for the worst"). Even if a relationship does turn out for the worst, you may have experienced some good times along the way.

The previous chapter, which discussed overcoming shyness and making initial contact, emphasized being clear about rewards as well as risks. This chapter, on choosing long-term relationships, emphasizes being realistic about risks as well as rewards. Forewarned is forearmed. The following are some reasons that the quality of your decision making when choosing a partner may be less than desirable.

- *Poor decision making skills.* Even at the best of times, you may not be good at making decisions in a systematic and rational way. Samuel Butler once said, "Life is the art of drawing sufficient conclusions from insufficient premises." You may possess a decision making style that interferes with the mature fusion of head and heart necessary to wisely choose a partner. You may get too anxious and hypervigilant. In this process you may fail to take into account or to weigh relevant information adequately. Alternatively, you may make decisions impulsively or passively conform to what others expect of you. Good decisions depend not only on collecting sufficient information but also on your ability to perceive and assess that information accurately.

- *Insufficient sense of your identity.* Paradoxically, most people have to make critical decisions about choice of partner and career when young and inexperienced. Your level of security and knowledge of your own wants and wishes may be insufficient at this stage. When choosing a relationship, my personification of me chooses my personification of you. However, I may not really know myself. Instead, what I call "I" or "me" may be a clutter of attitudes, values, and rules taken over from other people, such as my parents, as if these values were my own. I may perceive you in terms of others' values, not mine; you may do the same to me. The risk of such behavior is that, as either or both of us grow into more autonomous persons, we may get badly out of step with one another. Our relationship, instead of being built on the rock of stable yet flexible identities, has been built on the sand of unstable and possibly rigid identities.

- *Falling victim to impression management.* When people date they package themselves to get the other to perceive them favorably. Imagine getting ready for a new date. To some extent, each person is "out to get" the other. Depending on how far out of touch they are with their own valuing processes and identities, the people you date sell themselves, as though they were commodities. They emphasize their assets or selling points and strictly control the flow of information about their perceived liabilities. It can be hard to get to know another person well when, both consciously and unconsciously, that person is putting on an act for your consumption. Appearances can be deceptive. For example, conflicts may be smoothed over so as not to interfere with the goal of winning the other's affection; but later on, in the routine of daily living, these conflicts are likely to surface. Some people are very adept at manipulating appearances to conceal their negative points. However, others have hidden assets that become more apparent as you get to know these people better.

• *Idealization of the other.* A combination of the myth of romantic love, your own insecurities, and your date's skills of impression management may lead you to idealize your date. You see in him or her what you want to see. You may fail to acknowledge adequately messages that contradict your ideal picture. Furthermore, you may fail to realize that the other person may not be as interested in you as you are in him or her.

• *Unrealistic relationship expectations.* A number of other unrealistic expectations, besides the myth of the ideal partner, may build hidden weaknesses into your relationships. The following are some of them.

"People who are in love live happily ever after."
"Love overcomes all."
"Love lasts forever."
"I can change him or her."
"My marriage or partnership is not going to run into trouble; it can't happen to me."
"People will always be the same."
"My partner and I should meet all of one another's needs."
"Real love involves the complete fusion of two separate individuals."

Partners who enter relationships may be unaware of some of their hidden assumptions and expectations. They may fail to realize that because they expect too much, they set themselves up for a fall. Furthermore, they may remain unaware that a conflict between each partner's interdependence and autonomy is at the heart of all close relationships. To pretend that this conflict does not exist is a huge step away from being able to manage it constructively.

• *Looking for a role.* Some people may be heavily influenced to get married because they have been brought up to see marriage as their main role in life. They seek to marry a role rather than a person. They get married to secure the structure and trappings of married life without paying sufficient attention to the realities of having loving relationships with their spouses. Because of the traditional emphasis on females being the homemaker, women especially may feel the pressure to get into the married role, including motherhood and raising a family. Disparaging remarks like "old maid" and "on the shelf" are made about single females after a certain age. Males also may get married to present a more socially acceptable image to the world—for instance, to advance their careers.

• *Immature loneliness.* People search for companionship to avoid loneliness. The pain of loneliness is a major way by which nature ensures that people relate. However, people are lonely for different reasons. Some of these reasons may make you vulnerable to making poor relationship choices. For example, some people possess neither the security nor the skills to be able to spend much time on their own. Because they are more incomplete than they need be, they risk unwisely saying yes to a relationship. Young people who leave their homes and family networks may especially feel under pressure to establish a substitute home before they are emotionally ready to do so. Getting into a relationship on the rebound, when you feel undervalued and your self-esteem is low, is another example of loneliness contributing to poor choosing. Also, getting into a permanent relationship when you are geographically isolated and have little opportunity for adequate choice of a partner carries with it distinct risks.

• *Transference.* The psychoanalytic movement in particular has emphasized that people relate to others on the basis of their past experiences with similar people. For example, children who have had difficulty with their parents subsequently may react negatively to authority figures. In close personal relationships, without being aware of it you may both perceive and react to the other in terms of a previous relationship—an example for a male may be his mother or a former girlfriend. Transference reactions can be positive or negative. Either way, such reactions are not a sound basis on which to make relationship choices. You need to react to others as they are, not because they remind you of other people.

• *Infatuation.* If you are infatuated with another you are inspired with extravagant and unreasoning passion. Physical attraction is probably the main stimulus for people starting relationships. However, although it is very important, physical attraction is only one criteria for choosing a permanent relationship. Infatuation is a state of heightened emotionality that burns itself out. Infatuation and lovesickness are part of being alive. However, protect yourself when possible from making major commitments until you have come down to earth and made a more realistic appraisal. Strong sexual attraction makes it all too easy to misperceive one another and to rationalize away potential difficulties in your relationship.

• *Giving in to family pressures.* The previous discussion of an insufficient sense of identity mentioned that you may have internalized parental values. Even though your parents physically may not be around, you may still *psychologically* choose a partner to suit them. Trying to suit your parents may restrict your field of choice as well as build instability into your relationship. The same results can ensue when families openly put pressure on children not to marry out of their culture, class, religion, or whatever else, even though the children may strongly prefer someone different from themselves. Conformity and rebellion are two maladaptive ways to handle this kind of pressure. By conforming, you inhibit or bury your true feelings and settle for being less than you might have been. By rebelling, you overreact and may enter an unstable relationship you later regret. Although it is difficult, having the courage of your convictions and using assertion skills are the best ways to manage family pressures to act against your interests. With the trend toward later marriages and independent incomes for females, family pressures on mate selection probably carry less weight now than they did in the past.

The preceding list of possible distortions in choosing long-term partners is not exhaustive; you may think of others. The chances of making distorted choices double if you take into account that both you and your partner may misperceive each other. The discussion has focused on choosing long-term partners rather than friends for a number of reasons. Friendships are easier to end. They do not involve children. Also, you are less likely to be so sexually and emotionally involved when choosing your friends. Exercise 28 encourages you to explore whether you have some skills weaknesses when it comes to choosing a long-term partner.

Exercise 28
Exploring my possible skills weaknesses in choosing a long-term partner

Instructions: Write down your assessment of how each of the following skills weaknesses might interfere with your capacity to choose a suitable long-term partner.

Skills Weakness	My Assessment
Poor decision making skills	
Insufficient sense of my identity	
Falling victim to impression management	
Idealization of the other	
Unrealistic relationship expectations	
Looking for a role	
Immature loneliness	
Transference	
Infatuation	
Giving in to family pressures	
Other weaknesses not listed here	

1. Summarize your possible skills weaknesses in your ability to choose a long-term partner realistically.

_____

_____

_____

_____

2. To what extent are your possible skills weaknesses influenced by your biological sex and by your culture?

_____

_____

_____

_____

_____

Making More Realistic Choices

> There can be little liking where there is no likeness.
> *Aesop's Fables*

This section explores some considerations involved in realistically choosing a long-term partner. Especially if marriage is contemplated, your choice is a choice for all seasons. What matters to you in the short term may be different from what matters in the long run. Sternberg considers that among the things that increase in importance as relationships grow are willingness to change in response to one another and willingness to tolerate one another's imperfections (Trotter, 1986). Sharing values, especially religious ones, also becomes more important. Others have observed a shift over time from initial passionate love to eventual compassionate love (Cunningham & Antill, 1981).

Choosing a long-term relationship is a process that takes place over an extended period of time. Although you may initially say yes to another human being on first sight or initial meeting, it takes time to gather appropriate evidence to justify your initial choice. Also, you have to feel ready for a relationship. Intuition as well as physical attraction plays a large role in starting relationships. The intuitive little child inside you may feel an emotional attraction to the intuitive little child inside another. You may feel unexpectedly safe and comfortable in another's presence, as though you have been friends for some time.

Couples tend to be similar in many ways. Argyle and Henderson observe: "They are more similar than by chance in age, social class, religion, height, intelligence, values and beliefs and in some measures of personality" (Argyle & Henderson, 1985, p. 105). These similarities are not surprising, since people tend to meet one another in fairly circumscribed social settings. Although complementarity may add spice and interest, most relationships need to be grounded in a high degree of similarity.

The following are a series of considerations in choosing a long-term relationship. You cannot assess another person's suitability in isolation from yourself. There is no such thing as the perfect partner or the perfect relationship. Trade-offs, compromises, and negotiations are inevitable. Each person and each couple will weigh the importance of the following considerations differently, and their importance for either or both partners is likely to change over time. This change can either enhance closeness or result in partners who are badly out of step.

• *Physical attractiveness or sexual compatibility.* As memorialized in the film *10,* many people measure physical attractiveness on a simple scale ranging from 1 ("not at all attractive") to 10 ("extremely attractive"). Especially for males, physical attractiveness may be a very important consideration in starting a relationship. Individuals tend to match themselves on physical attractiveness. People who consider themselves less likely to be accepted may trade down to a less attractive partner. Physical attractiveness is not just a matter of natural attributes. How an individual uses body language—for instance, gaze and eye contact—also contributes to attractiveness.

With the increase in premarital sex, sexual compatibility is becoming more important in the choice of a long-term partner. Passion, as expressed by kissing, hugging, touching, and making love, needs to be satisfactorily given and received. Furthermore, partners need to be able to talk freely about their sexual relationship, including sharing their fantasies.

• *Emotional responsiveness.* Each partner needs to be emotionally responsive to the other. Warmth and caring need to be openly given and received. Partners also need to be sufficiently in touch with themselves that they can be spontaneous and express a range of feelings. Genuineness in the expression of feelings is very important. Verbal, voice, body, touch, and action messages should speak in the same direction. If you experience someone as either cool and unresponsive to you or "blowing hot and cold"—warm one moment and pushing you away the next—some further exploration, at least, is called for.

• *Capacity for intimacy.* Erich Fromm's 1956 book, *The Art of Loving,* emphasized the importance of knowledge in loving relationships. Your willingness to be known can help me relate to you as you are, rather than in terms of my inaccurate personification of you. Your openness and ability to reveal yourself as a fallible human being helps me to know you. It also makes it easier for me to drop my social masks and defensive facades. Capacity for intimacy and emotional responsiveness are related in that if you can feel free to disclose not only personal information but also your feelings you share the flow of your being with me, and I am encouraged to respond in the same way. Our relationship becomes a vibrant process rather than something static and dull; we have an open rather than a closed communication system.

• *Respect.* Your respect for me is your concern that, within our interdependence, you see me as I am and allow me to grow as a separate human being. Possessiveness and control are the antithesis of respect. When you respect me, you are secure enough in yourself that you allow me the psychological space to be myself. You are capable of helping me and taking pleasure in my unfolding. You do not need me to constrict myself so that you can sustain a false picture of yourself. I am a person in my own right and not an object for your use. A good test of whether another respects you is how well they listen to you. Poor listeners tend to be too bound up with their own agendas to respect you fully.

• *Considerateness and caring.* Considerateness means thoughtfulness and having regard for another's feelings. It entails both the presence of the desirable qualities of care and kindness and the absence of the undesirable quality of insensitivity to others. Considerateness involves being aware of another's needs and when reasonable trying to meet them; this can involve being positive in finding out the other's needs as well as reacting. Being considerate shows that you care. Caring plays a very important role in people's judgments of love (Steck, Levitan, McLane, & Kelley, 1982). Caring was one of the three main components in Rubin's Love Scale. Illustrative items included "I would do almost anything for [that person]"; "One of my primary concerns is [that person]'s welfare"; and "I feel responsible for [that person]'s well-being" (Rubin, 1980).

Considerateness also involves avoiding inconsiderateness. If someone does not try to minimize the negative consequences of their actions for you, he or she is inconsiderate and lacks the sensitivity to avoid hurting you unnecessarily. What counts for him or her is "me" rather than either "you" or "you and me." Such people behave like spoiled children.

• *Sense of humor.* Does the child in the other person appeal to the child in you? Does the other person have a similar sense of fun and humor? Do you enjoy kidding and playing together? Enjoying one another's sense of humor can both enhance the good times and ease the bad times in your relationship. In a British opinion survey, having a good sense of humor was rated above looks as a quality thought desirable in a partner (MORI, 1983).

• *Openness to experience.* If you are open to your experience, you are able to perceive incoming information without distorting or denying it. Openness is highly relevant to a person's capacity to maintain a long-term relationship in a number of ways. First, the more each of you can perceive yourself and the other accurately, the sounder the information base you have for transacting your relationship. Second, if a person is rigid, defensive, and not willing to look at his or her own behavior, he or she is sending you a critical danger signal in regard to entering a long-term relationship with that person. Rather more frequently than you would like, you may find yourself being held solely responsible for conflicts and misunderstandings. Third, openness to experience allows another person to change and grow, to be responsive to your changes and growth, and to renegotiate how you wish to relate in light of these changes.

• *Trustworthiness and commitment.* All relationships involve contracts, implicit and explicit. These contracts or agreements relate to such matters as not engaging in sexual activity with others, not criticizing and standing up for the other in public, keeping confidences, keeping promises, and generally acting in a reliable and dependable way. Another aspect of trust is trusting another not to reject or hurt you needlessly. The notion of commitment is closely allied to that of trust. A committed partner does not breach trust. Instead, a committed partner keeps trust by staying with the relationship through the inevitable hard times.

• *Relationship skills strengths.* Although most people do not think of their relationships in skills terms, there is no reason you should not. This book describes various skills for initiating, maintaining, and developing relationships throughout its text. You can assess the relationship skills of a person with whom you are considering a long-term relationship. You may consider such an assessment to be somewhat calculating. However, the success of your relationship depends heavily on how well each of you sends and receives messages and manages your anger and differences. Instead of rushing into a relationship, it may pay to spend some time allowing conflicts to emerge and then trying to deal with them. The engagement period is a time of increased commitment, when couples can assess one another's relationship skills more closely. Cohabitation offers a further opportunity for this.

• *Shared pleasant activities.* One of the main approaches to helping depressed individuals is to encourage them to increase the number of pleasant activities in which they are involved (Lewinsohn, Munoz, Youngren, & Zeiss, 1986). Similarly, if relationships are to remain happy, you need to engage in a reasonable number of shared pleasant activities. You can still enjoy individual activities as well. You need space apart from one another as well as together. Frequent conversations, both intimate and less intimate, are an important way of keeping in touch with one another both emotionally and practically. Couples vary in the activities they enjoy. Some illustrative pleasant activities include going for a walk, eating together informally, playing games indoors or out, gardening, having friends over, going to the movies or theater, and going to nightclubs. Enjoying doing things together is a good omen for your relationship. However, the activities each of you enjoy are likely to change over the course of your relationship. You may then need to work to keep sharing some pleasant activities.

   • *Compatibility of values.* Values are the underlying principles and priorities on which people base their lives. They constitute people's philosophies of life. At any time you and your partner have a profile of values, some of which are more important than others. Differences in values are inevitable. However, you need to feel comfortable with one another's major values to sustain a long-term relationship without great strain. The following are some values you may or may not share with a person you are considering as a long-term partner.

> *Friendship:* being joined to others outside your relationship by mutual intimacy and interests.
> *Family Life:* having and being part of a family; valuing parenthood.
> *Religious:* acknowledging the need for connectedness to some ultimate and superhuman power.
> *Materialistic:* values centered on the accumulation and control of money.
> *Aesthetic:* appreciating beauty and good taste, with special reference to the arts such as music, literature, and painting.
> *Intellectual:* valuing analytic and rational pursuits.
> *Social:* helping others; showing social concern.
> *Sensual:* valuing the pleasures of the flesh.
> *Hedonistic:* valuing fun and having a good time.
> *Career:* valuing having a career.
> *Practical:* valuing practical pursuits and, where practical matters are concerned, self-reliance.
> *Outdoors:* appreciating and valuing being outdoors; enjoying being in communion with nature.
> *Athletic:* valuing participation in sports.
> *Autonomous:* valuing independence and thinking for yourself; valuing enterprise.
> *Conventional:* appreciating tradition; valuing obedience and conformity to the status quo.
> *Self-actualizing:* being committed to personal growth and development.

Values are the basis on which you and your partner develop goals for your relationship. You may discover on closer examination that each of you wants and expects different things. Such differences need not constitute an insuperable obstacle to your relationship if you can resolve the value conflicts to your mutual satisfaction. However, major unresolved value conflicts are unlikely to go away.

When such conflicts are present, you should consider whether it is worth the risk of committing yourself to a long-term relationship.

• *Compatibility of personal rules.* Chapter 2 mentioned that each individual possesses an inner rule book of personal rules for living that he or she brings to relationships. These rules are of varying degrees of flexibility and represent a person's values. Rules manifest themselves in every area of a couple's functioning—for example, how the family income is earned and spent, use of leisure time, time spent with friends, sex, how to communicate with one another, how to manage anger and conflict, household chores, visiting relatives, and raising children. Sometimes, given flexibility on both sides, differences in personal rules can be negotiated to arrive at a mutually satisfactory solution. On other occasions, the differences may be more intractable—for instance, differences concerning size of family and education of children. When possible, find out in advance whether either partner feels unable or unwilling to work through a major difference. What you find out may influence your decision about making a long-standing commitment to the relationship.

• *Sex role compatibility.* We are now living through a transitional period in which traditional sex roles are being challenged. People enter heterosexual relationships with different personal rules about sex roles. In a transitional period, the differences may be greater than in a period when sex roles are to a great extent dictated by tradition. Sex role issues permeate every area of heterosexual relationships, from making love and doing the dishes to earning and spending a couple's income. Differences in how partners perceive sex roles can often be worked through by discussion and negotiation. However, when major differences remain, these are best acknowledged and taken into account in any decision about a long-term commitment.

• *Other Considerations.* You may wish to take other considerations into account as well. These considerations include the differences in your ages, your partner's earning capacity, whether you like his or her relatives and friends, and how you see him or her as a parent of your kids. Also, a host of day-to-day living considerations may be important: what sort of music and food the other likes, his or her sleeping habits, how tidy the other is, and so on. Think through what is important in a long-term partner. Then be prepared to compromise.

Exercise 29 enables you to explore how important each of these considerations is for you.

Exercise 29
Choosing a long-term partner

Instructions: Write down your assessment of how important each of the following considerations is for you in choosing a long-term partner. For each consideration indicate what in particular you should look out for.

(continued)

Exercise 29 (continued)

Consideration	*Importance and What to Look Out For*
Physical attractiveness/sexual compatibility	
Emotional responsiveness	
Capacity for intimacy	
Respect	
Considerateness and caring	
Sense of humor	
Openness to experience	
Trustworthiness and commitment	
Relationship skills strengths	
Sharing pleasant activities	
Compatibility of values	
Compatibility of personal rules	
Sex-role compatibility	
Others	

Write out a summary of your main priorities in choosing a long-term partner.

_____

_____

Concluding Self-Talk

I can increase my chances for happiness and fulfillment if I develop my skills in choosing a long-term partner. Many factors may contribute to my making a poor choice. These include poor decision making skills, an insufficient sense of my identity, falling victim to impression management, and unrealistic relationship expectations.

Partners may value different qualities in one another at different stages in their relationships. Consequently, I need to make a choice for all seasons. Making such a choice requires taking into account not only physical attractiveness, sexual compatibility, and how well we get on now, but also longer-term considerations. Considerations relevant to the long term include how open the other is to new experience and how compatible our values are. I need to look closely before I leap into a long-term relationship, especially one that will involve children.

Notes

8
Deepening Relationships

Only connect!
E. M. Forster

Choosing and deepening relationships are interrelated. At each stage of your relationships, you and those to whom you relate may choose either to develop or not to develop your relationships further. This chapter explores some of the ways bonds between people may be deepened and strengthened.

Rewardingness, Reciprocity, and Rules

Rewardingness, reciprocity, and rules are the three R's of developing and deepening relationships. Let us examine each in turn.

• *Rewardingness.* The main goal in life of most people is to be happy (Nelson-Jones & Strong, 1977). People seek out experiences that are rewarding for them. Furthermore, it is a fundamental psychological principle that people are more likely to repeat behaviors that have rewarding consequences for them than those that do not.

The notion of rewardingness permeates relationships in a number of ways (Argyle & Henderson, 1985). First, each partner looks for rewards. In close relationships these include the rewards of giving as well as of taking. Many of these rewards involve voice, body, touch, and action messages rather than just words. Second, relationships are likely to deepen if partners can increase the range and depth of their rewardingness for one another. Areas of mutual rewardingness include intimacy, caring, and sex. However, if either partner perceives and resents an imbalance in the exchange of rewards, the relationship is put at risk. Third, relationships are more likely to be maintained if partners are able to sustain a high level of rewardingness for each other. At the very least, the rewards or satisfactions of staying in the relationship must exceed the perceived rewards of getting out of it. Finally, relationships are likely to end when the rewards of being free of them consistently exceed the rewards of staying in them.

• *Reciprocity.* Most long-standing relationships are grounded in some form of reciprocity in the giving and receiving of rewards (Azrin, Naster, & Jones, 1973). Cunningham and Antill observe, "It is indisputable that most human relationships are based on considerations of equity and exchange" (Cunningham & Antill, 1981, p. 31). Put simply, you meet my needs and I meet yours. Happy relationships involve a preponderance of positive reciprocity, or mutual rewardingness. Where each partner genuinely cares for the growth and development of the other, positive reciprocity is especially likely to characterize the relationship. Sometimes a relationship may be imbalanced because one partner *willingly* donates his or her strength to draw out the potential of the other partner. For example, Carl

Rogers's 1973 book *Becoming Partners* recounts the moving story of Joe's steady trust in his partner Irene's potential for growth freed her from the unhappiness of her upbringing and two previous marriages. Distressed relationships are characterized either by a preponderance of negative reciprocity, in which partners trade negative behaviors, or by an imbalance in the exchange of positive behaviors, which is resented. Figure 8-1 is a schematic representation of reciprocity of rewardingness.

The analysis of reciprocity in Figure 8-1 is a simplification for many reasons. For example, you could be trying to show your positive feelings for me and I might either not perceive it or else push you away. Alternatively, you might not know how to show your affection for me because I am inhibited in telling you how to do it. Furthermore, when I appreciate what you do I may not be good at expressing this appreciation. Moreover, we may be mutually rewarding in some areas and not in others or offer different levels of reward in different areas. Many other disclaimers could be offered about this schematic representation. However, the basic point remains: some degree of reciprocity of rewardingness is critical to deepening and maintaining long-term relationships between equals.

• *Rules.* Each of you brings your personal rules to your relationships. However, your relationships also have their own formal and informal rules or contracts. The purposes of these relationship rules are to provide guidelines and to clarify

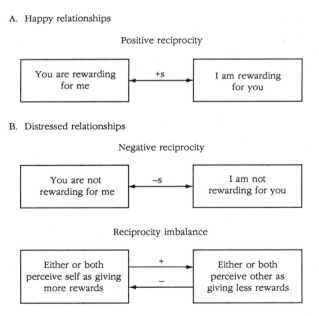

Figure 8-1.   Schematic representation of reciprocity of rewardingness in happy and distressed relationships.

expectations for your own and your partner's behavior. They prevent your having to think each issue through from scratch every time it arises. Argyle and Henderson observe that relationship rules are of two main kinds: those about providing rewards and those about avoiding inflicting costs (Argyle & Henderson, 1985). Rules about intimacy (for example, "share news of success"), about caring (for example, "show emotional support"), and about exchange of specific rewards (for example, "give birthday cards and presents") come under the first category. Rules about faithfulness (for example, "restrict sexual activity to the other partner") and privacy (for example, "respect one another's privacy" and " keep confidences") come under the second category.

Relationships take place in social contexts. Consequently, many rules will reflect cultural, social, and family customs. However, relationships also take place between two unique individuals who have the capacity to choose which relationship rules work for them. Thus partners have the potential to move beyond playing out roles in relation to each other in order to create rules that allow them to express their individuality as persons. These rules are likely to emphasize concepts such as reciprocity and rewardingness. However, they can be fresh, spontaneous, and negotiated between equals rather unthinkingly taken on from others, for good or ill.

The Intimacy Bond

> Things are seldom what they seem,
> Skim milk masquerades as cream.
> Externals don't portray insides,
> Jekylls may be masking Hydes.
> *Sidney Jourard*

By means of what he considered an atrocious verse, Jourard made the point that of all forms of life, humans are capable of being one thing and seeming from their actions and speech to be something else (Jourard, 1964). He emphasized that effective loving involves both partners knowing and relating to one another as they are. People who do not truly know one another cannot love one another.

Deepening relationships involves having the courage to discard impression management, social masks, and defensive facades. It involves the movement toward dropping all those concealing, as opposed to revealing, behaviors that protect you from knowing yourself and being known to another. Self-disclosure involves both revealing personal information and expressing your feelings. Chapter 3 discussed these dimensions of self-disclosure from the viewpoint of sending verbal messages. Here, the effects of self-disclosure on how relationships develop are explored.

Revealing Progressively More Intimate Information

> Raoul and Connie have been dating for a month. At first Connie thought Raoul was the strong, silent type. As he disclosed more of himself, she was surprised to find out how sensitive and emotional he was, how much he valued his close friendships, and how willing he was to listen to her talk about her goals in life. Raoul, on the other hand, was learning that Connie was a very determined person who wanted to combine having her own business and raising a family. He admired her openness and willingness to share her doubts about her femininity. Her openness made it easier for him to share his doubts about not being the typical male and his feelings of hurt at the teasing he had received because of this. Both Connie and Raoul were also able to share their doubts about their physical attractiveness.

In choosing whether to deepen a relationship, one of the main ways in which you psychologically feel each other out is by making progressively more intimate disclosures. Altman and Taylor indicate that as relationships develop there is both increasing breadth of disclosure and increasing depth (Altman & Taylor, 1965). The process of deepening a relationship involves matching the intimacy level of one another's disclosures prior to disclosing at a still more intimate level. You move beyond safe talk to talk that has increasingly more risk attached to it. The main risk is that of rejection. Another major fear is lack of confidentiality. In short, two important ways that you deepen a relationship are either by first making a more intimate disclosure or by matching a more intimate disclosure when another takes the first risk. If you both wish to develop your relationship, you are likely to coordinate the deepening of the intimacy level of your disclosures. More often than not, relationships do not make a smooth progression to more intimate disclosures but instead trace a jagged line in that direction.

Progressively sharing more intimate information involves you in revealing your vulnerabilities as well as your strengths. Some of you may feel the need to present yourselves in a positive light all the time. The effect this "boasting" can have on others is at least threefold. First, others may fail to get to know you properly since you wear a mask. Second, others may find themselves in a psychologically negative exchange with you since they alone in the relationship are vulnerable and make mistakes. Third, because they feel threatened, others may edit what they say to you.

The progressive matching of the intimacy level of disclosures deepens relationships for a number of reasons. One explanation is that your disclosure is a reward to another, indicating liking. This disclosure needs to be matched if the relationship is to remain in balance. Another explanation emphasizes how disclosures are received. If your disclosure is met with acceptance by another, this acceptance not only establishes the other as less threatening and more like you, but also gives the other permission to make a similar disclosure. Consequently, by accepting disclosures as well as by disclosing, trust is developed in the relationship.

Expressing Your Feelings About the Relationship

Acknowledging, owning, and openly expressing your feelings is a major way to develop the intimacy bond. Partners increasingly feel free not only to talk about themselves but to express themselves. As such they move beyond playing two-dimensional roles to relating to each other as three-dimensional persons. Furthermore, the relationship becomes an active process rather than a matter of relating to one another in rigid and stereotyped ways.

Although you should always acknowledge all your significant feelings, you have a choice as to when and how best to express them. You need to work toward an open communication system in which each partner feels free to express his or her feelings; avoid assuming that such an open system exists from the start. Expressions of feelings can damage as well as enhance relationships.

An important aspect of expressing feelings is the giving and receiving of feedback. Egan calls this skill immediacy, or "you–me" talk. He distinguishes between relationship immediacy, ("Let's talk about how we've been relating to each other recently") and here-and-now immediacy ("Let's talk about what's going on between you and me right now as we're talking to each other") (Egan, 1977, p. 235). "You–me" talk involves the giving and receiving of feedback either about our relationship or about what is perhaps left unsaid between us right now. The focus is mainly on expressing feelings about a relationship in ways that may do more good than harm.

The following are a few guidelines for expressing feelings about a relationship.

• *Become aware of your feelings.* Try to get in touch with what you truly feel. Avoid parroting other people's feelings as if they were your own. If you are confused about your feelings, be prepared to share this confusion. Your feelings about your relationship may become clearer as you discuss them with the other person involved.

• *Send "I" messages.* Feelings by definition are subjective. By your use of words, own your feelings and avoid making others responsible for them.

• *Be genuine.* Use voice, body, touch, and action messages that match what you say. As with all communication, giving feedback is not just a matter of what you say but how you say it.

• *Express positive as well as negative feelings.* Psychologist Irene Kassorla stresses the power of stating "honest positives" (Kassorla, 1984). Honest positives are genuinely held positive thoughts and feelings about another person. A valuable form of feedback in their own right, honest positives can also be interspersed with negative feelings to prevent the other person from feeling attacked by a barrage of negative comments. Here is a brief example.

Negative feelings only: "I'm seeing too much of you."
Positive and negative feelings: "I want to keep seeing you but I need more space for myself."

• *Share persistent negative feelings.* Rogers stresses the importance of sharing persistent negative feelings. He observes that if this sharing "is firmly based in the attitude, 'I want to share myself and my feelings with you, even when they are not all positive', then a constructive process can almost be guaranteed" (Rogers, 1973, p. 209). Negative feelings might include boredom with your sexual relationship, annoyance with the way the household chores are distributed, or disappointment that a partner is failing to take adequate care about his or her appearance.

• *Invite discussion.* Don't give hit-and-run feedback. Respect the other person's right to respond. "You–me" talk involves two-way sharing and discussion of feelings about your relationship. Relationships where communication goes only one way are headed for problems, if they are not already on the rocks.

• *Be prepared to look at your own behavior.* Your feelings take place in the context of a relationship in which you and your partner influence one another. You may have contributed to your negative feelings either by misperceiving your partner or by behaving negatively. When confronted, you need to be open enough to acknowledge any role you may have played in generating your negative feelings.

Experiment 9 gives you an opportunity to try out these guidelines.

Experiment 9
What happens when I am more open about sharing
my feelings in a relationship?

1. *Expressing positive feelings*

   Part A: Assessment
   1. Think of a relationship you think you could improve if you shared more of your positive feelings toward the other person.

   _____

   2. For an appropriate period, say three days, monitor how you send positive and negative messages to the other person.

   _____

   _____

   _____

   3. List all the positive feelings that are left unspoken in your relationship.

   _____

   _____

   Part B: Make an "If . . . then . . ." Statement
   Make an "If . . . then . . ." statement along the lines of "If I express these positive feelings (specify), then these consequences (specify) are likely to follow."

   _____

   _____

Experiment 9 (continued)

> *Part C: Try Out and Evaluate Your Changed Behavior*
> Try out your changed behavior. Assess its positive and negative consequences for yourself and the other person. Have your predictions been confirmed or disconfirmed? Has this experiment taught you something about the power of expressing positive feelings rather than leaving them unsaid? If so, what?

_____

_____

_____

> 2. *Expressing negative feelings*
> If appropriate, carry out the above experiment, but this time focus on expressing a negative rather than a positive feeling. Follow the guidelines for expressing feelings about another person.

_____

_____

The Caring Bond

All truly close relationships are characterized by a high degree of caring. This caring involves affection, interest in, and concern for one another's welfare and growth. The quality of caring is important. It can represent what Maslow terms "B-love (love for the Being of another person, unneeding love, unselfish love) and D-love (deficiency-love, love need, selfish love)" (Maslow, 1962, p. 39). When caring represents deficiency love it may be manipulative ("I show caring to you because I want something in return"), oppressive ("I care for you whether or not you want my care"), dependency-engendering ("I care for you because I do not want you to be free"), or aggressive ("I care for you so you should darned well show more caring for me"). Caring based on deficiency love is pseudo-caring. In the early stages of dating, you have insufficient information to know whether the caring expressed by another is superficial or the real thing. As you get to know one another better, you collect more evidence with which to make an accurate assessment.

When caring represents Maslow's being-love, your reward is in the giving as well as the receiving of caring. Fromm observes, "Love is the active concern for the life and growth of that which we love" (Fromm, 1956, p. 22). You prize the being of the person you love and are motivated by a consideration of their interests. A happy fusion between what is best for them and what you want for yourself takes place. Your caring is an end in itself and not the means to an end.

You respect the individuality and separateness of your partner and do not seek to manipulate, possess, or control him or her.

As relationships develop, you find out whether you and your partner reciprocate a satisfactory level of caring. You discover not only how much your partner cares for you but also how much you care for your partner. You need to cut through your own pseudo-caring as well as that of your partner. It is easy to think that you care for another person more than you do when you are in a romantic haze of infatuation and idealization. When you have to deal with the day-to-day realities of curlers and dirty shirts, you may feel otherwise. You will also be challenged to care for your partner when you are in conflict, and you do not like his or her behavior.

Since caring plays such a central role in the deepening and maintenance of relationships, it is described more fully in the following. Examples of statements about caring are given first, followed by discussion of verbal, voice, body, touch, and action messages showing caring.

• *Statements about caring.* The following are statements people might make to describe how they care for a partner.

"I try to be there for him/her when he/she is upset."
"I want him/her to feel emotionally supported by me."
"I try to tune into what he/she is going through and to show that I understand."
"If he/she ever really needs me, I will come running."
"I feel responsible for his/her welfare."
"I feel protective about him/her."
"His/her happiness is important to me."
"I try to avoid doing things that hurt him/her."
"I try to show him/her that I care."
"I like doing things to brighten his/her life."
"I like standing up for him/her in his/her absence."
"I always remember birthdays and anniversaries."
"However hurt and angry I feel, I always try hard to understand his/her position."
"I value his/her growth as a separate person within the context of our relation-
     ship."
"I want to help him/her attain his/her goals."

These statements of caring contain the themes of emotional support, showing understanding, concern for another's welfare, desire to give happiness and to avoid hurt, and respect and support for the other's individuality.

• *Verbal messages.* Verbal messages of caring include obvious statements such as "I love you," "I care for you," and "I want to help you." You may also pay one another compliments. Each partner in a relationship may have difficulty openly expressing his or her caring for the other. In such a situation, the other person may wrongly conclude that he or she is not cared for. Unless rectified, this perception damages the relationship. Furthermore, words of caring need to be matched by actions. The development of a relationship can flounder if either party is perceived as insincere. Another way you can show caring is through the quality of your listening responses. Do they indicate that you care enough to understand the internal viewpoint of your partner? In addition, confrontations, in which you challenge another to grow and not settle for less than their full humanity, can be very caring.

• *Voice messages.* Voice messages are extremely important in expressing caring. If your vocal music is wrong, you negate the effect of your fine words. Characteristics of caring voice messages include warmth, sympathy, expressiveness, and interest. Your voice should convey kindness rather than harshness and disinterest.

• *Body messages.* Your body messages can support or negate your verbal messages of caring. When sending caring verbal messages, your gaze, eye contact, body orientation, and facial expression all need to demonstrate your interest and concern for the other. Similarly, when others share their problems, you need to show good attending and listening body skills.

• *Touch messages.* Support and caring can be expressed by a hug, a half-embrace, an arm over the shoulder, a touch on the arm, or a hand on top of or holding a hand, among other ways. As with all touch messages, you are in another's close intimate zone and consequently must be very sensitive to picking up cues about their willingness to be touched. Nevertheless, touch can be a wonderful way to express your caring.

• *Action messages.* Action messages indicating caring include looking after the other when he or she is ill; being prepared to do your share of the household chores; giving birthday cards and presents; initiating pleasant events, such as going out to dinner; showing affection through flowers, poems, and other spontaneous gifts; and being available to help out in time of need. Additional action messages include the presence of small, helpful daily behaviors and the absence of unhelpful ones—for instance making the other person a cup of tea or coffee in the morning, or not leaving the bathtub dirty. These small repetitive indications of caring, or lack of caring, can have a large cumulative effect on how rewarding relationships are perceived to be. This perception in turn affects a relationship's future development, for good or ill.

Sex Roles and Caring

In Western cultures males are brought up to be more dominant, individualistic, and independent than females. They are also brought up to be less nurturing, sympathetic, and sensitive to others' feelings. Furthermore, some of the ways in which males show caring in their traditional sex roles have to do with providing things—for instance, the family income—rather than verbally supporting and showing affection to people. Thus, males more than females may have difficulties in both openly showing and receiving caring. Some males are very good at showing and receiving caring. Others may be better at showing than receiving caring, or the reverse. Some are good at neither.

Women may have their problems in showing and receiving caring, too. However, it is more part of the traditional female sex role to be rewarding in these ways. Disharmony can develop in relationships when partners experience a lack of reciprocity in the giving and receiving of caring. Despite their conditioning to be carers, females may be more dissatisfied with the quantity of expressions of caring they receive than males are. This dissatisfaction may be due to a lack of appreciation of their partners' true feelings for them or an accurate perception of their partners' lack of caring. Many males need to be both more expressive in showing caring and also more relaxed about receiving it. Exercise 30 helps you explore how you show caring.

Exercise 30
Assessing my showing caring behaviors

Instructions: Take one or more relationships that are important for you and for each fill out a worksheet made in the following format.

My assessment of my strengths and weaknesses in showing caring in my relationship with _____		
Skills Areas	*My Strengths*	*My Weaknesses*
Verbal messages		
Voice messages		
Body messages		
Touch messages		
Action messages		

1. Do you think your ability to show caring has been influenced by either sex role or cultural considerations? If so, give examples.

   _____

   _____

2. Do you think your ability to receive caring has been influenced by either sex role or cultural considerations? If so, give examples.

   _____

   _____

3. Do you think you need to develop your skills at showing caring? If so, set yourself specific goals and develop and implement a plan to attain them.

   _____

   _____

   _____

The Trust Bond

> Most people want security in this world, not liberty.
> *H. L. Mencken*

If you can develop a relationship with a deep level of trust, you reciprocate the reward of security. Trust means a firm belief in the honesty and reliability of another. It implies a confident belief in their trustworthiness. As you develop relationships, especially close ones, a major underlying question you ask yourself is "Can I trust this person?" When the answer becomes no, the relationship will certainly deteriorate, if not terminate.

Trust as Acceptance

One way of looking at trust in personal relations centers around your fears of rejection. The question becomes: "Can I trust this person to accept me?" Against this criterion, progressively disclosing more intimate information, revealing vulnerability and strength, and giving and receiving honest feedback all become ways of testing the trustworthiness of the other in relation to you.

Let us look at the progressive disclosure of personal information as part of the process of building trust. You show some trust in another by making a disclosure that is a little risky. If the other accepts and is supportive about your disclosure, trust is likely to be enhanced. Trust may be further enhanced if the other risks disclosing at a similar level of intimacy. However, if the other person rejects your initial disclosure, you are unlikely to risk deeper disclosures and may even end the relationship. Where both of you feel relatively safe, you may be prepared to continue testing and building trust by disclosing at a slightly deeper level, and so on. Relationships end up at different levels of trust. Moreover, some people can be trustworthy about certain areas of disclosure but not other areas.

Although it is not so obvious, the same process takes place in relation to the expression of feelings. Do not underestimate the role anxiety can play in distorting communication, even in the closest of relationships. People need to feel safe to get truly in touch with themselves and to be genuinely emotionally expressive. This aspect of building trust can be subtle, complex, and lengthy. Initial feelings of safety in the glow of romance may fade when differences surface. It is nearly impossible for people to wear permanent "nice" masks.

Trust as Commitment

Betsy had been married 15 years and had four children, ages 1 to 14. One evening at dinner her husband Howie, a managing director of an import company, announced that he had fallen in love with Jane, whom he had interviewed for a secretarial position. A few weeks later, when they were making love, Howie asked Betsy if he could call her Jane. Betsy has now divorced Howie, who has set up house with Jane a few blocks from his former family home. Howie just cannot understand why Betsy is so against taking up his offer to remain good friends despite their divorce.

Another way of looking at trust is to ask the question "Can I trust this person to honor his or her commitments?" Betsy could not trust Howie, although she tried to prevent herself from realizing her distrust for as long as she could. Trust involves confidence that the other person will abide by the formal and informal rules of your relationship even when out of your presence. Obvious untrustworthy behavior includes breaking promises and commitments that you can check on. Untrustworthy behavior that may deceive you includes lying, breaking confidences, and cheating on you with a third party.

Another aspect of trust as commitment is being willing to work on your relationship in the hard times as well as when times are good. There is much to be said for a crisis or catastrophe approach for understanding the development of trust. Misunderstandings, conflicts, arguments, and crises occur in all close relationships. Depending on how these difficulties are handled, partners can learn to trust themselves, one another, and the relationship. The partners can find out that their relationship is not fragile, that each is prepared to accept the nastier part of the other without quitting, and that each is committed to making the relationship work. Difficulties in sound relationships provide challenges that the partners tend to constructively work through together, despite the pain these challenges entail. In weak relationships, either or both partners do not have this level of commitment. Unresolved conflicts may lead to alienation, which in turn can lead to involvement with third parties and thus to the further breakdown of trust.

Being Trustworthy

In developing and maintaining a relationship you also need to demonstrate your own trustworthiness. You need to show characteristics like honesty, reliability, acceptance, and commitment. If you are mean, suspicious, uncaring, hostile, selfish, and competitive, people are unlikely to view you as trustworthy. Furthermore, given the tendency of partners to reciprocate one another's behavior, you may make it more difficult for others to be trustworthy for you. For instance, if you persist in being aggressive, you sow the seeds of your own rejection. Exercise 31 helps you to explore trusting and being trusted.

Exercise 31
Developing trust and being trustworthy

1. List some of the main ways that you assess whether you can trust another person enough to have a close relationship with him or her.

Exercise 31 (continued)

2. How easy do you find it to trust people? List some of the main positive and negative influences in your background that bear on your ability to trust people appropriately.

_____

_____

3. How trustworthy are you? Take a piece of paper and draw a line down the middle. At the top of the left column, write "Skills strengths" and, at the top of the right column, "Skills weaknesses." Then list what you perceive as your strengths and weaknesses in being a trustworthy person.

4. If appropriate, set yourself specific goals for being more trustworthy in your relationships, then monitor and evaluate your progress.

_____

The Pleasure Bond

> Nature knows no indecencies: man invents them.
> *Mark Twain*

Physical attraction is a major stimulus for long-term relationships. Nevertheless, you still have to coordinate how and when you integrate increased levels of sexual intimacy into your relationship. What Masters and Johnson call the pleasure bond is one of the main areas of reciprocity and rewardingness in the development and maintenance of relationships (Masters & Johnson, 1975). Traditionally, intimate sexual behavior was considered the preserve of marriage. Nowadays, sexual intercourse often takes place outside marriage, although a couple may later get married. A study by James showed that the frequency of sexual intercourse was highest in the two months after marriage, about four or five times a week, falling to just over twice a week during the second through the twentieth years of married life, followed by a further decline (James, 1983). Traditionally, the male was viewed as the expert in sexual behavior (Masters & Johnson, 1975). This view is increasingly being challenged, and now both sexes are encouraged to be equally responsible for expressing and sharing their sexuality (Alberti & Emmons, 1986). Effective sexual relationships take place *with* partners, not *to* them. Each partner needs to be actively involved in the process of giving and receiving pleasure. For this reason, you need to extend your skills of disclosing and listening to your sexual relationships. Sending or disclosing skills include taking initiatives, being playful, expressing wants, sharing fantasies, giving feedback, showing vulnerability, expressing pleasure and enjoyment, and showing gentleness and tenderness. Receiving skills include being responsive to verbal, voice, body, and touch messages that help you give and receive pleasure and have a mutually satisfying experience.

This book's major focus is not on sexual relating. However, the importance of trying to develop open communication in the sexual as in all other areas of your relationship should be stressed. Despite the sexual revolution, many people are still inhibited from talking openly about sex. Both males and females have fears and anxieties over matters like body image and sexual performance. Furthermore, many males need to become much more sensitive to women's feelings of vulnerability on account of their relative physical weakness.

There is no definite answer to the question whether sexual satisfaction leads to emotional closeness or the reverse. Argyle and Henderson indicate that whereas sex leads to love for men, the reverse may be true for women (Argyle & Henderson, 1985). Both sexes need to realize that effective sexual relating is not merely "doing what comes naturally" but requires the development and use of many skills of giving and receiving pleasure and of open communication. Those seeking more detail on sexual relating may wish to consult Comfort, 1972 and 1973; Kaplan, 1974; Masters and Johnson, 1975; or Brown and Faulder, 1977, to name a few useful works.

The Companionship Bond

Celia and Brad have been living together for two months. Every evening when they come home from work they spend at least an hour having a drink and talking over the main events, thoughts, and feelings of their days. On fine days they sit out on their deck to do this.

Jasmine and Francisco went out for six months. The relationship ended because, whenever they went out with Francisco's friends, Jasmine was very critical of them.

Doug and Janet met because they were members of the same choral society. They enjoy singing together both informally at their homes and during the rehearsals and concerts of their choir.

Diane is an ambitious young lawyer very wrapped up in her career. Her boyfriend Mark is getting fed up because she appears to put her career far above spending time with him.

An important skill is being a good companion with whom to share activities. Your relationship is more likely to stay fresh and be fun if you are sensitive and creative about doing things together. There is a limit to the number of intimate conversations you can have before these conversations become repetitive and boring. Much of your relationship is centered around activities of varying degrees of routine and enjoyment. Some of these activities are household chores, which you both may decide to do. Others may be more enjoyable parts of your daily routine, like having meals together, being in bed, watching television or listening to music. Still others may be special events—for instance, eating out or going to a concert. Table 8-1 is an illustrative list of activities you can do together (the home-based column does not necessarily assume that you live together). You are also likely to want to do things on your own since neither of you can be expected

Table 8-1. An illustrative list of companionship activities.

Home-Based	Outside the home
Eating informally	Going for a walk
Having a drink	Going swimming
Having a coffee	Going to the beach
Watching television	Going on vacation
Listening to music	Playing outdoor games
Listening to the radio	Going to the movies or the theater
Playing indoor games	Going to a concert, opera, or ballet
Being in bed	Going to a nightclub
Doing household chores	Going to a party
Preparing food	Going for a drive
Reading together	Going to the races
Interior decorating	Going to a baseball game
Gardening	Going to a talk
Sitting in the sun	Going to church
Massaging one another	Going shopping
Planning your finances	Visiting relatives
Having friends over	Visiting friends

to meet all of one another's needs. Your joint relationship may profit from the stimulus each of you gets from your independent activities.

How can doing things together help strengthen and deepen your relationship? First, you find out about one another's likes and dislikes and whether you are still compatible. Also, you discover whether each one of you is committed to spending time with the other. Second, your companionship helps both you and your partner avoid loneliness. Third, many of the dull activities become less wearisome and many of the pleasant activities more fun through having someone to share them with. Fourth, shared activities provide a vehicle for your ongoing relationship conversation. They have an emotional as well as a functional purpose. Fifth, if you do enjoyable things together, there is less room for potentially destructive third parties to enter your relationship. Sixth, sharing activities can be a source of strength during the rough times in your relationship. They may help you keep in contact despite feelings of hurt, pain, and anger.

The Decision Making Bond

> You cannot be friends upon any other terms
> than upon the terms of equality.
> *Woodrow Wilson*

Even when people start dating they have to negotiate numerous decisions with one another: what to do, where, when, and so on. As relationships develop, the number of these decisions increases—for instance, decisions about what type of food to eat when cooking for one another, how much to see friends, and how to use touch in the relationship. As time goes by, you develop relationship rules for many of these decisions so that you do not have to keep thinking about them.

Issues of power and influence are present in all relationships. As you get to know one another better, you also begin to learn whether power struggles and power plays—trying to get the other person to make decisions against his or her will—are likely to cause major disruptions. On the positive side, you also get an indication of whether together you can make most of the many decisions that are part of close relating without too much strife. The bond between you is likely to strengthen if you and your partner think that you can negotiate relationship decisions and rules to your mutual satisfaction—in other words, if you feel you can mesh with and adjust to one another without too much difficulty. Your relationship comes under strain if either or both of you feels dissatisfied with how power and decision making are handled in the relationship.

In traditional relationships the male tended to be more dominant in decision making than the female, although the female may have had certain areas in which she made most of the decisions—for example, in the kitchen. In the present times of sex role challenge and change, the traditional approach to decision making may build instability into your relationship. What happens if one of you (probably the woman) wants to move to a more equal distribution of power? Nowadays, relationships may be more stable—as opposed to seeming more stable—if partners have equal power. Equal power does not require that you share all decisions. You may either share virtually all decisions or divide the decisions into his and her spheres of influence. However, you willingly agree to the division and are prepared to renegotiate it if it does not work. In theory, equal power between partners is an ideal balance. In practice, the partner who commands the most financial resources is likely to have more power, especially when the other does not have an income.

Exercise 32
Assessing how good I am at deepening relationships

Instructions: Assess your skills strengths and weaknesses in each of the following areas of deepening a relationship. Answer either in general or in regard to a specific relationship.

Area	Skills Strengths	Skills Weaknesses
Intimacy		
Caring		
Trust		
Pleasure		
Companionship		
Decision making		

Exercise 32 (continued)

1. Summarize what you see as your main skills strengths and weaknesses in deepening relationships.

_____

_____

2. To what extent do you consider that your skills strengths and weaknesses have been influenced by either your cultural or your sex role upbringing? If possible, cite specific examples.

_____

_____

3. Where appropriate, set yourself some realistic goals for deepening a relationship, plan how to attain them, implement your plan, and evaluate the consequences. You may wish to discuss this exercise with your partner.

_____

_____

Postscript

Partners develop bonds in many other ways. For instance, as you get to know one another better, it may become clearer that you share similar values. As your relationship deepens, you may commit yourselves to parenthood or buying joint property. Deepening a relationship has risks as well as rewards. You may discover differences rather than similarities. Such discoveries can be either positive or negative; the outcome depends on the nature of the differences and on how well each of you copes with these differences.

Concluding Self-Talk

When deepening relationships, I need to pay attention to rewardingness, reciprocity, and rules. I am more likely to stay in a relationship when we are rewarding to one another and have negotiated mutually satisfying relationship rules.

I can try to deepen my relationships in a number of areas. Six important areas are intimacy, caring, trust, pleasure, companionship, and decision making. I need to assess my skills strengths and weaknesses in each of these areas and change my behavior accordingly. My attempts to deepen a relationship may create discomfort for either or both of us. How we cope determines whether the outcome is positive or negative for our relationship.

Notes

Assertion in Relationships

9

Nothing is so strong as gentleness and
nothing is so gentle as real strength.
Ralph W. Stockman

Abraham Maslow wrote "A person is both actuality and potentiality" (Maslow, 1962, p. 10). The same may be said about a relationship. Two people in a relationship are their own separate actualities and potentialities. They are also the actuality and potentiality of their relationship together.

In a close long-term relationship, I need to develop assertion skills in three interrelated areas.

• *Assertion for me.* I assert and define myself in regard to my personal goals. Here the emphasis is on preserving my rights, meeting my needs, and expressing my positive and negative thoughts and feelings. This individualistic form of assertion takes place in many situations other than my relationship with you—for instance, in my job. An assumption for this kind of assertion might be "I possess sufficient self-love to assert myself to fulfill my potential."

• *Assertion for you.* In a deep relationship I have a commitment to your happiness, growth, and fulfillment. Consequently, I endeavor to help you assert and define yourself in regard to your personal goals. I do not wish to possess or control you; instead, I try to help you become more of what you are capable of becoming. An assumption for this kind of assertion might be "I possess sufficient love and concern for you to help you assert yourself to fulfill your potential."

• *Assertion for us.* I am concerned not only for each of us as separate individuals but also for the quality, health, and vitality of our relationship together. When I assert myself within our relationship, I am sensitive to helping us attain our relationship goals. Our happiness and development is important not just in the context of our separate lives but in relation to one another. We are an interdependent team committed to nurturing and building our relationship. An assumption for this kind of assertion might be "I possess sufficient love and concern for each of us that I want both of us to assert ourselves to fulfill the potential of our relationship." The following are two examples of assertion for us.

Hank and Pam, both in their late 40s, are approaching their 25th wedding anniversary. Both are committed to open communication in their relationship. Pam considers that the timing of her assertion is very important. For example, if she knows that Hank is under great pressure to meet work deadlines, she will wait for an opportune moment to request that he meet her needs for more time, companionship, and back rubs. She listens carefully to his reactions to her assertion, and they work through its implications together. Hank values Pam both for her openness in stating her wishes and also for her considerateness. She is firm yet tactful.

Emilio and Maria have been going steady for five months. Early in their relationship Maria sensed that Emilio had difficulty in saying no to her and in standing up to her when their views differed. Maria was very fond of him. Consequently, she showed her love by encouraging Emilio to be more open and direct and by demonstrating that she could handle his assertion and also his anger. Their relationship has deepened because both now feel they are able to be more honest in it.

Here is a brief definition of assertion for us: assertion in a close, long-term relationship entails developing an open communication system in which, for the benefit of our relationship, we strive honestly and considerately to express our positive and negative thoughts and feelings and to act constructively toward one another.

Nonassertion, Aggression, and Assertion

Alberti and Emmons make useful distinctions among nonassertion, aggression, and assertion (Alberti & Emmons, 1986). When dealing with perceived negative behavior on the part of your partner, nonassertion implies being inhibited, submissive, and possibly not mentioning that you perceive a problem at all. Aggression implies unnecessarily putting your partner down, often by means of "you" statements. Assertion means standing up for yourself and honestly expressing your feelings without either being inhibited or engaging in character assassination.

The following are some examples of nonassertion, aggression, and assertion.

• You have cooked a special dinner for your partner, who arrives an hour late without contacting you.
Nonassertive: "It's all right. Good to see you."
Aggressive: "Damn you. Now the dinner is spoiled."
Assertive: "I'm concerned at your being so late without contacting me. Was there a reason for this?"
• You live with somebody who rarely cleans your apartment.
Nonassertive: You say nothing, but resent it deeply.
Aggressive: "You lazy idiot. Do you think I'm your servant?"
Assertive: "I'm annoyed because you almost always leave the cleaning to me. I want us to work out an arrangement so that we share the chores more evenly."

You may also express your positive thoughts and feelings in nonassertive, aggressive, and assertive ways.

• You have been wanting your partner to cut the lawn for some time and he or she finally keeps his or her word and does it.
Nonassertive: You are pleased but say nothing.
Aggressive: "That's great. It's about time you kept your word."
Assertive: "The lawn looks lovely. Thank you."

The preceding examples focus on the verbal component of nonassertive, aggressive, and assertive statements. However, the voice and body messages are also very important. Furthermore, to behave assertively you need to think assertively. It is to these thinking skills that we now turn.

Thinking Assertively

A number of key thinking skills enable you to behave more assertively. These are the same thinking skills necessary for combating shyness, although they are somewhat modified.

Attributing Cause Accurately

You may fail to be as assertive as you might be because you take a passive rather than an active stance in your relationship. Rather than assuming active responsibility for meeting your own and your partner's needs, you may hinder your effectiveness through misattributing cause. Examples of misattributing cause include the following.

"I'm naturally unassertive."
"I'm the victim of my past."
"My partner is there to meet my needs."
"My partner should know what I think and feel."
"I've tried before to improve our relationship."
"It's my partner's fault that I'm like this."
"Nobody loves me, so why bother?"
"My partner should not need to be told that I love him or her."
"My problems are so bad that I can't do anything about them."
"My partner should be able to assert himself or herself without much support from me."
"My partner and I should be able to communicate effectively without having to work at it during the rough times."

The danger of all of these potentially faulty explanations for how you behave is that they are dead ends. You need to become aware of both your misattributions and their consequences for you and your relationship. You then need to distinguish between fact and inference and formulate attributions that are more conducive to the health of your relationship. Such attributions make two main assumptions: first, that each of you is responsible for your own thoughts, feelings, and actions; and second, that you are jointly responsible for actualizing the constructive rather than the destructive potential of your relationship.

Using Coping Self-Talk

You may engage in negative self-talk that blocks your assertiveness. Negative self-talk that impedes assertion includes the following.

- *Emphasizing mastery rather than coping.* "Unless my assertion succeeds totally, it is a failure."
- *Catastrophizing.* "If I assert myself and then do not get what I want, it will be a catastrophe."
- *Negative self-labeling.* "If I assert myself, then I am being selfish." Butler states that "most women venturing into androgynous areas face a barrage of negative self-labels they must overcome before asserting themselves" (Butler, 1981, p. 60). These negative self-labels include such adjectives as nagging, castrating, unfeminine, bossy, pushy, bitchy, menopausal, and frigid. Men who assert their nurturing and tender characteristics also may have to overcome negative self-labels. These labels may include adjectives like weak, emotional, pansy, soft, wimpish, and effeminate.

Coping self-talk is the antidote to negative self-talk. In coping self-talk, calming and coaching elements tend to be interspersed. The following is an example of coping self-talk before, during, and after Pam asserts herself in requesting that Hank spend more time with her.

> *Before:* "Calm down. What are my goals? Just think through what skills I need to use to attain my goals."
> *During:* "I feel anxious. However, I know Hank cares for me and for the welfare of our relationship. I need to keep cool and say what I have to say."
> *After:* "I feel good that I said what was on my mind in a way that he could hear. I don't need to feel so anxious next time."

The goals of coping self-talk are to help you contain your anxieties and to stay focused on what you want to achieve. If you have a difficult assertion situation in your relationship, rehearsing and practicing your coping self-talk before your face-to-face assertion may help. You can rehearse by visualizing the scene and talking yourself throught it. When possible, visualize potential difficulties and setbacks and talk yourself through them as well.

Choosing Realistic Personal and Relationship Rules

As you grew up, you may have been subject to many pressures not to assert yourself. Furthermore, you may have lived with people who demonstrated inhibited or aggressive ways of attempting to meet their needs within their relationships. Rightly or wrongly, you may have internalized faulty assertion rules from many sources. The following are some of the sources that may have pressured you to become nonassertive in your relationships, along with some illustrative unrealistic rules that may later interfere with your achieving open relationships.

- *Your family.* "You must avoid conflict and commenting on unusual behavior." "You must not openly talk about sex."
- *Your religion.* "You should care for others rather than look after your needs." "You should always be gentle and self-effacing."
- *Your gender.* "Women should not be strong and independent." "Men should not be tender and nurturing."
- *Your culture.* "You must be very conscious of saving face" (Asian). "You should not express emotions too openly" (Anglo-Saxon).
- *Your race.* "Whites are better than blacks." "Whites are less smart than Asians."
- *Your peer group.* "You must conform to group norms." "You must be popular."
- *Your age.* "Children should be seen and not heard." "Parents know better than children."
- *Your schooling.* "Teachers know better than pupils." "Older children are better than younger children."

Probably everyone possesses some unrealistic personal rules that impede their capacity for assertion. These may be reflected in "mustabatory" demands on yourself and your partner. The following is a list of some of these rules.

I/my partner must be nice.
I/my partner must avoid conflict.
I/my partner must be liked.
I/my partner must be feminine.
I/my partner must be masculine.
I/my partner must not wear the pants.
I/my partner must not have wishes of my/his/her own.
I and my partner must never hurt one another.
I/my partner must not seem vulnerable.
I/my partner must not show anger.
I/my partner must not make a mistake.
I/my partner must not admit a mistake.

The first step in overcoming unrealistic personal rules that hinder assertion is to become aware that you possess them. Then you can logically analyze how realistic these rules are and their positive and negative consequences for you. In addition, you can reformulate your rules into flexible ones that work better for your relationship. The following is an example.

Inflexible rule: "I and my partner must never hurt one another."
Flexible rule: "Although we prefer not to hurt one another, we think it is important to our relationship to confront significant issues between us, even though this may sometimes cause pain."

In addition to each of you striving to possess realistic personal rules, it is important that partners subscribe to assertion rules supportive of their relationship. The following are some suggestions of beneficial assertion rules for a relationship.

"It is important to let one another know where we are."

"Each of us cares sufficiently about the other to want to know the other's thoughts and feelings."

"Each of us wants to meet the legitimate needs of the other."

"Each of us cares enough about the other to be considerate in the way we assert ourselves and to allow time and attention to process together the implications of our assertions."

Predicting Gain and Loss

Sometimes in the context of a deep relationship, assertion can seem even more risky than it seems in relationships where you have much less to lose. You may find you are testing the limits of your partner's commitment to your relationship. On the bright side, you may find that you have a fuller awareness both of your partner's commitment to you and of the extent of openness possible in your relationship.

An earlier section mentioned catastrophizing as a form of negative self-talk. In catastrophizing the consequences of assertion, you greatly overestimate the probability of negative outcomes. Furthermore, you may minimize your resources for coping with negative consequences. However, many of you may fail to be assertive less because you overestimate the negative consequences than because you underestimate the positive consequences of assertion. Minimizing the potential for reward, rather than maximizing the potential for loss, holds you back. Because you inadequately perceive the reward side of the loss/gain ledger balance, you are unwilling to take risks that might have a good chance of bringing genuine gains to your relationship.

The following are some of the general rewards of being assertive in your relationships.

You build more equal relationships.

Each of you is able to be more open.

Each of you has a greater knowledge of the other.

You have a greater appreciation of the strengths and weaknesses of your relationship.

You are able to show your concern for one another by taking action to correct unhelpful behaviors.

You are able to clarify misperceptions.

You are able to affirm the positives in your relationship as well as express the negatives.

You have a clearer idea of the degree of commitment in your relationship.

Awareness of any tendency you may have either to overestimate the negative or to underestimate the positive consequences of assertion is the starting point for working on these thinking skills weaknesses. For each weakness, you have to challenge your existing thinking by making sure you achieve a realistic appraisal of the potential gains *and* losses your assertion may cause. If you underestimate the gains, you may have to work hard to generate and assess the realistic benefits of being more assertive. Exercise 33 helps you explore your skills in thinking assertively.

Exercise 33
Assessing my strengths and weaknesses in thinking assertively

Instructions: Assess your skills strengths and weaknesses in each of the following areas of thinking assertively in your relationships.

Thinking Skill	My Strengths	My Weaknesses
Attributing cause accurately		
Using coping self-talk		
Choosing realistic rules		
Predicting gain and loss		

1. Summarize your strengths and weaknesses in thinking assertively.

   _____

   _____

2. To what extent do you consider that your strengths and weaknesses in thinking assertively reflect your sex role upbringing and your cultural upbringing? If relevant, illustrate with specific examples.

   _____

   _____

3. Set yourself specific goals for overcoming any skills weaknesses you may possess in thinking assertively.

   _____

   _____

Behaving Assertively

Behaving assertively involves showing commitment to your relationship not only by trying to be a rewarding person for your partner but also by helping your partner to be more rewarding for you. Chapter 8 dealt with the role of caring in deepening relationships. With caring, you assert yourself by offering rewards to your partner. In this chapter, the emphasis is on initiating, making requests for behavioral changes, handling power plays, ending a relationship, and encouraging one another's assertion.

Dimensions of Assertive Behavior

Behaving assertively follows from thinking assertively. Furthermore, assertive behavior involves not simply what you do but how you do it. Table 9-1 is a grid for looking at the choices involved in nonassertive, aggressive, and assertive behavior. In assertive behavior your thinking is disciplined, realistic, and goal-oriented; your basic feeling is of adequacy, and you keep in check any self-defeating feelings; your verbal message is clear; your voice and body messages back up your verbal message with an appropriate degree of muscle, and if necessary so do your actions. Nonassertive and aggressive behavior is deficient, to a greater or lesser degree, on each of these dimensions.

When being assertive, your voice and body messages can greatly add or detract from your overall message. For instance, a firm tone of voice may communicate to others that your verbal assertion is to be taken seriously, whereas a weak tone dilutes your assertion. Assertion is not only a matter of the presence of desirable verbal, voice, and body messages but also involves the absence of undesirable messages. Above all, verbal, voice, and body messages that put down others should be avoided.

- *Voice messages.* Some voice messages likely to support an assertive verbal message include the following.
Volume: reasonably loud.
Tone: firm, not putting on a "little girl" or "little boy" voice.
Inflection: presence of positive inflections and absence of negative inflections that indicate aggression and are put-downs.

Table 9-1. A grid for looking at the choices involved in nonassertive, aggressive, and assertive behavior.

	Your Thoughts	*Your Feelings*	*Your Verbal Messages*	*Your Voice Messages*	*Your Body Messages*	*Your Actions*
Nonassertive behavior						
Aggressive behavior						
Assertive behavior						

• *Body messages.* Some body messages likely to support an assertive verbal message include the following.

Eye contact: looking another directly in the eye.
Facial expression: being genuine—for instance, not smiling when you are angry.
Body posture: erect posture if standing or sitting, not a slouch or a slump.
Gesture: using hand and arm movements to help express yourself in a constructive fashion.
Proximity: not avoiding another, not hitting and running.
Absence of negative body communication: head shaking, door slamming, fist shaking, finger pointing.
Absence of distracting body communication: hair pulling, fiddling with fingers.

A Six-Step Framework for Assertive Behavior

The following is a six-step framework for behaving assertively in specific situations in your relationship.

1. *Be aware.* Become aware of when you may be acting either nonassertively or aggressively. Listen to feedback from your partner as well as to your own thoughts and feelings.

2. *Specify goals.* You may fail to be assertive through lack of clarity concerning your goals. Be specific as to what you want and assess whether it is in the best interests of your relationship. During this process you may generate and evaluate many goals before deciding which is best.

3. *Develop a plan.* Develop a plan to attain your goals. Your plan is likely to focus on how to change your thinking as well as your behavior. Take into account appropriate voice, body, and action messages.

4. *Rehearse and practice.* Especially if you anticipate finding your assertion difficult, rehearse and practice it in advance. You may role-play with another how you want to behave. Alternatively, you can use visualized rehearsal and practice. Remember to anticipate setbacks and difficulties in your practice.

5. *Implement your assertion.* Pick an appropriate time to give your assertive message, and go ahead and do it.

6. *Evaluate.* Evaluate how well you used assertion skills and their positive and negative consequences for yourself, your partner, and your relationship. Learn from both your successes and your mistakes.

When learning to be more assertive, you may find it helpful to work on easier problems before moving on to more difficult ones. With luck, your success in being assertive in the "shallow end" will give you the confidence to move on to the "deep end." In close relationships, your partner can be an invaluable resource in helping you to become more assertive. He or she can assist you with your assertion skills both in general and also in specific situations. Furthermore, you can gain confidence if you know your attempts at assertion are likely to be met with respect if not always with agreement.

Initiating

In equal relationships, each partner feels free to initiate. Taking or suggesting an initiative means assuming responsibility for making things happen rather than waiting for your partner to make the first move. Butler considers that a couple's first date frequently sets up an unequal relationship between a man and a woman that may last for the whole of their married life. She considers that a woman "waits for a phone call, waits to be asked out on a date, allows a man to initiate sexual contact, and yokes her expression of affection to his" (Butler, 1981, p. 16).

Many women feel that they are controlled by men in their relationships. Frequently, these women consider that they are expected to behave passively, to wait for the male to take a lead, to buttress the male ego, and not to have their own competence and authority fully acknowledged. However, the reverse is also true: some men feel controlled and dominated by women. Men tend to feel less dominated than women do for reasons such as men's larger physical size and their greater control over financial resources. In reality, both sexes allow themselves to be controlled by their role expectations not only of one another but also of themselves. In certain areas, women traditionally expect and are expected to take the lead—for instance, cooking, looking after the house, and harmonizing family relations. In certain areas, men traditionally expect and are expected to take the lead—for instance, being the breadwinner, looking after the car, and taking the initiative in bed. Traditional relationships are permeated with double standards for both sexes, with different permissions and prohibitions regarding taking and suggesting initiatives.

You can be nonassertive, aggressive, and assertive in initiating.

Nonassertive: "Do you want to go to the movies tonight?"

Aggressive: "Come on. We're going to the movies tonight whether you like it or not."

Assertive: "I would like to go to the movies tonight. Do you want to come?"

Note that in this example, the assertive initiative is expressed as an "I" message and invites discussion. This verbal message is accompanied by appropriate voice and body messages.

The following suggestions about initiating may be important if you do not want a relationship based on traditional sex role expectations. First, both of you have to be strongly committed to relating on an equal basis. Second, listen carefully to your own wants and wishes and help your partner do the same. Third, respect one another's right to suggest initiatives. Fourth, respect one another's right to say no. Fifth, develop the skills of working through and negotiating differences. Experiment 10 offers you an opportunity to try out these suggestions.

Experiment 10
What happens when I initiate?

Part A: Assessment

Assess the degree to which you are prepared to initiate in each of the following areas of a male–female relationship.

Asking for a date _____

Making phone contact between dates _____

Ordering a meal _____

Paying the bill after eating out _____

Providing transportation _____

Driving _____

Bringing up topics of conversation _____

Touching in an affectionate way _____

Initiating sexual activity _____

Taking responsibility for contraception _____

Initiating variations in lovemaking _____

Initiating recreational activities _____

Initiating caring _____

Requesting support _____

Showing affection _____

Initiating discussion of money matters _____

Any other areas you consider important _____

Part B: Make an "If . . . then . . ." Statement

Choose an area in a specific relationship in which you wish to initiate more. Make an "If . . . then . . ." statement along the lines of "If I implement my changed behavior (specify), then these predictions (specify) are likely to come true."

_____

_____

Part C: Try Out and Evaluate Your Changed Behavior

Try out your changed behavior. How well did you do it? What were its positive and negative consequences for yourself, the other person, and for your relationship? Have your predictions been confirmed or disconfirmed? Has this experiment taught you something about how you can use initiating skills more to attain your relationship goals? If so, what?

_____

_____

Requesting Changes in Behavior

People in relationships build up patterns of behavior. When you request a change in your partner's behavior you may have one of three goals: getting him or her (1) to do something that they are not already doing, (2) to do something they are already doing to a greater extent and/or better, or (3) to decrease or stop an unwanted behavior. You may be nonassertive, aggressive, or assertive in each of these three areas. The following are some examples.

• *Requesting a new behavior.* Doris wants Tim to bring her flowers on birthdays and anniversaries.
Nonassertive: Doris keeps commenting on how other people bring their partners flowers on birthdays and anniversaries.
Aggressive: "You've got no imagination. Don't you know that a woman likes flowers on birthdays and anniversaries?"
Assertive: "One thing that would give me a lot of pleasure is if you could bring me flowers on birthdays and anniversaries."
• *Requesting more of an existing behavior.* George wishes Wanda would caress his body more in their lovemaking.
Nonassertive: George says nothing but feels bad.
Aggressive: "You only seem interested in receiving pleasure. Why don't you take more interest in giving it to me?"
Assertive: "I love it when you caress my body with your fingertips. I feel wonderful all over. Please keep doing it."
• *Requesting less of or an end to an existing behavior.* You study for an exam and your partner plays the stereo very loud.
Nonassertive: You thump the table and curse to yourself.
Aggressive: "Turn that goddamn stereo down. Don't you realize that I have work to do?"
Assertive: "I'm upset because I can't concentrate with the stereo so loud. Would you please turn it down?"

A number of considerations are involved in making behavior change requests in a relationship. These include the following.

• *Assume cooperative intentions.* When possible, assume that your partner is committed not only to his or her own welfare but also to yours and to that of your relationship. This assumption may lessen unwanted inhibition and aggression.

• *Ask yourself "Is it worth being assertive?"* Assertion can be overdone. Some behaviors may not be worth bothering about. In a primary relationship, it is hard to get away from irritating behaviors. However, with other relationships you have more choice. Another issue is how realistic it is to be assertive when you know the other person is highly threatened and potentially destructive when challenged. It is naive to expect that assertive messages, however well sent, always bring happy outcomes.

• *Watch out for your own defensiveness.* When your view of yourself is threatened, you may be very tempted to strike back under the guise of being assertive. Especially when you feel strongly, you may label your behavior as assertive when in reality it is aggressive and destructive to your relationship.

• *Pay attention to timing.* If you want your partner to hear your assertive message, be sensitive to timing. Sometimes, as in the example of the loud stereo, you may not have much choice. On other occasions, you may be able to wait until your feelings are more under control.

• *Make "I" statements.* Locate the source of your requests directly in you, allowing them to remain requests rather than to become demands. Demands are much more likely to threaten and create resistance.

• *Be specific.* A basic rule of making requests is to be specific. Trite as it sounds, this rule is frequently violated. For instance, Gary sulks and plays the victim rather than telling Mary Beth that he prefers her not to wear hair curlers at breakfast.

• *Consider using honest positives.* It is very easy to initiate a cycle of negativity when requesting a behavior change. You may soften your requests if you comment on some positives as well as on the negative aspects of your partner's behavior (Kassorla, 1984).

• *Make requests positively.* Where possible, emphasize the positive by stating what you want rather than what you do not want. A simple example is to rephrase "You look awful when you wear curlers at breakfast" to "I like seeing your hair without curlers at breakfast."

• *Pay great attention to voice and body messages.* Voice and body messages have already been stressed. Firmness need not be at the expense of consideration and kindness.

• *Use listening skills.* Listen carefully to the feedback generated by your assertive messages. Regard your assertive messages as invitations to discuss your requests rather than as demands. It is also important that your partner feel understood.

• *Use FER messages.* You can follow the FER (feeling, explanation, request) format when confronting negative behavior, though not always slavishly in that order. "F" stands for how you feel. "E" signifies your explanation of why you feel that way, which should specify the behavior you find negative. "R" stands for your request that the negative behavior be ended or at least explained.

• *Use the minimum necessary muscle.* Basically, muscle is a message of how forceful to be (Butler, 1981). As a rule of thumb, assertive messages should use the minimum level of muscle to achieve their objectives. There are two main reasons for using the minimum muscle necessary. First, the more muscle you use, the more likely you will elicit resistance from the other person. Second, even if you get what you want, the more muscle you use, the more likely you will leave a residue of resentment. This unfinished business may later hinder your relationship.

• *Deal with defensiveness as best you can.* You have inner and outer agendas when faced with defensiveness. The inner agenda concerns how you handle your own thoughts and feelings. Defensiveness is a common initial reaction to assertive messages. It does not necessarily indicate either that you have asserted yourself poorly or that you may not ultimately be successful. Even if unsuccessful, you can only be responsible for your own behavior. The expectation that your partner will always do what you want is unrealistic. Such an expectation can only contribute to your denigrating yourself when your partner does not conform to your wishes.

The outer agenda concerns how you behave toward your partner. Assuming you decide to persist in the assertion, you have a number of options. First, you may pause after the negative response and then calmly yet firmly repeat your behavior change request. Second, you may reflect your partner's feelings before repeating your request.

Partner A: "I'm upset because I can't concentrate with the stereo so loud. Would you please turn it down?"
Partner B: "Why the hell are you complaining?"
Partner A: "I realize you're angry at my request, but I badly need to concentrate on my schoolwork and would be grateful if you could turn the stereo down."
Partner B: (still not too pleased): "OK."

A third option is to use more muscle. For instance, you may both use a firmer voice and strengthen your verbal message by saying "I'm serious, please turn the stereo down." A fourth option is to try to negotiate a mutually acceptable solution—for instance, negotiating times when your partner can play the stereo and times when you can study without it. The skills of managing conflict are covered later in this book.

• *Take cultural considerations into account.* When relating to someone from a non-Western culture, you must be especially careful to tailor your requests for behavior change so that they can understand them and still be prepared to listen. You need to be aware of cultural differences in assertion. For instance, in Indonesia submissiveness is valued more than assertiveness (Argyle, 1983), gaze is much more sparingly used in Japan than in North America, and in Asia great value is placed on not losing face.

Exercise 34 and Experiment 11 help you explore the process of making an assertive request for behavior change.

Exercise 34
Making assertive requests for behavior change: writing scripts

Example
John uses the FER (feeling, explanation, request) format to request that Belinda

Exercise 34 (continued)

change her behavior and call him when she is going to be late for dinner.
John: "I'm angry [feeling] because I've put a lot of work into preparing our dinner and now it's not so nice [explanation]; would you please phone and let me know when you are going to be late [request]?"

Instructions: Using the FER format, write out assertive requests for behavior change to a real or imaginary partner in the following areas:

Not leaving the bathroom so dirty ⎯⎯⎯⎯⎯⎯⎯⎯⎯⎯⎯⎯⎯⎯⎯⎯⎯

⎯⎯⎯⎯⎯⎯⎯⎯⎯⎯⎯⎯⎯⎯⎯⎯⎯⎯⎯⎯⎯⎯⎯⎯⎯⎯⎯⎯⎯⎯⎯⎯⎯⎯

Spending more time with you ⎯⎯⎯⎯⎯⎯⎯⎯⎯⎯⎯⎯⎯⎯⎯⎯⎯⎯⎯

⎯⎯⎯⎯⎯⎯⎯⎯⎯⎯⎯⎯⎯⎯⎯⎯⎯⎯⎯⎯⎯⎯⎯⎯⎯⎯⎯⎯⎯⎯⎯⎯⎯⎯

Not coming home drunk ⎯⎯⎯⎯⎯⎯⎯⎯⎯⎯⎯⎯⎯⎯⎯⎯⎯⎯⎯⎯⎯⎯

⎯⎯⎯⎯⎯⎯⎯⎯⎯⎯⎯⎯⎯⎯⎯⎯⎯⎯⎯⎯⎯⎯⎯⎯⎯⎯⎯⎯⎯⎯⎯⎯⎯⎯

Expressing affection more openly ⎯⎯⎯⎯⎯⎯⎯⎯⎯⎯⎯⎯⎯⎯⎯⎯⎯

⎯⎯⎯⎯⎯⎯⎯⎯⎯⎯⎯⎯⎯⎯⎯⎯⎯⎯⎯⎯⎯⎯⎯⎯⎯⎯⎯⎯⎯⎯⎯⎯⎯⎯

Not leaving all the initiating of sex to you ⎯⎯⎯⎯⎯⎯⎯⎯⎯⎯⎯⎯⎯

⎯⎯⎯⎯⎯⎯⎯⎯⎯⎯⎯⎯⎯⎯⎯⎯⎯⎯⎯⎯⎯⎯⎯⎯⎯⎯⎯⎯⎯⎯⎯⎯⎯⎯

Initiating conversations more often ⎯⎯⎯⎯⎯⎯⎯⎯⎯⎯⎯⎯⎯⎯⎯⎯⎯

⎯⎯⎯⎯⎯⎯⎯⎯⎯⎯⎯⎯⎯⎯⎯⎯⎯⎯⎯⎯⎯⎯⎯⎯⎯⎯⎯⎯⎯⎯⎯⎯⎯⎯

Any other areas relevant to your current relationships ⎯⎯⎯⎯⎯⎯⎯⎯

⎯⎯⎯⎯⎯⎯⎯⎯⎯⎯⎯⎯⎯⎯⎯⎯⎯⎯⎯⎯⎯⎯⎯⎯⎯⎯⎯⎯⎯⎯⎯⎯⎯⎯

Experiment 11
What happens when I make an assertive request for a behavior change?

Part A: Assessment
Take a relationship that is important to you and assess your skills strengths and weaknesses in making requests for behavior change in the following areas.

	Skills Strengths	*Skills Weaknesses*
Requesting a new behavior		
Requesting more of or improvement in an existing behavior		
Requesting less of or trying to stop a behavior		

Part B: Make an "If . . . then . . ." Statement
Choose a specific area in which you wish to make an assertive request for a behavior change in a relationship. Make an "If . . . then . . ." statement along the lines of "If I implement my changed behavior (specify), then these predictions (specify) are likely to come true."

Part C: Try Out and Evaluate Your Changed Behavior
Try out your changed behavior. How well did you do it? What were its positive and negative consequences for yourself, the other person, and your relationship? Have your predictions been confirmed or disconfirmed? Has this experiment taught you something about how you can use assertive requests for behavior change in your relationships? If so, what?

Handling Power Plays

Power plays are attempts by others to get you to do what they want rather than what you want (Berne, 1964; Steiner, 1981). Jeff uses his anger to get what he wants. Juan obscures the issue to avoid dealing with his partner directly. Vera finds that tears are very effective in getting her partner to bend to her wishes. Marie withdraws affection if her partner does not give her the feedback she wants. In all these instances, people are using power plays—anger, mystification, tears, and withdrawal of affection—to get what they want at their partners' expense. Sometimes a whole relationship has underlying assumptions placing one of the partners at a disadvantage—for example, when a man discourages a woman from pursuing her career on the basis of traditional sex role assumptions.

Being aware of others' attempts to operate on your self-definition and to manipulate you is the first step in being able to handle their power plays. You then have a number of options. First, you can be submissive and at least tacitly acquiesce in others' false definitions and manipulations. Second, you can be aggressive and perhaps escalate the tension and emotional temperature by counterattacking. Third, you can be assertive by quietly yet firmly persisting in your definition of yourself, the situation, or both. This option may also include working on your own tendencies to either acquiescence or escalation. In addition, you may confront your partner with how he or she behaves and invite discussion of the behavior.

Fourth, if you find you are relating to a highly manipulative person, you can get out of the relationship. Ending a relationship may also be viewed as an assertive option.

Ending a Relationship

A relationship can be ended in nonassertive, aggressive, or assertive ways. To start, you need to be clear that ending the relationship is really what you want. For example, Nanette asks Peter not to come around to her place anymore. However, each time he does come, she lets him in and has a long conversation with him. Here Nanette is giving Peter a very mixed message about ending the relationship.

Some of you may be nonassertive about ending a relationship because you take on responsibility for another person's life. For instance, Enrico does not come right out and tell Eva that he thinks they have no future because he tells himself he is afraid that she will not be able to handle being on her own. In reality, Enrico may be afraid of the confrontation. After a period of adjustment, Eva might manage very well on her own. Many relationships end with hurtful arguments, after which the participants are not on speaking terms. Aggressive endings to relationships can add to the pain of parting for either or both of you. Furthermore, they can negate the good times you may have had in the relationship.

Several factors may make it difficult to end a relationship assertively, especially if you are married and have children and shared property. Here the focus is on ending nonmarital relationships assertively. Already you may have set some limits in the relationship—for instance, by restricting the intimacy level of your disclosures or by limiting the amount of physical contact. Many of the assertion considerations mentioned in the section on requesting a behavior change apply to ending a relationship. These include the use of "I" messages, the minimum necessary use of muscle, the use of honest positives when possible, and firm yet kind voice and body messages as an accompaniment to your verbal message.

Although sometimes relationships end abruptly, most often some prior signal indicates that they are in trouble. If both of you are coordinated in your wish to end the relationship, the ending is eased. Where you are the person who initiates the ending of the relationship, it is generally better to come right out and say what you want rather than fudge the issue. You may be asked for an explanation for your decision or feel it appropriate to give one. Alternatively, you may be the recipient of a tirade of abuse. In either event, you may be able to show your strength by doing minimal damage to the self-esteem of the person with whom you have been involved. Ending a relationship assertively entails showing respect for yourself and the other person rather than being brutal and ruthless. Although you may well be contributing to another's pain, you have a responsibility for your own happiness and fulfillment. Provided that you have not raised another's expectations dishonestly, part of the implicit contract in your relationship was probably that either of you could withdraw and seek your happiness elsewhere. Exercise 35 helps you explore how you might end a relationship assertively.

Exercise 35
Ending a relationship: saying goodbye assertively

1. Write down what you think are the main considerations in ending a relationship assertively.

   _____

   _____

2. Do you experience or anticipate any special areas of difficulty in ending a relationship?

   _____

   _____

3. If relevant, pick a relationship that you have ended or would like to end. Take a sheet of paper and draw a line down the middle. At the top of the left-hand column, write "past/present behavior" and at the top of the right-hand column, "proposed assertive alternative." Fill in both columns.

4. Do you think you are influenced by any special sex role or cultural considerations in the way you might end a relationship? If so, please specify.

   _____

   _____

Encouraging One Another's Assertion

In a close, long-term relationship based on assumptions of teamwork and equality, you feel responsible for one another's happiness and fulfillment and are not constantly absorbed with securing your own rights. Assertion for "us," rather than for either just "me" or just "you," is motivated by your positive feelings for one another. Such assertion can involve both of you in demonstrating quiet strength, caring, and vigilance on a daily basis.

The following are some of the many ways you can encourage one another's assertion for the sake of your relationship.

• *Possessing realistic relationship goals and rules.* You can openly discuss the goals of your relationship—for example, a commitment to honest and open communication on the basis of equality. You can also try to clarify the relationship rules most likely to attain them—for example, "Each of us cares enough about the other to be considerate in the way we assert ourselves and to allow time and attention to process together the implications of our assertions." In short, you give each other permission to be assertive.

• *Providing rewarding consequences.* The consequences you provide for one another's assertions can either encourage or discourage these assertions. You can provide rewards for assertive messages in various ways. Perhaps the main way is by treating assertive messages with respect and concern. Respect and concern are demonstrated by the quality of your listening and understanding. At times, you may even praise one another for having the courage to be assertive in difficult areas. Another way of providing rewarding consequences is to acknowledge caring assertions—for instance, a compliment—with gratitude.

• *Demonstrating assertive thinking and behavior.* Assertive thinking and behavior can be contagious. If you are open and honest, it generally makes it easier for your partner to be the same way. This mutuality is a protection against destructive cycles of mutual inhibition or aggression.

• *Providing openers and confrontations.* You can show you care for one another's views by asking what the other's views are. If you think your partner holds back and requires encouragement to be assertive, you can offer this encouragement. If necessary, you can confront your partner with the need to keep being assertive.

• *Showing understanding.* If either of you thinks you have a problem with assertion, the other can be there to offer assistance and support as you explore being assertive. Sometimes this assistance and support may involve working through painful past experiences that have contributed to present difficulties in being assertive.

• *Encouraging outside assertion.* If each of you adopts assertion as a way of life outside your relationship, it may be easier to be assertive within the relationship. You can support one another in your attempts to be assertive in your outside contacts.

Assertion for "us" requires constant vigilance. It is easy to settle for less than your relationship's full potential for happiness and fulfillment. Working together as a team, you are more likely to attain the potential than you are if each of you is always bound up with your own assertion agendas.

Concluding Self-Talk

In a close, long-term relationship, as well as being assertive for myself I can be assertive for my partner and for the well-being of our relationship. We are a team, and as such we help one another both to develop and to use assertion skills. We also strive to avoid being nonassertive or aggressive.

Assertion involves both thinking and behavior. Four important thinking skills I can use to support my assertive behavior are attributing cause accurately, using coping self-talk, choosing realistic personal and relationship rules, and predicting the consequences of my behavior as accurately as possible. I can use my assertion skills in suggesting and taking initiatives in my relationships. I can also be tactful yet firm in making requests for behavior change. In addition, I can handle power plays and end relationships assertively. I and my partner can work through the issues raised by our assertive messages in a spirit of mutual respect and caring.

10
Managing Anger

Love's best habit is a soothing tongue.
William Shakespeare

Anger, a major manifestation of psychological pain, features prominently in virtually all close relationships. It is often intense, repetitive, and violently expressed. Furthermore, it can be combined with a high level of defensiveness, which involves unwillingness to examine one's own behavior. All of you carry psychological pain from hurtful events in your upbringing into your relationships. You are also subject to current stresses from outside your relationship. Thus, from both past and current sources you import the potential for anger. Then you face the further stresses of one another's negative behaviors.

The destructive consequences of anger scarcely require stating. Anger can be directed either at other people (anger *out*) or at yourself (anger *in*) (Tavris, 1982). When directed out, anger's two main negative forms are hostility and withdrawal. These behaviors can lead to alienation and distress in relationships, to the point of total breakdown.

Anger can also have positive consequences. Possessing angry feelings does not in itself destroy relationships, but handling them poorly may. Anger can be a signal for yourself and your partner that something is wrong and requires attention. Such

anger should be a cue to examine your own behavior, not just your partner's. Anger can be an energizer, leading to assertive requests for behavior change and to confronting festering conflicts. Anger can also be a purge; after expressing it, you may calm down and be more rational. In a close relationship, partners can work out rules that allow their anger to be used for constructive purposes such as these rather than as a means to tear one another apart.

Thinking and Action Skills

Since anger can be the mortal enemy of relationships, it is important to develop the skills of both regulating and expressing anger. Although they overlap, you need to focus on both your thinking and action skills. Some thinking and action skills for managing anger are listed in Table 10-1. In a close relationship the best way to handle unnecessary anger is to prevent it. Your use of thinking skills may help you avoid laying your own trips on your partner. Furthermore, how you think can support your taking positive actions when angry as well as avoiding negative ones. This chapter reviews the skills listed in Table 10-1. Often you may use these skills in combination rather than singly.

Thinking Skills

To paraphrase Shakespeare, "Love's best habit is a soothing mind." A soothing mind is the precondition for a soothing tongue. On many occasions, you can

Table 10-1.   Some thinking and action skills for managing your anger.

Thinking Skills	Action Skills

Owning responsibility for your anger
Realistic personal rules
Perceiving provocations differently
Coping self-talk
Using visualization
	Assertion skills
	  – expressing anger
	  – requesting behavior changes
	Handling aggressive criticism
	Relaxing yourself
	Managing stress
	Helping one another

exhibit your concern by disciplining your thinking so that you either prevent, do not express, or dilute your expression of anger. On the one hand, you can choose to think yourself into hating, aggressive blaming, nursing resentments, wanting to cause psychological pain, and acting violently. On the other hand, you can choose to think yourself into a calmer and more problem-solving frame of mind.

Owning Responsibility for Your Anger

Anger is a complex emotion. It is often combined with other emotions such as hurt, jealousy, anxiety, low self-esteem, powerlessness, frustration, irritability, and depression. Owning responsibility for your angry feelings is a starting point for working on them.

You may be reluctant to own your anger and its related feelings for many reasons. For example, you may have learned that it is not feminine to be angry or that it is not masculine to admit to feeling hurt and vulnerable. Furthermore, people of both sexes—possibly especially males—may be reluctant to admit how they use anger to control others. You may have been brought up in a home where expressing anger was considered inappropriate. Moreover, your angry feelings may have been so strong that you found it easier to repress them than to face the consequences of acknowledging and acting on them. In addition, your religion and culture may have taught you that being angry was wrong.

Currently you may possess skills weaknesses that block you from fully being aware of and owning your anger. These weaknesses include the following.

• *Deficient inner listening skills.* You may not be good at becoming aware that you are angry. Your angry feelings may go unacknowledged or only partially acknowledged. Your body may experience anger through heightened blood pressure, tension, ulcers, or insomnia. However, you may be deficient in understanding the meaning of these physical reactions.

• *Faulty use of language.* The way you use language may distance you from owning responsibility for angering yourself (Glasser, 1984). For example, you may say "He/she/you/it/they make(s) me angry," locating the cause of your angry feelings outside of yourself. You may also use phrases like "It's only natural to react with anger" or "I had no choice but to be angry."

• *Unrealistic personal rules.* You may have personal rules that make it difficult for you to acknowledge your anger—for example, "Women should not get angry" or "Christians should not get angry."

• *Defensive processes.* You may have ways of handling your anxiety that let you avoid assuming responsibility for acknowledging and managing your angry feelings and being fully aware of their consequences. These defensive processes include the following.

Denial: for instance, either hating someone and not being prepared to acknowledge this or being unwilling to realize the consequences for someone of your psychological or physical violence.

Projection: for instance, hating someone but pretending that they hate you.

Reaction formation: forming reactions that are the opposite of what you really feel—for instance, love that masks intense anger.

Misattributing responsibility: an overemphasis on making others responsible for how you feel; blaming someone for making you angry is perhaps the prime example.

Defensive lying: making up stories about yourself and others intended to make you seem right and the other person seem wrong; giving way to the Nelson-Jones Reality Principle—"If you can't accept reality, create it!" Defensive lying differs from deliberate lying in that you yourself believe your own dishonest distortions of reality.

Attack: attacking another who provides unwelcome feedback concerning your anger and its consequences; trying to control another's feedback by putting overt and/or subtle emotional pressure on them.

Avoidance: avoiding issues that will likely make you have to confront your own angry feelings; withdrawing emotionally and physically.

Exercise 36 enables you to explore how you handle anger in your relationships.

Exercise 36
Exploring how I handle my anger in relationships

Instructions: Write out your answers to the following questions.
1. To what extent is managing your anger a problem for you in your relationships?

2. How good are you at tuning in to your angry feelings?

3. To what extent do you get angry with yourself (anger in) rather than with other people (anger out)?

4. How confident a person are you, and to what extent does this affect your proneness to anger?

_____

5. To what extent do you consider that other people make you angry? Give reasons for your answer.

_____

_____

6. Do you believe you are less of a person because you have angry feelings? If so, please explain.

_____

_____

7. Are you aware of engaging in any of the following defensive processes to avoid assuming responsibility for your anger and its consequences?

_____ Denial

_____ Projection

_____ Reaction formation

_____ Misattributing responsibility

_____ Defensive lying

_____ Attack

_____ Avoidance

8. What other feelings—for instance, hurt or anxiety—do you experience when you are angry?

_____

9. What physical reactions—for instance, tension—do you experience when angry?

_____

10. List the kinds of thoughts you have when you are angry concerning the other person involved.

_____

11. What verbal, voice, body, and action messages do you send when you are angry?

_____

_____

Exercise 36 (continued)

12. Have you ever been or do you consider you have the potential to be physically violent when angry? If so, please elaborate.

_____

_____

13. When in a relationship, do you and your partner take a teamwork approach to helping each other manage anger? If so, please explain.

_____

_____

14. What positive and negative consequences for yourself and your relationships stem from how you currently handle your anger?

_____

_____

15. Assess the extent to which you are effective in owning responsibility for acknowledging and managing your anger in your relationships.

_____

_____

_____

Choosing Realistic Personal Rules

Like any feeling, anger can be viewed within the ABC framework.

A: The activating event (provocation or trigger).
B: Your thoughts.
C: Your feelings and actions.

Possessing unrealistic personal rules contributes to destructive anger (for example, Lopez & Thurman, 1986). You can set yourself up for feeling angry by mustabatory rules about how you, your partner, and your relationship should be. Mustabatory demands you may place on yourself include the following.

I must never make mistakes.
I must always be right.
I must be rational and consistent all the time.
I must always get my revenge.
I must never make a fool of myself.

Mustabatory demands you may place on your partner include the following.

My partner must never make me feel angry.
My partner must never disagree with me.
My partner must never criticize me.
My partner must always let me be right.
My partner must always let me have my way.
My partner must always be able to read my mind.
My partner must not in any way attempt to restrict my freedom.
My partner must always be feminine or masculine.
My partner must meet 100% of my needs.
Where cultural differences exist, my partner must always adjust to my culture.

Mustabatory demands you may place on your relationship include the following.

Our relationship must never have conflict in it.
Our relationship must seem free of conflict to outsiders.
We must compete rather than collaborate with each other.

When you find yourself getting angry, it helps to not act impulsively. Instead, stop and think whether any of your unrealistic personal rules contribute to your anger. You can develop the skill of backtracking from your angry feelings to the thoughts that generate and sustain them. Then you can evaluate how realistic these rules are and their positive and negative consequences for you and your relationship. You can also reformulate unrealistic, anger-evoking personal rules into rules that are more self-supporting.

As mentioned in Chapter 6, some of the main characteristics of self-supporting personal rules are that the rules (1) express preferences rather than demands, (2) emphasize coping rather than perfectionism, (3) are based on your own valuing process, (4) are flexible and amenable to change in light of new information, and (5) lead to a functional rating of specific characteristics and not to a global self-rating of your personhood.

Here are some examples of reformulating anger-evoking personal rules into more realistic rules. Exercise 37 gives you an opportunity to reformulate your own personal rules.

Unrealistic rule: "I must always get my revenge."
Realistic rule: "My interests are not best served by thinking in terms of revenge. I can work out more appropriate strategies for meeting my needs and keeping my relationship intact."

Unrealistic rule: "My partner must not criticize me."
Realistic rule: "Feedback is important in our relationship. I would prefer that my partner is tactful when giving feedback."

Exercise 37
Managing anger: identifying and reformulating unrealistic personal rules

Instructions: Think of one or more recent situations in your relationships when you have felt angry. For each situation write out:

1. The activating event, trigger, or provocation. _____

   _____

2. Your thoughts: focus on identifying both realistic and unrealistic personal rules.

   _____

   _____

3. How you felt and how you acted. _____

   _____

4. A reformulation of each unrealistic personal rule into a more realistic personal rule.

   _____

   _____

5. Any changes in how you feel and act that might result from your more realistic personal rules.

   _____

   _____

It may help to record your reformulated rules with a cassette player and play them back to yourself at least once a day for the next week.

Perceiving Provocations Differently

> How strange it is to see with how much passion
> People see things only in their own fashion.
> *Molière*

This section focuses on not being unnecessarily hard in the way you judge others' behavior, which can also help you to not be too hard on yourself.

Jimmy and Peggy had been going out for two months. Every time Peggy said that she found another man attractive, Jimmy felt jealous, put down, and angry with her.

Cindy and Drew were newlyweds. When Drew started coming home from the office a little later than usual, Cindy concluded that he was becoming bored with her. She resented this.

Lucy and André had been living together for six months. Lucy was becoming extremely uptight because André was not more openly affectionate. She concluded that he did not love her anymore.

Chapter 6 discussed how jumping to perceptual conclusions contributes to shyness. The same is true for anger (for example, Feindler, Marriott, & Iwata, 1984). Let us assume that the explanations Jimmy, Cindy, and Lucy chose to give themselves were erroneous. Their errors may have resulted partly from their own insecurities and partly because they have insufficiently developed their skills of perceiving accurately. The outcome of their misperceptions was that each of them felt angry with his or her partner.

An obvious but often overlooked skill of trying to explain another's behavior is simply to ask the other person what is going on and to check out their reasons before jumping to conclusions. Another skill is to generate alternative explanations and then choose the one that best fits the factual evidence. Exercise 38 gives you an opportunity to explore this skill; but first, here are some examples.

1. Alternative explanations Jimmy might have given himself for Peggy's behavior.
   - "I tell her when I find other women attractive, so why shouldn't she tell me the same about other men?"
   - "Peggy would not make such comments to me if she did not feel safe with me."
   - "Our relationship is deteriorating and she does not try to be tactful anymore."

2. Alternative explanations Cindy might have given herself for Drew's behavior.
   - "He told me that they have a big job on at work. It's my own insecurity talking when I feel he is bored with me."
   - "Drew has a girlfriend at the office and our marriage is already on the rocks. He is being unfaithful."
   - "Drew is working extra hard to ensure that we are on a sound financial footing."

3. Alternative explanations Lucy might have given herself for André's behavior.
   - "He never has been openly affectionate, but he has always been there for me when I want him."
   - "André is good at showing affection. It's just that I am very demanding."
   - "André came from a family where neither parent was openly affectionate, and he needs help in becoming more expressive."

If you become aware that you have a tendency to become unnecessarily aggressive, a useful skill you may try to acquire is to curb your knee-jerk reactions to perceived provocations and to search for alternative and better ways of explaining them. Sometimes this process is called reframing or reappraising. Like combating shyness, this skill of managing anger involves you in the following kinds of self-talk.

"Stop and think. What are my perceptual choices?"

"Are my perceptions based on fact or inference?"

"If my perceptions are based on inference, can I perceive the situation in other ways that are more closely related to the factual evidence?"

"If necessary, what further information do I need to collect?"

"What perception do I choose because it fits best with the factual evidence?"

Exercise 38

Managing anger: generating and evaluating different perceptions

1. Choose one or more situations in your relationships in which you have felt angry, possibly without due cause.

2. For each situation make a worksheet in the following format.

Situation	Upsetting Perception(s) (initial explanation(s))	Different Perceptions (alternative explanations)

3. Write down the situation and, in the "upsetting perception(s)" column, any perceptions associated with your anger. Assess the realism of your upsetting perception(s) by logically analyzing them.

_____

_____

4. In the "different perceptions" column, write down as many different perceptions of the situation as you can generate. Then evaluate which has the best fit for explaining the situation.

_____

_____

5. Assess the ways in which the emotional and behavioral consequences of your best-fit perceptions would have been different from those of your initial perceptions.

Using Coping Self-Talk

Those of you with a tendency to be impulsive when angry and to shoot your mouth off might consider using coping self-talk. Anger-evoking situations may be viewed as challenging you to respond in task-oriented rather than in impulsive and self-defeating ways. Simple self-instructions, like "Calm down," "Cool it," "Count to ten," and "Take it easy," can often give you the time and space to get your feelings more under control (Goldstein & Keller, 1987). Once your feelings are more controlled, you have considerably more choice concerning whether and how to express your anger.

> Beth is angry with Joe because he said he could pick her up from work, but he has kept her waiting for half an hour. When he finally arrives, looking tired and rushed, she tells herself, "Take it easy. Count to ten. He is obviously tired and this is no time for either of us to have a fight." Joe apologizes and says that he was delayed by a flat tire.

In many relationships, provocations are relatively predictable. You know that your partner may tease you, leave his or her clothes lying around, not do a domestic chore, or act in some other way that you dislike. Here you can use coping self-talk to help achieve your goal of managing a specific provocation better. Managing a provocation entails making choices that increase your sense of mastery and lessen the likelihood of your anger being both unpleasant for yourself and counterproductive in your relationship (Novaco, 1977; Meichenbaum, 1983). Coping self-talk involves both calming self-instructions—for instance, "Stay calm"—and coaching self-instructions that help you stay focused on how you can best perform the task at hand.

Possible coping self-talk statements that you might tell yourself before a potentially anger-evoking provocation include the following.

"Keep calm and remember what I want to achieve in this situation."
"Remember, stick to the issues and avoid put-downs."
"I can handle this situation if I don't let my stupid pride get in the way."

Possible coping self-talk statements that you might tell yourself during an anger-evoking provocation include the following.

"Stay cool. I'm not going to let him or her have the satisfaction of getting to me."

"Relax. My anger is a signal telling me to calm down and keep my goal in mind."
"Just because he or she is being competitive, I don't have to get sucked into behaving the same way."

Possible coping self-talk statements that you might tell yourself after an anger-evoking provocation include the following.

"I'm learning to cope better without being aggressive."
"Even though the situation is unresolved, I'm glad I didn't come on too strong."
"Using my coping self-talk prevents me from feeling powerless and over-whelmed."

Along with using coping self-talk, you can diminish your physical reactions to provocation by breathing slowly and regularly. Sometimes it also pays to defer dealing with a provocation until your feelings are more under control. Exercise 39 and Experiment 12 help you explore how you can use coping self-talk to manage anger.

Exercise 39
Managing anger: using coping self-talk

1. Make a list of your anger-evoking self-statements. If you have difficulty doing this, keep a diary and record your anger-evoking self-talk.

   _____

   _____

2. Identify a specific situation in your relationships where you consider that your anger is harmful. Write down: (a) your goals in this situation; and (b) at least three coping self-talk statements each for before, during, and after the situation. It may help to write each statement on an index card for practice and use-in-emergency purposes.

   _____

   _____

   _____

Experiment 12
What happens when I use coping self-talk to manage anger?

Part A: Assessment
Look back at your answer to Exercise 39 and use the situation for which you formulated coping self-talk statements.

Part B: Make an "If . . . then . . ." Statement
1. The "If . . ." part of your statement relates to rehearsing, practicing, and using your self-talk statements before, during, and after an anger-evoking situation. Rehearsal and practice is important. Spend at least two separate periods rehearsing and practicing your coping self-talk as you imagine yourself before, during, and after your anger-evoking situation.

---

2. The "then" part of the statement indicates the specific consequences you predict will follow from the changes in your behavior. In brief: "If I use coping self-talk, then these consequences (specify) will follow."

Part C: Try Out and Evaluate Your Changed Behavior
Try out your changed behavior. How well did you use coping self-talk? Assess its positive and negative consequences for yourself and your relationship. Have your predictions been confirmed or disconfirmed? Has this experiment taught you something about how you can stay more in control of your feelings and behavior by using coping self-talk? If so, please specify what you have learned.

Using Visualization

You think not only in words but also in pictures or images. You can use visualization—consciously changing the images in your mind—to help you manage anger better. Ways that you can use visualization include the following.

• *Visualized rehearsal.* When preparing yourself to handle an anger-evoking provocation, you can visually go through the various steps involved in the way you want to behave. Once you have worked these steps out, you can repeatedly imagine yourself handling the provocation competently. When you play these "movies in your mind," you may also have a soundtrack of coping self-talk.
• *Visualized relaxation.* Visualization is best done in a quiet and comfortable place, where you can shut your eyes and relax. You may visualize restful scenes not only as a prelude to other forms of visualization—for example, visualized rehearsals—but also as a way of calming yourself down when angry. Visualized relaxation may be used independently of or in conjunction with muscular relaxation, which is described later in this chapter. Each of you probably has one or more special scenes that help you feel relaxed—for instance, looking at a valley

with lush green meadows or sitting in a favorite chair at home. The following is an example of a visual relaxation scene.

> I'm lying on an uncrowded beach on a pleasant, sunny day, enjoying the sensations of warmth on my body. A gentle breeze blows. I can hear the peaceful noise of the sea lapping against the shore nearby. I haven't a care in the world and enjoy my feelings of peace, calm, relaxation, and well-being.

• *Visualizing the opposite.* When you are in the grip of anger, hatred, and resentment, switching from a verbal to a visual mode of thinking may help disrupt your negative ruminations. You can use visualizing to help you get in touch with your kinder feelings about the person with whom you are angry. When angry, it is very easy to allow yourself to erect negative stereotypes of others.

At their cancer clinic in Dallas, Texas, the Simontons have used an imagery process to help patients let go of resentments and forgive people who have hurt them. Patients are asked to get a clear picture in their minds of the person about whom they feel resentment. They are then instructed to "picture good things happening to that person. See him or her receive love or attention or money, whatever you believe that person would see as a good thing" (Simonton, Matthews-Simonton, & Creighton, 1978, p. 152). The Simontons report that as patients continue to use the process of visualizing good things happening, they begin to get a different perspective on the person they resented. Consequently, they begin to feel more relaxed, less resentful, and more forgiving. Some other ways of using visualizing to access more loving feelings are included in Exercise 40.

• *Visualizing another's viewpoint.* You can use visualization to help you understand how the other person might view a situation in which you become angry. By taking their perspective, you may gain insight into your own contribution to the conflict.

Exercise 40 gives you the opportunity to try out visualization as a skill of managing anger.

Exercise 40
Managing anger: using visualization to become more forgiving

Instructions: Find a quiet place where you can be uninterrupted. Sit in a comfortable chair, and after you read each instruction close your eyes.

1. Visualize a restful and relaxing scene. Evoke not only the sights but the sounds, smells, and other sensations that make this such a calm and peaceful scene for you. Stay in this scene for at least two minutes.

2. Visualize a clear picture of a person toward whom you feel anger. Then do each of the following visualizations. Spend at least two minutes on each, and take note of your reactions.

(a) Visualize good things happening to that person, the sort of things that make them happy.
(b) Visualize one or more happy times in your relationship that you have both enjoyed.
(c) Visualize yourself doing good things for that person.
(d) Visualize that person doing good things for you.
(e) Visualize characteristics of the other person that you like.
(f) Visualize your saying to the other person that you love them and value your relationship.

After going through these visualizations, review which if any helped you feel better about the other person and more relaxed. Which of them might help you become more forgiving and behave more appropriately? You are likely to have to repeat these visualizations a number of times to gain their full benefit.

Action Skills

Being Assertive

Chapter 9 emphasized being assertive in both initiating and making requests for changes in behavior. These assertion skills can be skills of preventing anger as well as of managing it. The following are some examples where people's failure to be assertive contributes to their anger.

• *Not initiating and saying what you want.* On some occasions, you may be angry because you are too timid about sharing your thoughts and feelings.

> Paul and Barb usually do what Paul wants. Paul is very positive about initiating and stating his wants and wishes. Barb is very inhibited about stating what she wants. She resents Paul because she thinks he is too domineering and should know what she wants without having to be told.

• *Not making requests for behavior change.* In some instances, you may disapprove of another's behavior and either bottle up your anger or let some out indirectly—for instance through cynicism or gossip. Until you have made a genuine effort to change another's behavior, you may be colluding in situations that help you to feel resentful.

> Rita and Luz are sisters. Rita does not like lending Luz money. Every time Luz asks, Rita grudgingly lets her have the money and then nags Luz until she is repaid. Rita gets furious with Luz both because of her continual requests and also because Luz is poor at meeting repayment deadlines. Rita could prevent her anger if she made it clear to Luz that she wanted no more loan requests. If Rita backed up her words by not lending money, after a period of adjustment Luz might stop asking her.

Chapter 9 reviewed nonassertive, aggressive, and assertive ways of initiating and making requests for behavior change. Turn back to that chapter if you would like further details on how to be assertive in those areas.

Handling Aggressive Criticism

When you think someone is aggressive in criticizing you, you can react in a nonassertive manner ("I'm sorry. It's all my fault. I won't do it again"), an aggressive manner ("How dare you say that to me? You fool"), or an assertive manner. Though you may not always have time in the heat of the moment, examine your thinking choices. For example, your unrealistic personal rules may contribute to your perceiving accurate feedback as aggressive criticism. You may also have jumped to the conclusion that the criticism is unjust without having reviewed the evidence to determine whether your perceptions are accurate. Moreover, you may react impulsively without thinking through whether the criticism is worth bothering about. You may not be using coping self-talk to stay calm and stick to the issues.

You can make numerous action choices in dealing with aggressive criticism. Some of these choices involve the skills of trying to stay calm. For instance, you can keep quiet and avoid an impulsive knee-jerk reaction when your emotions are aroused by criticism. Instead, you can give yourself time and space to compose your thoughts and feelings. You may also regulate your breathing. You may tell yourself to relax, calm down, and breathe slowly and regularly until you feel more under control.

The following are five verbal strategies for dealing with aggressive criticism. You need to accompany your verbal messages with appropriate voice and body messages. These strategies may be used in combination as well as singly.

1. *Reflective strategy*. Here you allow the other person to vent their strong feelings and respond in a way that shows you have understood both their feelings and their reasons—for example, "You feel mad at me because you think I am not pulling my weight in doing the household chores." Often, people stuck in their anger sound like broken records because they rightly or wrongly believe that they are not being heard. Reflecting their anger gives them the message "I hear your anger and criticism and I accept it as being your internal viewpoint." Reflecting another's anger does not mean that you automatically agree with the person.

2. *Deflective strategy*. The object here is to blunt the thrust of the aggressive criticism by agreeing with part of it. This strategy is especially applicable where you actually do agree with part of the criticism. Examples of this strategy include "You may have a point, I can be rather untidy at times" or "I'm not always as considerate as I would like to be." Once you have allowed the other person to establish the legitimacy of his or her area of criticism, he or she may be more prepared to review with you whether the criticism is justified in this specific case.

3. *Inquiry strategy*. After a reflective or a deflective response, or both, you may follow up with an inquiring response: "Would you please be more specific about what I've done to upset you?" The inquiry response may further defuse the

aggressiveness of the criticism, since it shows you are willing to allow the other to elaborate on his or her internal viewpoint. Furthermore, the inquiry response may provide you with information to clear up any misunderstandings that may have arisen. However, in some instances the inquiry response may ignite rather than defuse anger. Some people become threatened when asked to specify the reasons for their anger.

4. *Feedback strategy.* After showing that you have heard another's criticism, you may choose to give feedback both about the criticism and the manner in which it was given—for example, "I feel very uncomfortable when you criticize me so harshly. I am so late in picking you up because I had a flat tire on the way over." Sometimes when another person attempts to talk you down, you may calmly and firmly repeat your position while at the same time acknowledging that he or she feels differently.

5. *Deferral strategy.* Often, you have the option to back off now and react to criticism at a later date. Backing off does not mean backing down; instead, you husband your resources for a more effective moment. You may say something like, "I've heard what you're saying (if necessary, specify). I would like some time to think about it." Alternatively, if it becomes clear that you disagree, you might say, "It's obvious that we disagree. I think we both need some time to think about it. Could we fix a time to discuss it again?" Deferral strategies are not intended to avoid issues. Instead, they should allow either or both parties time to cool down and later to deal with the emotions and issues raised by the criticism more rationally. The skills of managing conflict discussed in Chapter 11 can be highly relevant here.

Exercise 41 helps you explore using these strategies to deal with aggressive criticism.

Exercise 41
Managing anger: dealing with aggressive criticism

1. Write down how you see yourself feeling, thinking, and acting when you are aggressively criticized. Give specific examples.

---

2. The following is a hypothetical situation in which you are being aggressively criticized. The other person, shouting and pointing his or her finger, says, "Why don't you ever pull your weight with the household chores? Do you expect me to be your servant? You never keep your side of our agreements." For each of the following strategies, write out a response to this aggressive criticism of you.

   Reflective strategy ——————————————————————

Exercise 41 (continued)

Deflective strategy ——————————————————————

————————————————————————————————————

Inquiry strategy ————————————————————————

————————————————————————————————————

Feedback strategy ————————————————————————

————————————————————————————————————

Deferral strategy ————————————————————————

————————————————————————————————————

Which, if any, of these strategies do you think might be effective used either singly or in combination?

————————————————————————————————————

3. If appropriate, choose a situation from your current relationships where you are or are at risk of being aggressively criticized. Write out (a) how you are or might be criticized; (b) responses based on each of the five strategies; and (c) which if any of these strategies you think might be most effective; state your reasons.

————————————————————————————————————

————————————————————————————————————

————————————————————————————————————

Relaxing Yourself

Mention has already been made of how you can try to counteract angry feelings by visualizing a restful scene. Progressive muscular relaxation is another method you can use to try to dissipate your anger. Progressive relaxation refers to the progressive cultivation of the relaxation response. You may use progressive muscular relaxation in conjunction both with visualized relaxation and also with other thinking skills—for example, coping self-talk (Deffenbacher, Story, Brandon, Hogg, & Hazaleus, 1988). Relaxation skills can help you to deal with the unpleasant and counterproductive aspects of heightened emotional arousal. Consequently, relaxation may help you think and act more rationally.

The first step in physically relaxing yourself is to find a quiet space where you will be uninterrupted. You may use a bed, a recliner chair, or a comfortable chair with a headrest. If possible, wear loose-fitting, comfortable clothing, and remove items such as glasses and shoes. Your arms should be either by your side if you are lying down or on the arms of your chair if you are seated. Your legs should be uncrossed and your eyes shut.

Progressive muscular relaxation involves you in tensing and relaxing various muscle groups. You go through a five-step tension–relax cycle for each muscle group (Bernstein & Borkovec, 1973). These steps are (1) *focus*—focus attention on a particular muscle group; (2) *tense*—tense the muscle group; (3) *hold*—maintain the tension for five to seven seconds; (4) *release*—release the tension in the muscle group; and (5) *relax*—spend 20 to 30 seconds focusing on letting go of tension and further relaxing the muscle group.

Table 10-2 lists the various muscle groupings and self-instructions for tensing them. You can make up a relaxation cassette for yourself that instructs you through the five steps for each muscular grouping. For example: (1) "I'm *focusing* on my right hand and forearm"; (2) "Clench my right fist and *tense* the muscles in my lower arm"; (3) "*Hold* for 5 to 7 seconds"; (4) "*Release*—let my body go back to its basic relaxed position"; (5) "*Relax*. Focus on the sensations of tension leaving my right hand and forearm for 20 to 30 seconds." At the end of your progressive muscular relaxation instructions, also instruct yourself to imagine a restful scene for three to five minutes and to forget all your cares. Throughout the process of making your relaxation cassette, speak in a slow, quiet, firm, and relaxed voice.

Progressive muscular relaxation requires regular practice to gain its full benefits. When learning the technique, you should practice daily for at least 15 minutes for a week. If you come back to it after a break, you should also practice until you find yourself deeply relaxed again. However, at times your anger may be unexpected and immediate. At such times, relaxing yourself with or without the use of a cassette player may still help you to cope with your heightened arousal. Exercise 42 allows you to explore how relaxing yourself can help you manage anger.

Exercise 42
Managing anger: relaxing myself

1. Make up a progressive muscular relaxation self-instruction cassette as described in the text.

2. Spend at least 15 minutes a day for the next week practicing your muscular and visual relaxation skills.

3. If practical, when you feel angry in your daily life go to a quiet room with soft lighting and no distractions. Sit or lie in a comfortable position and practice your relaxation skills. Afterward, note any changes in the way you feel.

Table 10-2.   Tensing self-instructions for progressive muscular relaxation.

Muscle Group	Tensing Self-Instructions*
Right hand and forearm	Clench my right fist and tense the muscles in my lower arm.
Right biceps	Bend my right arm at the elbow and flex my biceps by tensing the muscles of my upper right arm.
Left hand and forearm	Clench my left fist and tense the muscles in my lower arm.
Left biceps	Bend my left arm at the elbow and flex my biceps by tensing the muscles of my upper left arm.
Forehead	Lift my eyebrows as high as possible.
Eyes, nose, and upper cheeks	Squeeze my eyes tightly shut and wrinkle my nose.
Jaw and lower cheeks	Clench my teeth and pull the corners of my mouth firmly back.
Neck and throat	Pull my chin down hard toward my chest yet resist having it touch my chest.
Chest and shoulders	Pull my shoulder blades together and take a deep breath.
Stomach	Tighten the muscles in my stomach as though someone were about to hit me there.
Right thigh	Tense the muscles of my right upper leg by pressing the upper muscle down and the lower muscles up.
Right calf	Stretch my right leg and pull my toes toward my head.
Right foot	Point and curl the toes of my right foot and turn it inward.
Left thigh	Tense the muscles of my left upper leg by pressing the upper muscle down and the lower muscles up.
Left calf	Stretch my leg and pull my toes toward my head.
Left foot	Point and curl the toes of my left foot and turn it inward.

*With left-handed people, tensing instructions for the left side of the body should come before those for the right.

Managing Stress

Stress can come both from within and from without. Both sources can contribute to anger. It is important to develop your awareness of your stress signals and how well you listen to them. Also, try to become more aware of what stresses you. Such awareness may help you not only to prevent and manage your anger but also to avoid taking it out on other people.

Each of you has an optimal level of stress or a particular level of stimulation at which you feel most comfortable. At this level, you experience stress without distress (Selye, 1974). Below this level, you may be insufficiently stimulated or bored. Above this level, you are likely to experience physiological and psychological distress. Body reactions to too much stress include hypertension and susceptibility to heart attacks and ulcers. Psychological feelings of distress may include shock, depression, frustration, anger, disorientation, and fears of insanity or nervous breakdown. If the heightened stress is prolonged or perceived as extremely severe, you may feel you are in a state of excessive stress or crisis.

The following are two examples of people whose stresses make them more prone to anger. Kim has allowed herself to develop an excessively stressful lifestyle. Art is reacting to external pressures. However, in both examples internal and external sources of stress interact.

> Kim is a high-pressure stock and bond salesperson. She is always on the go, both professionally and personally. She lives on her nerves, burning the candle at both ends and in the middle. When things go wrong, she gets tense and irritable. She is like a tightly stretched rubber band, just waiting to snap with anger.

> Art has just received a promotion at work. He now has to supervise 15 people. Although pleased at the promotion, Art still needs to develop the skills of being a good supervisor. He feels under pressure because of his promotion and is very irritable when he gets home. Art does not sleep well and his appetite is poorer than usual.

Some of the skills of managing stress are peculiar to the specific situations in which people find themselves. For example, as Art develops supervisory skills he is likely to feel less under stress. Other skills for managing stress are more general. For instance, the more you can develop your relationship skills, the less likely you are to generate stressful reactions from others. In addition, by developing your thinking skills you can prevent stress. For example, people who set themselves perfectionist standards for achievement are excellent candidates for feelings of distress. They need to develop more realistic personal rules.

The following are further ways of managing stress so that you are less prone to anger.

- *Muscular and visual relaxation.* This topic has already been reviewed.
- *Developing adequate recreational outlets.* You may need to explore the extent to which you lead a balanced life based on meeting your needs as well as

others' demands. How much time do you spend on rewarding leisure activities? Knowing when and how to get some recreation is a most useful skill for preventing and managing anger.

• *Participating in your health.* Being physically unfit contributes to many people's feelings of being stressed. You may be failing to exercise regularly, smoking a lot, drinking too much, engaging in drug abuse, or eating too much. If so, you need to change your attitude toward assuming responsibility for your health. If you have physical symptoms attributable to stress—for instance, hypertension—you should see a doctor.

• *Developing a support network.* If your support network is inadequate, you may wish to spend time developing it. Your support network is likely to consist of trusted friends, colleagues, relatives, neighbors, and possibly people in the helping services. People without such networks are much more vulnerable to feeling isolated and powerless when things go wrong.

• *Developing skills for managing problems.* Life is full of hassles. The better you are able to deal with these, the less likely you are to be stressed. Your attitude toward problems should be that they are an ordinary part of life. When possible, break problems down into their component parts, so that they seem more manageable and you can define them accurately. Be creative about generating alternative solutions and realistic about evaluating the consequences of these. Then implement the best-fit solution, and monitor and evaluate its consequences. Be prepared to modify or change plans that do not work for you.

The message of this section is that sometimes the most effective way to manage your anger is to analyze the broader context of stresses in which it occurs. You may be able to make choices and develop skills for dealing with stresses outside a relationship that will free you to be happier and more relaxed within the relationship.

Helping One Another to Manage Anger

In a close relationship based on assumptions of teamwork and equality, you can help one another to manage anger. Some degree of anger in your relationship is likely to be a fact of life. You can each take responsibility for managing anger constructively rather than destructively. The following are some ways you may work together as a team to manage anger.

• *Possess realistic relationship rules.* Together you can formulate realistic rules for the expression and management of anger in your relationship. The following rules may be helpful.

"Each of us tries to become aware of and openly locate our anger in ourselves."
"Neither of us tries to control the other through the use of threats, anger, or physical violence."

"Each of us attempts to avoid hurting the other through aggressive put-downs and shutting the other out by withdrawing emotionally."

"Expression of anger in our relationship is a signal to explore our own thoughts, feelings, and actions, not just those of the other person."

"If either of us has been destructively hurtful in anger, we openly acknowledge our negative behavior when calmer."

• *Develop accurate and caring models of each other.* Each of you can attempt to move beyond superficial personifications of yourself and your partner in order to develop a more accurate understanding. You work to understand one another's fears and vulnerabilities, trigger points, stresses, burden of previous hurts, defenses, and ways of showing and avoiding showing anger. In addition, you strive to keep an awareness of one another's strengths and positive qualities.

• *Develop a soothing tongue.* You can discipline yourself to watch your mouth. You express your anger assertively and show an awareness of what your partner is going through before, during, and after your expression of anger. You give specific feedback that allows the other to understand the reasons for your anger, rather than just shooting your mouth off. Your expression of anger is an invitation for discussion and not an end in itself.

• *Use listening and helpful responding skills.* Ways in which you can use listening and helpful responding skills include the following. First, you can tune in to your partner and help him or her to express angry feelings that he or she may either have difficulty acknowledging or getting out into the open. Second, you can show that you have clearly understood your partner's feelings and reasons when he or she expresses anger. Third, you can help one another analyze and deal with the material underlying the anger. This kind of analysis may entail helping one another to articulate unmet needs and unstated requests in your relationship here and now, to work through hurtful there-and-then experiences prior to your relationship, and to deal with current there-and-now stresses outside your relationship. Another way of looking at this process is that you offer each other informal therapy. A risk here is that you may focus exclusively on your partner, when exploration of your contribution to his or her anger might also be fruitful.

• *Be prepared to admit to and change negative behaviors.* Defensiveness is probably more dangerous than anger in close relationships. If you are defensive, you risk fanning the flames of one another's anger. However, if you are open, capable of acknowledging hurtful behaviors when pointed out, and willing to change them, you not only defuse those situations but also make it easier for your partner to behave likewise. By your honesty and actions, ill will can be transformed into goodwill.

• *Develop a capacity for tolerance and forgiveness.* The German poet Schiller wrote, "Happy is he who learns to bear what he cannot change!" One of the reasons for the increased divorce rate in Western countries is that people have higher expectations of marriage than they once did (Argyle & Henderson, 1985). You may need to examine your personal rules to see whether your expectations are counterproductive to your own happiness and that of your partner. In addition, you may need to work on the fears and insecurities that make it difficult for you to forgive and let go of past hurts. Martin Luther King, Jr. observed that forgiveness does not entail ignoring what has happened but instead means that you choose not to allow the past to remain a barrier to your current relationship (King, 1963). Forgiveness may be partly enlightened self-interest. Understanding human frailty and valuing caring behavior may make it easier for you to forgive your partner. You may need to learn to forgive yourself, too.

In addition to using these teamwork skills, you can also help one another to manage anger by increasing your exchange of rewarding behaviors and by managing your conflicts collaboratively, rather than in competition. These additional skills are the subject of Chapter 11.

Concluding Self-Talk

I can use anger either constructively or destructively in my relationships. I need to develop my skills of tuning in to my angry feelings and owning responsibility for them. Thinking skills I can use to regulate angry feelings include identifying and reformulating unrealistic personal rules, perceiving provocations differently, using coping self-talk, and developing relevant visualization skills.

I can also use action skills to manage my anger. Assertion skills can help me both to prevent anger-evoking situations from developing and to express anger constructively. I can adopt a range of strategies to handle aggressive criticism, including reflection. I can also use muscular and visual relaxation skills to calm my heightened level of arousal. Furthermore, when I manage stresses better, I'm less likely to overreact to provocations.

In a close relationship, we can use teamwork so that our anger does not become destructive. For instance, we can possess realistic relationship rules and formulate accurate and caring models of each other. In addition, we can help one another express and understand the reasons for our anger. We can also watch our tongues!

Notes

11

Preventing and Managing Conflict

So that's what Hell is. I'd never have believed it. . . . Do you
remember, brimstone, the stake, the gridiron? . . . What a joke!
No need of a gridiron, [when it comes to] Hell, it's other people.
Jean-Paul Sartre

The best part of married life is the fights.
The rest is merely so-so.
Thornton Wilder

The word *conflict* comes from the Latin roots *com-,* meaning "together," and
fligere, meaning "to strike." Dictionary definitions of conflict emphasize words like
"fight," "struggle," "antagonism," and "sharp disagreement." These dictionary
definitions include three elements: first, a difference or disagreement; second, a
severe quality to the disagreement; and third, ill will. This chapter focuses on
managing differences in relationships. These differences need not be the cause of
severe ill will, although they frequently are.

Conflicts are inevitable in ongoing relationships. Argyle observes, "There is a
very high level of conflict in marriage, and violence is quite common" (Argyle,
1983, p. 155). Deutsch states that conflicts usually involve any of five basic types of
issues: control over resources; preferences and nuisances; values; beliefs; and the
nature of the relationship between the partners. People enter relationships with
differences in socioeconomic and possibly cultural backgrounds, sex role expectations, levels of self-esteem, ability to tolerate stress, tastes and preferences,
beliefs and values, interests, social and family networks, and capacity to change
and grow (Deutsch, 1973). Add to these differences the fact that many people are

deficient in their relationship skills, including those of managing conflict, and the inevitability of conflict becomes even more obvious.

Productive and Destructive Conflict

The negative effects of conflict scarcely need cataloging. Conflicts can cause immense psychological pain that may last well after the relationship has ended. Relationships that offer promising opportunities for both partners can founder because conflicts have not been managed effectively. Chapter 1 provided statistics on the high level of breakdown and distress in North American marriages. Unhappy homes—where parents' energies are diverted into fighting with one another and also sometimes displacing their frustrations onto their children—can adversely affect those reared in them. Parental unhappiness or divorce can contribute to children's delinquency, aggression, disobedience, conduct problems, social withdrawal, depression, anxiety, and bed-wetting. Children may also learn poor skills of managing conflicts in their own lives. On a more subtle level, conflicts can fester and contribute to withdrawal and distance in relationships that were once happy and close.

Work environments are also frequently characterized by destructive conflicts. Not only can these conflicts cause great stress and unhappiness, but they can also lower output, with the extreme case being a strike. A degree of conflict is inevitable

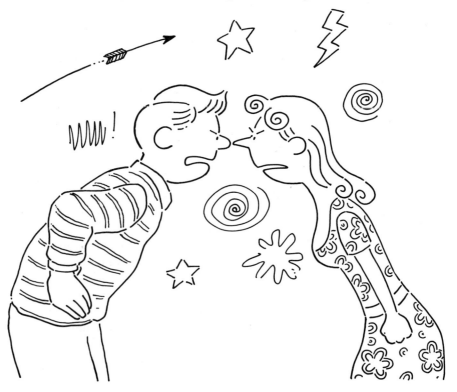

in work relationships, just as it is in personal relationships. Resources may be scarce, personal styles may clash, values and beliefs may differ, and you may have different expectations of one another and of the workplace. Moreover, you do not leave your relationship skills weaknesses at home. You take them to work, increasing the likelihood that conflicts will take a course destructive for both the individual participants and the attainment of group goals.

Conflict can be a good as well as a bad thing. The course of conflict may be productive rather than destructive. It is very easy to state the negative aspects of conflict. To redress the balance, four positive aspects of conflict in relationships are offered here.

- *Greater trust.* Conflict can build trust. People who can relate despite differences, as well as people who can work through differences together, may feel that their relationships are much less fragile than people who have not had such experiences.
- *Increased intimacy.* An important aspect of intimacy is the ability to give and receive honest feedback. A fuller sharing of self can occur when partners can reveal and work through their differences rather than just inhibit their disagreements.
- *Increased self-esteem.* Partners who manage their conflicts effectively may make gains in self-esteem. They know that their relationship is strong enough to withstand conflict. Each may feel better for being able to say what he or she thinks and feels. Problems may be identified, aired, and solved, rather than being allowed to fester. Each partner may gain a firmer sense of his or her own identity as well as greater knowledge of the other. Both may gain valuable practice in managing conflicts effectively.
- *Creative solutions.* The course of productive conflict can be viewed as a process of mutual problem solving. Creative solutions that meet both parties' needs, sometimes called win–win solutions, may be the outcome of this process. The opposite of a win–win solution is a lose–lose one, in which neither party's needs are met. In a win–lose solution, only one party's needs are met.

The remainder of this chapter presents some thinking and action skills for preventing and managing conflicts.

Thinking Skills

Emotions can run very high in conflicts. You may get so aroused that, temporarily at least, you may lose your capacity to be rational. Causing pain, being right, and ventilating your anger may become your main short-term objectives. The longer-term consequences of your behavior may be obscured in the heat of the moment. In close relationships, partners can get stuck in repetitive patterns of conflict that undermine trust and mutual rewardingness. You may drag one another down in cycles of recrimination and bitterness. The lows in your relationship may get longer and deeper and the highs shorter and fewer.

Many thinking skills are relevant to both preventing avoidable conflicts and managing unavoidable ones. These skills include the thinking skills covered in Chapter 10 to help you manage anger better: owning responsibility for your anger, choosing realistic personal rules, perceiving provocations differently, using coping self-talk, and visualization. This chapter develops two interrelated areas of perceiving accurately—namely, owning personal responsibility for your choices and perceiving the other more accurately. Conflicts are frequently caused and sustained by misperceptions in these areas.

Owning Personal Responsibility for Your Choices

> Seek not good from without: seek it within yourselves,
> or you will never find it.
> *Epictetus*

Look at the ways in which people may describe their choices in conflicts.

"Until she stops being nasty to me, I'm not going to stop being nasty to her."
"I had no choice but to tell him what I thought of him in no uncertain terms."
"He makes me so mad that I can't help hitting him."
"It's all your fault that our relationship is heading for the rocks."
"You tell me how we can get out of this mess."
"If you're not prepared to be reasonable, I don't give a damn what you think."
"I'm so hurt by all you've done to me that I find it impossible to forgive you."

In each of the preceding examples, the speaker is likely to stay stuck in conflict through inability to perceive and acknowledge responsibility for his or her feeling, thinking, and action choices. The speaker may worsen the conflict through aggressive voice and body messages. Numerous thinking errors in these statements indicate that the speakers inadequately own responsibility for their choices. These errors include the following.

• *Dependent thinking:* allowing your feeling, thinking, and actions to be controlled by another's behavior.
• *Lack of alternative thinking:* saying that you have no choice, rather than identifying where your areas of choice are.
• *Passive ("I'm the second to change") thinking:* needing the other person to make the first move before you can alter your behavior.
• *"Poor me" thinking:* allowing yourself to wallow in self-pity and other negative emotions rather than acknowledging your strengths and coping capacities.
• *Misattributing cause:* looking to blame another person rather than to assign cause accurately for what sustains the problem, including your own contribution to it.

- *Overemphasizing the past:* dwelling on past hurts and resentments rather than trying to ensure that you relate better in the present and future.
- *Insufficient consequential thinking:* inadequately thinking through the consequences of your thinking and action choices for yourself and others.
- *Competitive thinking:* thinking in terms of "you versus me" rather than collaborating to find solutions that work for "you," "me," and "us." The notion of replacing competition with collaboration is a recurring theme in this chapter.
- *Insufficient problem-management orientation:* not seeing the difficulties and differences in your relationship as problems to be managed rather than excuses to give and receive pain.

Reversing these errors results in a list of thinking skills that help you to own responsibility for your choices in relationship conflicts. These skills strengths are as follows.

Independent thinking
Flexible thinking that identifies alternatives
Active ("I'm prepared to be the first to change") thinking
"Adequate me" thinking
Realistically attributing cause
Emphasizing the present and future much more than the past
Consequential thinking
Collaborative thinking
Problem-management orientation

Exercises 43 and 44 are designed to raise your awareness that in conflicts you always have choices. Exercise 43 focuses on the thinking and action choices others make that may hinder their effectiveness. Exercise 44 assumes that sometimes you can get insight into how you might approach a conflict if you view the conflict in ways completely opposite to your current viewpoint.

Exercise 43
Exploring personal responsibility for managing conflict: some case studies

For each of the following conflict case studies write down: (1) some of the main thinking skills weaknesses that may get in the way of the main character or characters acting effectively; (2) the specific ways in which the main character or characters act ineffectively; (3) how each of them might think and act differently to attain their goals.

Case Studies
1. Steve is an 18-year-old who enjoys his girlfriend's company but has frequent fights with her. During their arguments, he tends to make comments like, "You

Exercise 43 (continued)

women are all the same. You just can't make the effort to understand the male viewpoint."

_____

_____

_____

_____

2. Mary and Jerome are 17-year-old twins who share the use of the second car in the family. Each is extremely touchy and jealous over the other's use of the car. Each believes the other is taking advantage of his or her own weaknesses. They get very emotional and argue a lot. Their parents are getting fed up with their arguments and are threatening to stop both of them from using the car.

_____

_____

_____

_____

3. Nancy is a 50-year-old widow who lives with her 18-year-old son, Eric, and 16-year-old daughter, Kate. Nancy is constantly nagging the children to help her more with the housework and to be less messy. She makes remarks like, "You are selfish children" and "If your father were alive he would not let you behave this way." Eric's reaction to Nancy's remarks is to get angry and sulky. Kate says that since Eric is not pulling his weight, why should she?

_____

_____

_____

4. Deryl and Russ are junior executives who both have very fixed ideas about how their unit should be run. They appear to be in a constant power struggle. In meetings with their boss, each tries to argue the strength of his own case. Each presents his own point of view as though it were the only way to get the job done, and each gets defensive when challenged by the other. Each is anxious for the approval of their boss, and they both view their meetings with him in win–lose terms. Their boss regards both of them as rather immature and not yet ready for promotion.

_____

_____

_____

_____

5. Cheryl and Lennie have been married ten years and feel they are drifting apart. They rarely go out together, and each increasingly resents the other. They argue about how to bring up the children, how much to see their in-laws, what friends each should have, how they should spend their money, and so on. Lennie's way of getting what he wants is to become emotional and angry. Often Cheryl gives in but carries around a residue of resentment that shows up in her snide remarks, deliberate failures to do things that would please Lennie, and tales she tells Lennie about how other people, like her friends and her mother, view him as difficult. Every now and then Cheryl explodes, and they have a blazing fight. During these arguments, they catalog one another's deficiencies. Each has lost the desire to give real happiness to the other. The emotional atmosphere in their home is tense and bitter. Their children welcome the opportunity to play in their friends' homes.

_____

_____

_____

Exercise 44
Choosing the opposite response in a conflict

This exercise is designed to help you become more aware that you choose how you respond to others when in conflict. The idea is to get you thinking and responding in a way opposite to the way you currently behave.

Think of someone with whom you either are or have recently been in conflict in a close personal or work relationship. Assume that you have been saying that this person is wrong, disparaging him or her, and sending hostile voice, body, touch, and action messages to him or her.

1. Imagine going up to that person and acknowledging the rightness of his or her position. How might he or she react?

_____

2. Imagine paying a number of honest compliments to that person. How might he or she react?

_____

3. Imagine speaking in a kind and considerate tone of voice to that person. How might he or she react?

_____

4. Imagine going up to that person looking relaxed, smiling, open, and friendly. How might he or she react?

_____

Exercise 44 (continued)

5. If appropriate, imagine either shaking hands with that person or giving him or her a hug, a kiss, or both. How might he or she react?

_____

6. Imagine going out of your way to give something to or do something for that person that he or she would really like. How might he or she react?

_____

Perceiving the Other More Accurately

> Two-thirds of what we see is behind our eyes.
> *Chinese proverb*

Even when they are not in conflict, people in close relationships may have distorted pictures of one another. With the anxiety, threat, and heightened emotionality generated in a conflict, these pictures may become even more distorted. Maslow distinguishes between "deficiency-motivated" and "growth-motivated" perception. He writes, "We may not be aware when *we* perceive in a need-determined way. But we certainly are aware when *we* ourselves are perceived this way. . . . We dislike being perceived as useful objects or as tools" (Maslow, 1962, pp. 37–38). In deficiency-motivated perception, your picture of me is likely to be distorted by your own needs and fears. You do not see me as I am. Instead, you see me in a way that will help you fulfill your own picture of yourself. For instance, if you need to see yourself as the victim, you need to see me as the persecutor.

Developing a more realistic, accurate, and caring model of the other person is a skill for both preventing and managing conflict. This skill helps prevent conflicts, because with a more realistic model of the other person, you are less likely to jump to erroneous conclusions concerning his or her motivation. Similarly, during conflicts you are more able to relate to the other person on the basis of balanced and accurate rather than distorted information.

How can you be more accurate in your perception of others? You may have to work hard to counteract destructive negative perceptions that are not completely based on reality. The first step is to become aware that your model of your partner may be inaccurate and that you may be perceiving him or her some of the time in a deficiency-motivated way.

The second step is to become aware of some of the specific ways in which you may distort your perceptions of your partner. These include the following.

• *Lack of information.* Many relationships get stuck at a level of self-disclosure that falls short of genuine intimacy. Partners tend to reciprocate one another's behavior, consolidating the impasse. However, the less actual information partners provide about themselves, the more room each has to supply make-believe information to fill this vacuum. Thus your models of one another may contain not only information gaps but also distorted pseudo-information designed to fill some of these gaps.

• *Perceptual errors.* Numerous perceptual errors may distort your vision of your partner, especially in the heat of conflict when you feel anxious and threatened. These errors include the following.

> *Selective attention to negatives:* focusing on your partner's negative behavior .and blocking out positive thoughts, feelings, and reactions to them.
>
> *Exaggerating negative characteristics:* trying to make a point through overstatement. For instance, in the statement "You are never around to help in the house," the word *never* may be a gross exaggeration.
>
> *Rating personhood negatively:* going beyond negative perceptions of specific behaviors to rate your partner negatively as a person—for instance, "The reason we keep having all these hassles in our relationship is that you have such a rotten personality."
>
> *Overgeneralizing:* drawing a broad conclusion from a specific observation—for instance, "You did not remember our anniversary, therefore you do not love me anymore."
>
> *Black-and-white thinking:* thinking in either/or terms—for instance, "Either you love me all the time or you do not love me at all."
>
> *Misattributing cause:* giving inaccurate explanations for your partner's behavior that lead to and sustain conflicts—for instance, "You did not pick me up when you said you would because you wanted to take out your anger on me."

The third step in trying to rid yourself of inaccurate and negative stereotypes of others is to work diligently to alter your thinking and behavior. Some suggestions for how to alter your thinking and behavior include the following.

• *Collect more information.* By using good listening and self-disclosing skills, you make it safer for your partner to reveal more of themselves. By taking more of an interest in your partner, including asking pertinent questions, you may amplify your model of them.

• *Understand the external contexts of your partner's behavior.* Get to know the past influences that have shaped your partner. What rules and directives did your partner receive from his or her family or origin and from other sources? Try also to understand current stresses on your partner outside your relationship—for instance, at work.

• *Correct your specific perceptual errors.* Try to identify how you distort your perceptions when you are anxious, angry, and in conflict. For instance, do you emphasize and exaggerate your partner's negative behaviors? If so, what are the consequences for you, your partner, and your relationship? When you catch yourself being unrealistically negative, consciously try to balance this negativity with more positive perceptions. When you catch yourself overgeneralizing, consciously try to draw more accurate inferences from the available facts.

• *Develop checking-out and clarifying skills.* Be willing to check out with your partner how he or she sees him- or herself as behaving and the reasons for this behavior. If you are still unclear, you may request further clarification from your partner.

• *Develop perspective-taking skills.* Check your tendencies toward egocentric thinking by trying to see how the other person views the conflict. How does the other person see you as behaving? How does the other person see him- or herself as behaving? What does the other want for your relationship?

• *Behave differently.* Try altering your behavior to see whether your negative perceptions of your partner are as much a function of your behavior as they are of his or hers. Just as partners tend to reciprocate negative behaviors, they also tend to reciprocate positive behaviors. You may both have realistic opportunities to behave differently and so lessen your negative perceptions of one another.

• *Work to eliminate a competitive attitude.* When partners compete with one another on an "I win, you lose" basis, each has a vested interest in perceiving the other negatively. You can develop a conciliatory and collaborative attitude to problems in your relationship. When possible, your goal is to find solutions acceptable to both of you. Such solutions may be better than simple compromises, in which each of you only gets part of what you want.

Exercise 45 helps you assess whether you have been distorting your perceptions of another in a relationship.

Exercise 45
Preventing and managing conflict by choosing
to perceive another more accurately

1. Regarding either your partner or some other person of your choice with whom you come into conflict, assess the extent to which you distort your picture of that person through: (a) lack of information; and (b) specific perceptual errors: selective attention to that person's negative characteristics, exaggerating his or her negative characteristics, rating his or her personhood negatively, over-generalizing, black-and-white thinking, and misattributing cause.

---

2. If you consider that some of your perceptions, of either your partner or some other person, are inaccurate in ways that generate and sustain conflicts, assess the extent to which each of the following might help you to perceive him or her more accurately: (a) collecting more information; (b) understanding the external contexts of their behavior; (c) correcting specific perceptual errors (already listed in this exercise); (d) developing checking-out and clarifying

skills; (e) developing perspective-taking skills; (f) behaving differently yourself; and (g) adopting a more conciliatory and collaborative attitude.

_____

_____

_____

3. Set yourself clear and realistic goals for perceiving either your partner or
   another person more realistically, then develop and implement a plan to
   achieve your goals.

_____

_____

_____

Action Skills

In addition to thinking less emotionally and more rationally, how can you act to
prevent and manage conflicts? Here the focus is on two important teamwork skills:
increasing the exchange of rewarding behaviors and collaborating to manage
conflicts.

Increasing the Exchange of Rewarding Behaviors

Chapter 8 introduced the notions of positive reciprocity, in which partners exchange rewarding behaviors, and negative reciprocity, in which they exchange
unrewarding behaviors. Most relationships involve a mixture of the two. However,
partners in distressed relationships reciprocate more unrewarding behaviors than
partners in happy relationships do.

Exchanging a great number of rewarding behaviors both prevents and contains
conflicts. Positive reciprocity prevents conflicts because happy people are less
likely to pick unnecessary fights. Positive reciprocity contains conflicts because it
creates an emotional climate of good-will, in which conflicts are more likely to be
approached productively than destructively. However, increasing your exchange
of rewarding behaviors is definitely not a substitute for developing the communication skills to manage conflicts collaboratively.

Partners in unhappy relationships may be well advised to take a systematic
approach to increasing their exchange of rewarding behaviors. This approach
involves six steps.

1. *Being aware* of the importance of exchanging rewarding behaviors.
2. *Acknowledging* existing rewarding behaviors.
3. *Making requests* for additional rewarding behaviors.
4. *Agreeing* to exchange specific additional rewarding behaviors.
5. *Implementing* your agreement.
6. *Evaluating* progress and making further agreements.

1. *Being aware of the importance of exchanging rewarding behaviors.* Although it may seem obvious, you may need to become more aware that people are more attractive to one another if they are rewarding rather than unrewarding. This basic point can easily be lost in the heat of a conflict. You may also need to remind yourself that how you act influences how the other reacts. Stuart observes that a basic principle of social interaction is that "POSITIVE ACTIONS ARE LIKELY TO INDUCE POSITIVE REACTIONS, FIRST IN THE ATTITUDES OF OTHERS, AND THEN IN THEIR BEHAVIORS" (Stuart, 1980, p. 194).

Humans may have a tendency to reciprocate negative behaviors more quickly than positive ones, on a tit-for-tat theory. Nevertheless, if you maintain rewarding behaviors, chances are good that such behaviors will soften your partner's attitude. In turn, this softening of attitude may result in both an increase in their positive behaviors and a decrease in their negative behaviors toward you. Furthermore, if you both agree that the insufficient exchange of rewarding behaviors is a problem in your relationship, the fact that each of you now makes an effort to please is likely to help rebuild trust.

2. *Acknowledging existing rewarding behaviors.* Partners in unhappy relationships tend to overemphasize one another's unrewarding behaviors. Conversely, they often misperceive, take for granted, or fail to show appreciation for one another's rewarding behaviors. Both of you may need to become more aware of the rewards that already exist in your relationship. You can share your perceptions of existing rewarding behaviors in two main ways. First, each of you can make a list of *your* behaviors that you perceive as rewarding for your partner. What do you do that pleases? What do you say that pleases? This process can help people find out for themselves not only what rewards they currently offer their partners, but also how few those rewards may be. Listing your own gaps in rewardingness may be less threatening than having them pointed out by your partner would be. These lists of "rewards I give you" can be exchanged and discussed. Second, each partner can make a list of *the other's* behaviors that they perceive as rewarding. Here it is important not to spoil your positive feedback with negative "hooks"—for instance, "I like it when you rub my back, but you could do it less clumsily." These lists of "rewards you give me" also can be exchanged and discussed. During this discussion, you should refrain from hostile criticism.

3. *Making requests for additional rewarding behaviors.* Each of you now answers the question "What rewarding behaviors would I like you to offer me that you don't currently offer?" The behaviors you list should be specific and stated positively. For example, "not to be such a messy person" is neither specific nor stated in the positive. "Not to leave your dirty socks on the bedroom floor" may be specific, but it is stated in the negative, not the positive. "Put your dirty socks

into the laundry hamper" is both specific and stated in the positive. It is important to include some small behaviors that are not necessarily in any of your areas of major conflict, to allow your partner to take some easy first steps. In addition, try to make some of these behaviors the sort that can be performed almost daily—for example, "Ask me how my day has been when I get home from work." You may list the rewarding behaviors you want from your partner in any area of your relationship—for example, companionship, sex, money, household chores, and so on. Take time and care in making your lists. Keep in mind that your purpose is to influence the other person to become more rewarding for you, not to humiliate them; be tactful. When both of you have had enough time to make your lists, exchange them.

4. *Agreeing to exchange specific additional rewarding behaviors.* Your goal here is to make an agreement in which you both state that you will perform some additional rewarding behaviors for the other for a specified time period—say the next two weeks. Each of you should feel free to choose what additional rewards you give. If necessary, clarify one another's requests. Sometimes both of you may make the same request—for example, "Spend more time talking to me." Much of the time each of you is likely to be agreeing to different requests.

A choice in making agreements or contracts is whether they should be quid pro quo ("If you do this, I'll do that") or instead based on good faith ("My behavior is independent of yours"). Good faith contracts are preferable in personal relationships, since they make each of you responsible for your own behavior. You can always review your partner's behavior at the end of the agreement. An example of a simple good faith contract made between a mother and her 17-year-old son Sam, both of whom wanted to improve their stormy relationship, was that, for the next two weeks, Mom agrees to:

Have a pleasant conversation for at least ten minutes each evening when both of us are home.
Say "I love you, Sam" at least once.

For his part, Sam agrees to:

Have a pleasant conversation for at least ten minutes each evening when both of us are home.
Say "I love you, Mom" at least once.
Say "Thank you" when Mom washes my clothes and chauffeurs me around.
Wash the dishes when asked.
Tidy my room at least once.

Each person should have a written copy of the agreement. The agreement can be signed and countersigned if you think that will help you keep it. Each person should post the agreement in a place where he or she is likely to be frequently reminded of its terms—for instance, on a bedroom door or on the refrigerator.

5. *Implementing your agreement.* Changing your behavior from a negative to a positive pattern may be difficult. If necessary, make a plan for how you are going to stick to your agreement. Remember that rewarding verbal messages need to be accompanied by rewarding voice and body messages if they are to have the desired effect. For example, you do not say "I love you" when you are deep in reading the

newspaper. Take a few risks in being more positive for the sake of your relationship. Your taking some risks may make it easier for the other person to reciprocate. If you wish to offer further rewarding behaviors outside your agreement, feel free to do so.

A skill involved in implementing your agreement is to acknowledge and reward one another's attempts to be rewarding by saying "Thank you," "That's great," "I like that," or "I'm pleased." A fundamental psychological principle is that behavior that is rewarded is more likely to be maintained than behavior that goes unrewarded. Possibly each of you may have been less rewarded in the past because you did not apply this principle adequately.

6. *Evaluating progress and making further agreements.* Take note of your efforts to be rewarding. Also acknowledge what each of you has achieved. If you wish, make this first agreement a stepping-stone to another, in which you agree to expand the scope of your rewarding behaviors. Even without agreements, you should develop the skills of monitoring your rewardingness for your partner and taking corrective action if you are not rewarding enough. You should develop the skill of helping your partner to be more rewarding for you—for instance, by making specific, tactful requests for behavior changes and by saying "Thank you."

Experiment 13 gives you an opportunity to try out being more mutually rewarding in a relationship.

Experiment 13
What happens when we increase our exchange of rewarding behaviors?

This experiment needs to be done with someone else when both of you want to improve your relationship.

Part A: Assessment
Work through the procedures described in the text for acknowledging existing rewarding behaviors and for making requests for additional rewarding behaviors.

Part B: Make an "If . . . then . . ." Statement
Together make an "If . . . then. . . ." statement along the lines of "If we formulate and implement an agreement to increase the amount of rewarding behaviors exchanged in our relationship, then these consequences (specify) are likely to follow."

Part C: Try Out and Evaluate Your Changed Behavior
Try out your changed behavior. Assess its positive and negative consequences for yourself, one another, and your relationship. Do you think developing the skills of increasing the exchange of rewarding behaviors will help you to prevent and/or

manage conflicts better in the future? If so, be specific in identifying how it will help.

_____

_____

_____

Collaborating to Manage Conflicts

> To jaw-jaw is better than to war-war.
> *Winston Churchill*

An important way partners can show their love and concern for one another is to work together on their differences, problems, and conflicts. You can adopt three main conflict-management styles: competitive, compliant, or collaborative.

• *Competitive.* Here you view the problem as involving scarce resources. Consequently, there has to be a winner and a loser, and the loser is not going to be you. You adopt an "I win and you lose" approach to the conflict and do all in your power to get your way. Your tactics may include manipulation; not telling the whole truth; not admitting mistakes; or sending aggressive verbal, voice, and body messages. The risks of such an approach include not arriving at the best solution and making your partner feel violated. Although you may win in the short term, you may pay a high price for your victory.

• *Compliant.* Here either or both of you are unassertive. You may collude with one another in not confronting problems in your relationship. You may wish to keep the peace for fear of the psychological discomfort of confronting problems. Each of you may deceive yourself as to your motivation for complying and not own your anxieties and fears. Compliant approaches to managing problems can involve either both partners avoiding the issues or one partner giving in much of the time.

• *Collaborative.* Here you relate on a basis of mutual respect. You work as a team both to prevent unnecessary conflicts and to arrive at mutually satisfactory solutions to real conflicts. Neither of you attempts to impose your wishes on the other. You seek "I win and you win too" solutions that maximize the gains and minimize the costs for each partner and your relationship. Furthermore, each of you is prepared to work on your own inner difficulties as well as with one another. Both of you strive to develop accurate models of one another and to avoid indulging in negative misperceptions.

It may be helpful for you to use CUDSA, a systematic five-step framework for managing conflicts in collaboration. Implementing the CUDSA framework involves using almost all the sending and receiving skills described in this book. The five steps in CUDSA are the following.

1. *Confront* the conflict.
2. *Understand* one another's positions.
3. *Define* the problem(s).
4. *Search* for and evaluate alternative solutions.
5. *Agree* upon, implement, and evaluate the best solution(s).

The five steps of this framework frequently overlap. Table 11-1 gives an overview of the central task and examples of the skills involved in each step of the framework. Although the table does not so indicate, participants in conflicts need to discipline themselves to avoid aggressive voice and body messages that are perceived as put-downs; this directive is relevant to all steps in the CUDSA framework.

CUDSA provides an easily memorized, comprehensible framework for you and your partner to use in managing your conflicts. Sometimes conflicts can be handled more informally. However, on other occasions you may need to work

Table 11-1.   CUDSA: a five-step framework for managing conflicts.

Task(s)	*Illustrative Skills*
Step 1 Initiate the collaborative process	CONFRONT *the conflict* Owning the existence of the conflict; deciding whether or not to confront; being calm and keeping the threat level low; timing your confrontation; inviting the other to work on the conflict with you; choosing an appropriate time and place for further discussion
Step 2 Clear up misunderstandings, clarify positions, defuse emotions	UNDERSTAND *one another's positions* Sending "I" messages; expressing feelings and stating wants and wishes assertively; giving specific feedback; stating honest positives; listening and responding helpfully; checking out and clarifying; taking the other's perspective; admitting to and changing misperceptions
Step 3 Arrive at mutually acceptable definition(s) of problem(s)	DEFINE *the problem(s)* Avoiding unfair fighting tactics; identifying and acknowledging areas of common ground; admitting your own mistakes and hurtful behaviors; identifying actions of the other that sustain the conflict; identifying hidden agendas; acknowledging and communicating changes in your positions; stating the problem(s) clearly and simply
Step 4 Generate and assess alternative solutions	SEARCH *for and evaluate alternative solutions* Generating solutions; evaluating the consequences of solutions; expressing reactions to solutions clearly; asking for the other's reactions; clarifying; making trade-offs and compromises
Step 5 Reach a clear agreement that can be renegotiated if necessary	AGREE *upon, implement, and evaluate the best solutions(s)* Stating agreements clearly; checking out that agreements are clearly understood; planning for, implementing, and evaluating consequences; making requests to renegotiate rather than breaking agreements; modifying and changing agreements

together more systematically. Even where only one of you is prepared to adhere to the framework, following it may help that person to influence the conflict-management process constructively. Unfortunately, some people are so prone to defensive thinking in conflicts that a framework that assumes you are both fairly rational may have only limited practicality.

Step One: Confront the Conflict

> Fred and Debbie had been dating for two months and each thought the other was special. However, both were aware of tensions in their relationship. They avoided talking directly about these difficulties for fear of hurting and then losing each other.

> Natalie was getting increasingly steamed because Bob was not doing his share of the dishwashing. She kept her resentment to herself until one evening she blew her stack and said a whole lot of things she later regretted.

Some of you, like Fred and Debbie, may find it easier to avoid confronting conflicts. Others, like Natalie, may collect trading stamps and one day cash them in by going for your partner's jugular. There are many skills of confronting conflicts in ways likely to initiate a rational rather than a destructive process.

When you are aware of and own a conflict, you may still choose whether to confront it openly. Many considerations are involved, including whether anything will be gained from confrontation and whether the conflict is important enough to either or both of you to bring it out into the open. Assuming that the conflict is not so obvious that your partner cannot ignore it and also that you decide to bring it into the open, the following skills may help.

• *Keep calm.* You want the other person to take notice of you, but you should avoid being unnecessarily threatening. Shouting or screaming is likely to alienate the other and may consolidate his or her unwanted behaviors.

• *Pay attention to timing.* You have to choose the best time for raising the issue that there is a problem between you. It is probably not a good idea to try to discuss problems when one or both of you are rushing off to work, when you have visitors, or when one or both of you have arrived home tired after a hard day. A good time may be after a meal when both of you have more energy.

• *Assert yourself.* Confronting a conflict involves assertion. You need to avoid the twin dangers of nonassertiveness and aggression. Furthermore, if the other person still resists owning that there is a problem in your relationship, you need to persist in your assertion to the point where your partner recognizes that there is a problem for him or her as well as for you.

• *Invite the other to work on the conflict.* Some conflicts may be resolved quickly and amicably once they are out in the open and discussed. If conflicts cannot easily be resolved, you can attempt to enlist the other in taking a collaborative approach to managing the conflict. In essence you say, "We have a problem in our relationship. Let's see if we can collaborate together to solve it for our mutual benefit." Both of you then need to set aside sufficient time and energy for dealing with it.

Ideally, you should also find a quiet and comfortable location free from interruptions and distractions.

Step Two: Understand One Another's Positions

> Jack and Lisa are unhappy in their marriage. When they argue, neither of them listens to the other closely. Instead they shout, point fingers, and make comments like "You *never* think of anyone but yourself" and "You have *always* been selfish."

Make an agreement that, at the start of discussing a conflict, each of you takes turns in having uninterrupted "air time" to state your position. During your air time, the only talking your partner should do is to reflect and ask you to clarify your internal viewpoint. Partners are likely to be more prepared to listen once they feel safe in the knowledge that they will have their turn. If your partner interrupts, you have a number of choices including pausing; saying something like "Please let me finish, you have had (will have) your turn"; or putting out your arm with your palm facing him or her, standard body language requesting silence.

Making the effort to try to understand one another's positions is critical to managing conflicts effectively for a number of reasons. First, you may discover that your so-called conflict is based only on misunderstandings and misperceptions. It need not exist in future. Second, making the effort indicates that each of you has a commitment to a collaborative approach to managing your conflict. You show respect for one another. Third, trying to understand one another may take some of the emotional steam out of the conflict. Often, when people feel they have been heard and understood they calm down and become less aggressive, helping them to think more rationally. Finally, trying to understand one another enables both of you to start identifying the real issues in the conflict, rather than focusing on imaginary issues.

The following are some of the sending and receiving skills involved in understanding one another's positions.

- *Sending "I" messages.* Own your perceptions by sending "I" messages instead of a competitive series of blaming "you" messages. Do not communicate as though you have a monopoly on the truth and wish to impose your definition of the conflict on your partner.
- *Expressing feelings and wishes assertively.* Share your feelings in an open yet tactful way. When you have wants and wishes, state these clearly. Do not expect your partner to read your mind.
- *Sticking to the issues.* Focus on the current issues and avoid both verbal personal attacks and putting your partner down by means of hurtful voice and body messages. Also avoid dragging in irrelevant past history.
- *Giving specific feedback.* Avoid sending general negative messages that lead nowhere. Give specific feedback so that your partner knows what behavior you would like changed. Furthermore, be willing to intersperse your feedback with honest positives. You are more likely to be listened to if you do, since you will lessen the risk of being perceived as doing a "hatchet job" on the other person.

• *Using listening and helpful responding skills.* Use good attending behavior. Listen to and observe voice and body as well as verbal messages. Help your partner to share his or her perceptions of the conflict. Use restatements and reflections to show you have understood. Pay particular attention to tuning in accurately to your partner's feelings; this, above all, may help them to feel understood by you.

• *Using checking-out and clarifying skills.* At the end of your partner's initial statement of his or her position, it may help for you to make a summary restatement of it to check out the accuracy of your understanding. Where something your partner says is unclear, tactfully request clarification—for instance, "I think I hear you saying . . . , but I'm not altogether certain." Endeavor to make your understanding of the other's internal viewpoint as accurate as possible; avoid making unwarranted assumptions and inferences.

• *Admitting to and altering misperceptions.* Where you have misunderstood your partner's actions and intentions, be prepared to let your partner know this. Update your model of your partner in light of any significant new information.

Step Three: Define the Problem(s)

> Tim and Ginger were both in their early twenties and had been seeing one another for more than a year. The moment they became engaged, their previously happy relationship became full of conflict. Whereas previously they made decisions easily, now they argued over practically everything: which restaurant to go to, what film to see, and so on. One evening when they were trying to become reconciled, Ginger redefined the conflict. She admitted that getting engaged symbolized the loss of her autonomy. She was panicking because she felt trapped. Once she identified her hidden agenda she and Tim were able to work through her underlying fears. They are now happily married with two children.

In step two, each of you may have been offering your own definition of the problem. Conflicts become extremely destructive when each partner competes to define the problem on his or her own terms. Both of you risk repetitively stating your positions and becoming increasingly frustrated and resentful. The task of step three is to try and arrive at a mutually acceptable definition of your problem(s). Some of the skills involved in defining problems include the following.

• *Avoiding unfair fighting tactics.* Unfair fighting tactics are competitive put-downs that show a lack of respect for your partner (Bach & Wyden, 1968). Such tactics may be viewed as power plays designed to influence the other's definition of you, him- or herself, and the problems between you. Unfair fighting tactics include the following.

Mindreading and ascribing negative motives
Unnecessarily attacking psychologically vulnerable spots
Engaging in overkill and coming on far too strong
Monologuing and dominating the conversation
Using threats that engender insecurity

Sending threatening body messages—for instance, pointing fingers, glaring, punching, or scratching

Sending threatening voice messages—for instance, shouting or screaming

Unnecessarily dragging in third parties' opinions to support your own

Using passive-aggressive tactics, such as attacking while making yourself out to be the victim

Using tears to engender guilt

Sulking and emotional withdrawal

Playing games, such as feigning collaboration yet always frustrating the search for mutually acceptable definitions of your problem(s)

• *Identifying areas of common ground.* Even in a real conflict not based on misunderstanding, you may still have considerable common ground. Often people polarize conflicts into a simple "good guy–bad guy" format, which obscures areas of agreement. Identify and acknowledge any common ground. An important way you can find common ground and defuse emotions is to acknowledge your own mistakes and hurtful behaviors. Acknowledging your own role in the conflict may make it easier for your partner to be less defensive, too.

• *Identifying hidden agendas.* Try to deal with the real agenda, rather than the surface agendas. For instance, if a spouse suspects his or her partner is having an affair, to pick on him or her concerning a whole range of other issues is not the best way to try to define and solve the problem. Ideally, both of you should be able to communicate your needs, including those that are unmet, simply and clearly. Being allowed to say "I want" and "I need" without recrimination can contribute to identifying the real agendas in a conflict.

• *Identifying specific actions that sustain the problem(s).* Focus on your and your partner's specific actions that maintain the conflict. In short, focus more on *how* the conflict is being sustained, rather than on who started it or why it arose.

• *Stating the problem(s) clearly and simply.* The end product of step three is a simple statement of the problem.

> Having raised three children, Monique wanted to return to work. Her husband, Henri, was unhappy about her desire to go back to work because he was already under terrific pressure at his job and did not want any extra work at home. Once they became calmer, they both agreed to define the problem as being how they would get the housework done. Henri admitted he had changed his position from not wanting Monique to have a job once they defined the problem in a way that allowed the needs of both of them to be met.

Step Four: Search for and Evaluate Alternative Solutions

Take the example of Monique and Henri just given. Having defined the problem, they could join in the collaborative search for mutually acceptable solutions. Such solutions might include getting a smaller house, paying someone to clean the house, eating out more, getting more take-out meals, and so on. Searching for alternative solutions is often best done in two distinct stages: first, generating solutions and, second, evaluating them. Generating solutions is a creative process that may be inhibited by premature evaluation of emerging solutions. Some of the skills of step four include the following.

• *Generating solutions.* The objective is to generate a range of options, among which may be some effective ones. Sometimes it helps to brainstorm. The object of brainstorming is to discover ideas. The rules for brainstorming include avoiding criticism and evaluation of ideas and coming up with the greatest quantity possible.

• *Evaluating solutions.* Evaluate solutions on the basis of what is best for both of you. Agree on which solutions seem feasible and assess the possible consequences of each of them. Each of you needs to state your reactions to the possible solutions as clearly as possible.

• *Using checking-out and clarifying skills.* Be prepared to ask the other person for his or her reactions to a proposed solution. Also, if necessary, get the other person to further clarify his or her reactions.

• *Making trade-offs and compromises.* As you evaluate alternative solutions, you may be faced with choices as to whether or not to modify your position. A useful skill is the ability to make realistic trade-offs and compromises. Acknowledge and show appreciation of any concessions made by the other person. Also, if necessary, be prepared to remind him or her of any concessions you make.

Step Five: Agree Upon, Implement, and Evaluate the Best Solution(s)

> Hal and Janet thought they had an agreement as to who would do the dishes on what evening. On Tuesday, the dishes remained unwashed, and each said that he or she did not do them because it was the other's turn.

Having evaluated the better of your possible solutions, you then make an agreement or contract. Agreements need to be implemented, evaluated, and if necessary renegotiated. Some of the skills of step five are as follows.

• *Stating agreements clearly.* If agreements are unclear, they are more likely to be broken, if only through misunderstanding. Breaking an agreement risks rekindling your conflict. Agreements vary according to the nature of the conflict. For instance, if your conflict has been about household chores, the contract will concern who is to do what, and when. It is generally desirable to put agreements in writing. Writing out your agreements helps you to verify that they are clearly understood and to avoid future conflicts over the terms of the agreement. Written agreements also can be posted in places where they serve as reminders to implement them.

• *Making a plan when necessary.* Some agreements involve planning. For instance, Ellie and Roberto have been in considerable conflict over how to spend their vacation. Having finally agreed to spend three weeks driving around Canada, they now need to plan how best to go about this. Possibly, their agreement should include who plans which aspects of the vacation by what time.

• *Renegotiating rather than breaking agreements.* If for whatever reason you cannot live with an agreement, it is much preferable to renegotiate it than to break it. Breaking your agreement is a breach of trust. Furthermore, your partner may consider that your breach gives them the right to do the same, which may further damage your relationship.

• *Modifying and changing agreements when necessary.* Some solutions may turn out to be inadequate when they are implemented. Frequently, only minor modifications to the initial agreement are necessary. However, on other occasions either or both of you may discover that the "best" solution has major weaknesses. Possibly, another reasonable solution is available from the list you generated in your earlier search for alternatives. Otherwise, you need to generate and evaluate further solutions.

A final point about CUDSA is that partners in a conflict may wish to monitor and evaluate the success of their procedures to manage conflict, and modify those procedures if necessary. The framework suggested here is not meant to be a straitjacket. You need to adjust it to suit your personal style. However, if the CUDSA framework has been helpful, you may be motivated to use it in managing future conflicts. Experiment 14 helps you explore the usefulness of the CUDSA framework for you.

Experiment 14
What happens when we collaborate to manage a conflict within the CUDSA framework?

This experiment needs to be done with someone else when both of you want to work through a specific conflict.

Part A: Assessment
What solutions to the conflict have you already attempted? What have been the consequences of your attempted solutions? What so far have been your skills strengths and weaknesses in trying to manage the conflict?

Part B: Make an "If . . . then . . ." Statement
Together make an "If . . . then . . ." statement along the lines of "If we collaborate in a sincere attempt to manage our conflict (specify) within the CUDSA framework, then these consequences (specify) are likely to follow."

Part C: Try Out and Evaluate Your Changed Behavior
Try out your changed behavior. How well did you implement it? Assess its positive and negative consequences for yourself, one another, and your relationship. Do you think that developing the skills of collaboratively managing your conflicts within a systematic framework will help you in the future? What parts of the CUDSA framework, if any, did you find particularly helpful?

_____

_____

_____

Concluding Self-Talk

Conflicts are inevitable in my close relationships. Conflicts may help as well as harm my relationships. What is important is that I develop the skills of both preventing and managing conflicts as effectively as possible. Developing these skills involves working on both thinking and action skills.

All the thinking skills that help me manage anger better are relevant to preventing and managing conflicts. When in conflict, it is easy to avoid responsibility for my choices—for instance by blaming or waiting for the other to make the first move at reconciliation. I need to discipline myself not to do this. I also need to perceive those to whom I relate accurately, rather than seeing them in terms of my own needs and fears.

Two teamwork skills my partner and I can use to prevent and manage conflicts are increasing our exchange of rewarding behaviors and collaborating to manage our problems in a systematic fashion. Increasing our exchange of rewarding behaviors involves being aware of the importance of rewardingness, making requests, and implementing and evaluating agreements to be more positive. Together we can approach areas of difference within the CUDSA framework for managing conflicts. The five steps of CUDSA are (1) *confronting* the conflict, (2) *understanding* one another's positions, (3) *defining* the problem(s), (4) *searching* for and evaluating alternative solutions, and (5) *agreeing* upon, implementing, and evaluating the best solution(s). This framework challenges each of us to use a range of relationship skills when the going gets rough.

12

Maintaining and Developing Your Relationship Skills

> Yes! to this thought I hold with firm persistence;
> The last resort of wisdom stamps it true:
> He only earns his freedom and existence
> Who daily conquers them anew.
> *J. W. von Goethe*

This chapter focuses on how you can maintain and develop your relationship skills. For the remainder of your life, you will be faced with the possibility of making good or poor relationship skills choices, choices that help you achieve your goals or choices that land you in trouble. You need to maintain your relationship skills daily. Moreover, for others' sakes as well as your own, you are responsible for developing your relationship skills.

Reassessing Your Skills

In Exercise 1 you were asked to give an initial assessment of your relationship skills. Exercise 46 asks you to reassess your relationship skills in light of your reading of this book. By now you will have completed some if not all of the exercises and experiments. Furthermore, you have probably tried to develop many of the skills by practicing them in your daily life. Take your time over the

251

exercise. Accurate assessment is vital in pinpointing strengths and weaknesses. Once you have clearly identified weaknesses, you have already made considerable progress in overcoming them. You may wish to use Exercise 46 periodically in the future to maintain and reassess your skills.

Exercise 46
Reassessing my relationship skills strengths and weaknesses

Using the following format, make a worksheet for reassessing your relationship skills strengths and weaknesses. For more detail about a skills area, see the relevant chapter.

Skills Area	My Strengths	My Weaknesses
Understanding what I bring to relationships		
Disclosing myself		
Being a rewarding listener		
Responding helpfully		
Making initial contact		
Choosing relationships		
Deepening relationships		

Skills Area	My Strengths	My Weaknesses
Asserting myself		
Managing anger		
Preventing and managing conflict		

Make a list of your main skills strengths. Then make a list of the specific skills weaknesses you most need to work on.

Maintaining and Developing Your Skills

Once you have acquired some relationship skills strengths, how can you keep them going? You face numerous pressures not to maintain your relationship skills. Some of these pressures come from within yourself. For instance, you may feel the pull of long established weaknesses when your skills strengths have only recently been learned. Some of you may give up too easily because you have not fully learned that maintaining your relationship skills—perhaps in times of conflict—involves inner strength and toughness. Some of you may play the comparison game and think that because someone else fails to use good skills, you are legitimized in relinquishing your skills, too.

Some of the pressures not to maintain your skills come from outside of you. Relatives, friends, and colleagues may reward some of your weaknesses rather than your strengths—for instance, they may be more comfortable around you if you are nonassertive. The media constantly bombard you with messages conducive to superficial relationships. Moreover, the notion of people working hard on their relationship skills has still to gain widespread acceptance. This kind of personal excellence tends to be left to individuals to develop as best they can.

Whether the pressures come from yourself, others, or both, it is easy to give in to them, backslide, and translate some of your relationship skills strengths into weaknesses. However, you should be going in the other direction if it is at all possible. The following are some suggestions for maintaining and developing your relationship skills.

• *Remember to view relating in terms of skills.* Chapter 1 stressed both the importance of viewing relationships in skills terms and that these skills represent choices, which may be well or poorly made. Because many of you have not been brought up to see your relationships in terms of skills, you may lose not only this perspective but also the benefits you can derive from it. Viewing relationships in terms of skills gives you a set of skills "handles" with which to work on relating better. Furthermore, this perspective assumes that you are personally responsible for making the skills choices most conducive to your happiness and fulfillment.

The skills perspective keeps relationships out of the realm of magic and places them firmly in the realm of practicality.

• *Clarify your values.* Some people approach their relationships as though the others involved are objects to be manipulated or conquered, rather than treating them as persons worthy of respect. Others treat themselves as objects and scarcely allow themselves enough time and energy to relate well. Neither approach places sufficient value on affirming others and oneself through the quality of relationships. Both groups need to confront themselves with the consequences of their choices. You are more likely to commit yourself to developing your relationship skills if you set a high value on your own and others' personal growth. If you value other goals—such as making money or sexual conquests—more highly, these other goals are likely to interfere with the actualization of your full humanity. If this is the case, you need to reassess and clarify your values. It is a contemporary tragedy that large numbers of people are fully committed to neither their own development, nor that of their partners, nor that of their children. A recognition of more fundamental values, sometimes with the aid of religion, can release many people to become more caring and compassionate.

• *Remain open to inner and outer feedback.* Being an effective human animal involves both inner and outer listening. You require inner responsiveness to your significant feelings and physical reactions. You are also faced with a constant struggle to avoid misperceiving yourself, others, and the outer feedback you receive. One important way of motivating yourself to maintain and develop your relationship skills is to be mindful of the positive consequences that result from using them. You are more likely to repeat behaviors you perceive as bringing rewards than those you perceive as unrewarding.

> Ramón was a married man with three teenage girls. As he worked on his tendencies to be violent in getting his way at home, he felt he was losing some of his power. However, when he thought of the positive consequences of treating his wife and family in a more democratic and considerate way, he realized the importance of continuing to curb his temper and to use his skills in managing anger and conflict.

• *Make a contract.* Commitment and motivation are crucial to maintaining and improving relationship skills. Relationship skills contracts can be created for individuals, couples, or families. A relationship skills contract establishes a written commitment among the parties to it to use, maintain, and develop their own relationship skills and also to help the other to do so. Table 12-1 is an example of an individual contract, which can be amended when others are involved. It may be a good idea to reword the contract in your own language.

• *Work together with a partner.* This book has emphasized the importance of partners working together in various relationship skills areas—for instance, in managing anger. When one of you uses your relationship skills strengths, you encourage the other to do likewise. By relating in a more open and direct way, you make it easier for your partner to reciprocate. By helping one another to work through specific difficulties in your individual lives or in your relationship, you demonstrate your active concern for one another's welfare. By making an implicit

Table 12-1.   An individual relationship skills contract.

The Contract

1. I am ultimately responsible for my feelings, thoughts, and actions in my relationships.
2. I commit myself to using, maintaining, and developing my relationship skills.
3. When appropriate, I commit myself to helping the other people in my relationships to use, maintain, and develop their relationship skills.
4. The relationship skills I commit myself to using, maintaining, and developing include being in touch with my feelings; starting relationships, when appropriate; being prepared to develop relationships through openness and honesty; listening to others and helping them to feel understood; responding helpfully to others; managing my feelings of anger constructively; managing conflict constructively.
5. Although I may have shortcomings and make mistakes, I commit myself to persist in trying to honor this contract.

Signed ————————————————————

Date ————————————————————

This contract should be posted in an obvious place as a reminder.

---

or explicit relationship skills contract and by endeavoring to implement it in your daily life, you increase your chances of maintaining a high degree of mutual rewardingness in your relationship. Your joint use of relationship skills is likely to increase the good times and lessen the bad times. Furthermore, you help one another avoid destructive negative spirals.

• *Use co-counseling.* Co-counseling is an approach to working together. You may choose to co-counsel either with your partner or with someone else. The latter approach has risks if your partner disapproves of your discussing sensitive material with third parties. Co-counseling involves regular joint counseling sessions. You decide who will start off as "counselor" and who will be the "client." The counselor gives the client air time to examine his or her relationship concerns and skills and supports this exploration by responding helpfully. This air time may last for 10 or 15 minutes or longer if necessary. Afterward, you reverse roles. A sharing and discussion session may follow. Co-counseling with a spouse or partner has much to recommend it. It can help maintain communication as well as assist you in working together to improve your own and the other's relationship skills.

• *Practice your skills daily.* The old saying "Practice makes perfect" is relevant to relationship skills, even though a perfect relationship is more of a myth than a reality. By practicing your skills conscientiously, not just in crises but all the time, you are likely to improve them. You may become more confident and also more flexible in applying your skills. You often face a very important gap between learning a skill and putting it into practice. Psychologists call overcoming this gap "transfer of training." However, transfer of training can go beyond maintaining a skill to improving it with continued practice.

• *Improve your support network.* People exist in support networks, which have varying degrees of adequacy. In reality, an individual's network comprises participation in many different networks: family, friends, work colleagues, clubs, church, and so on, as well as access to volunteer or professional helpers. With luck, your support network contains people who model and reward the skills you wish to maintain and develop. You may possess an adequate support network but not use it to its best effect. Alternatively, you may need to develop your skills of giving as well as receiving support. Your support network may be insufficient or inadequate, which may require you to actively seek out more rewarding contacts.

• *Participate in a peer support group.* You may choose to meet on a regular basis with a group of other people to work on your relationship skills. Being in a support group has the advantage of enabling you to practice your skills, observe others' skills, and obtain feedback. Peer support groups can be specifically focused on discussing relationships and helping one another with problems in them. Alternatively, in the context of another focus—for instance a women's or men's group or a bereavement group—you can work on the relationship skills pertinent to that group's main task.

• *Participate in workshops and training courses.* There are no hard and fast distinctions between training courses and workshops. However, training courses are usually spread out over a longer period, say a month or more, whereas workshops are ordinarily relatively intense experiences lasting from a day to a week. Means of finding out about relationship skills workshops and training courses include contacting a counseling service or personnel office; getting in touch with professional associations in psychology, counseling, and social work; and keeping an eye on relevant journals and newsletters. In all instances, look before you leap. Since acquiring good relationship skills requires much work and practice, courses and workshops offering miracle cures should be avoided. Table 12-2 provides a checklist for assessing training courses and workshops.

• *See a professional counselor.* Some of you may consider that you need the services of a professional counselor to help you improve your skills. A training course or workshop may offer little chance for the trainer to spend much time on

Table 12-2.   Checklist for assessing training courses and workshops.

1. What are the goals?
2. What methods will be employed?
3. What is the pertinent training and experience of the trainer(s)?
4. What is the size of the training course or workshop? Is there a screening process prior to entry?
5. When does the course or workshop start? How long is each session? Over what period will the course or workshop continue? Where will it be held? Are the facilities adequate?
6. What is the fee for the course or workshop, if any? Will it involve additional expenses?

Table 12-3. Names and addresses of North American national professional associations in counseling and psychology

United States	
Counseling	American Association for Counseling and Development, 599 Stevenson Ave., Alexandria, Va. 22304
Psychology	American Psychological Association, 1200 Seventeenth St. N.W., Washington, D.C. 20036
Canada	
Counseling	Canadian Guidance and Counselling Association/Société Canadienne d'Orientation et de Consultation, P.O. Box 13059, Kanata, Ontario K2K 1X3
Psychology	Canadian Psychological Association/Société Canadienne de Psychologie, 588 King Edward Ave., Ontario K1N 7NX

individual problems. Moreover, some people are so lacking in confidence that they require a safer environment. Group counseling may be desirable for some of you instead of, concurrently with, or after individual counseling. Counseling groups tend to comprise a leader and about six to ten members. They provide a more sheltered environment for working on emotional and relationship issues than that found in many training groups and workshops. All the items in the Table 12-2 checklist are relevant to assessing counseling groups.

Choosing a counselor can be a difficult process. Counselors differ greatly in their personalities, knowledge, skills, and theoretical orientations. The kind of counselor who reflects the theoretical orientation of this book would combine an existential-humanistic perspective with a cognitive-behavioral one. In layperson's language, this sort of counselor would believe in the concept of relationship skills, focus on thinking and action skills as well as on feelings, and consistently encourage personal responsibility and self-help. Look for a counselor with whom you feel comfortable and who both supports and challenges you to attain more of your potential. Be prepared to change your counselor if you are dissatisfied.

You may not be immediately aware of a suitable counselor. You may find the name of someone appropriate by asking a helping service professional—for instance, a psychologist, social worker, doctor, or priest. You could look up the relevant occupational listings in the phone book. You could also contact an advice hotline. In addition, you could inquire at the relevant county or provincial, state, or national professional associations. Table 12-3 lists some national associations.

• *Avoid burnout.* People who face a combination of difficult environments and poor skills in looking after themselves and managing relationships tend to be excellent candidates for burnout, if not for breakdown. Freudenberger defines burnout as follows: "To deplete oneself. To exhaust one's physical and mental resources. To wear oneself out by excessively striving to reach some unrealistic expectation imposed by one's self or by the values of society" (Freudenberger, 1980, p. 17.) The better your relationship skills, the less likely you are to create unnecessary problems in your relationships. Bad relationships are exhausting.

They can lower your energy level so that your effectiveness is diminished and you find it harder to use your skills.

Many other skills weaknesses may contribute to your feeling burned out. These include the following.

Perfectionistic personal rules in any area of your life
Undue need for external approval
Poor skills at listening to how stressed your body is
Inability to set limits on others and to say no to unreasonable requests
Inability to set limits on yourself and the need to be superwoman or superman
Assuming too much responsibility for others' lives and too little for your own
Poor skills at leading a balanced life and having adequate recreational outlets
Poor skills at looking after your health and physical fitness
Poor time management skills
Poor skills at managing problems and making decisions

People who are punch-drunk with exhaustion often lack the energy to use good relationship skills. They are cranky and irritable and can become highly abusive. Their perceptions of others are colored by their own distress, and they are more likely to be disappointed in others. Chapter 10 mentioned some skills of managing stress—for instance, mental and visual relaxation, developing adequate recreational outlets, and developing skills in managing problems. Feelings of exhaustion, excessive stress, and lack of resilience can result from numerous causes, both within and outside your relationships. Consequently, you may need to use a wide variety of skills to deal with these conditions adequately. When you are thoroughly run-down, you do not feel at your most skilled. Consequently, when possible, it is far preferable to prevent burnout than to try to cure it.

• *Read relevant material.* Although supplemental practice is always necessary, reading relevant books and articles is a further way to develop your relationship skills. The bibliography at the end of this text marks books and articles likely to be of interest to the self-help reader with an asterisk. You may also view this book as an ongoing resource. One approach is to go through the whole book every now and then as a refresher. Another approach is to focus on specific chapters, exercises, and experiments when you think you need further work to maintain and develop a skill.

Exercise 47 helps you assess these methods of maintaining and developing your relationship skills.

Exercise 47
Maintaining and developing my relationship skills

Instructions: A number of different methods you can use to maintain and develop your relationship skills are listed here. Using the worksheet provided, assess whether and how you might use each method.

Method	My Assessment of Whether and How I Can Use Each Method
Viewing relating in terms of skills	
Clarifying my values	
Remaining open to inner and outer feedback	
Making a contract	
Working together with a partner	
Co-counseling	
Practicing my skills daily	
Improving my support network	
Participating in a peer support group	
Participating in workshops and training courses	
Seeking a professional counselor	
Avoiding burnout	
Reading relevant materials	
Other methods not mentioned here	

Develop a plan for maintaining and improving your relationship skills.

The Challenge of Relationships

The stark truth is that many if not most close relationships in North America end in hatred, pain, and mutual recrimination and often hurt innocent parties such as children. Many workplaces are also characterized by considerable hostility. Each person possesses his or her past and present pain and skills weaknesses. However, the challenge of relationships is to affirm yourself and others despite these adverse factors. The answer to the challenge is to strive to use, maintain, and develop your relationship skills. Whatever progress you make, however slight, is a triumph, because you are choosing to increase your own, other people's, and the world's store of happiness.

Concluding Self-Talk

I am responsible for maintaining and developing my relationship skills. I am constantly being challenged to make good choices in my relationships.

Pressures not to do so can come from both within me and outside me. Reassessing my skills can help me to pinpoint weaknesses and to do something about them.

I can maintain and develop my relationship skills using many methods. These methods include viewing relating in terms of skills, clarifying my values, remaining open to inner and outer feedback, making a contract, working together with a partner, co-counseling, practicing my skills daily, improving my support network, participating in a peer support group, participating in workshops and training courses, seeing a professional counselor, avoiding burnout, and doing relevant reading.

Maintaining and developing my relationship skills involves me in affirming my strengths despite adverse circumstances. This is hard work and I need to hang in there. I can and will develop the strength and skills to relate better!

Notes

Bibliography

References likely to be of special interest to the self-help reader are indicated with an asterisk.

*Alberti, R. E., & Emmons, M. L. (1986). *Your perfect right: A guide to assertive living* (5th ed.). San Luis Obispo, CA: Impact Publishers.

Altman, I., & Taylor, D. A. (1965). Interpersonal exchange in isolation. *Sociometry, 28,* 411–426.

Argyle, M. (1983). *The psychology of interpersonal behavior* (4th ed.). Harmondsworth, England: Penguin.

Argyle, M. (1984). Some new developments in social skills training. *Bulletin of the British Psychological Society, 37*(12), 405–410.

*Argyle, M., & Henderson, M. (1985). *The anatomy of relationships.* Harmondsworth, England: Penguin.

Azrin, N. H., Besalel, V. A., Michalicek, A., Mancera, M., Carroll, D., Shuford, D., & Cox, J. (1980). Comparison of reciprocity and discussion-type counseling for marital problems. *American Journal of Family Therapy, 8,* 21–28.

Azrin, N. H., Naster, B. J., & Jones, R. (1973). Reciprocity counseling: A rapid learning-based procedure for marital counseling. *Behaviour Research and Therapy, 11,* 365–382.

*Bach, G. R., & Wyden, P. (1968). *The intimate enemy.* New York: Avon.

*Bach, G. R., & Torbet, L. (1983). *The inner enemy.* New York: Berkley Books.

Bandura, A. (1977). *Social learning theory.* Englewood Cliffs, NJ: Prentice-Hall.

Baucom, D. H., & Lester, G. W. (1986). The usefulness of cognitive restructuring as an adjunct to behavioral marital therapy. *Behavior Therapy, 17,* 385–403.

Beck, A. T. (1976). *Cognitive therapy and the emotional disorders.* New York: New American Library.

Bem, S. L. (1974). The measurement of psychological androgyny. *Journal of Consulting and Clinical Psychology, 42*(2), 155–162.

Bem, S. L. (1981). Gender schema theory: A cognitive account of sex typing. *Psychological Review, 88*(4), 354–364.

Berensen, B. G., Mitchell, K. M., & Laney, R. C. (1968). Level of therapist functioning, types of confrontation and type of patient. *Journal of Clinical Psychology, 24,* 111–113.

*Berne, E. (1964). *Games people play.* New York: Grove Press.

Bernstein, D. A., & Borkovec, T. D. (1973). *Progressive relaxation training: A manual for the helping professions.* Champaign, IL: Research Press.

Besalel, V. A., & Azrin, N. H. (1981). The reduction of parent-youth problems by reciprocity counseling. *Behaviour Research and Therapy, 19,* 297–301.

*Bianchi, S. M. (1984). Wives who earn more than their husbands. *American Demographics, 6*(7), 19–23, 44.

*Bianchi, S. M., & Seltzer, J. A. (1986). Life without father. *American Demographics, 8*(12), 43–47.

*Bloom, D. E. (1986). Women and work. *American Demographics, 8*(9), 25–30.

*Bolton, R. (1979). *People skills: How to assert yourself, listen to others, and resolve conflicts.* Englewood Cliffs, NJ: Prentice-Hall.

*Bower, S. H., & Bower, G. H. (1976). *Asserting your self: A practical guide for positive change.* Reading, MA: Addison-Wesley.

*Brown, P., & Faulder, C. (1977). *Treat yourself to sex.* Harmondsworth, England: Penguin.

*Burley-Allen, M. (1982). *Listening: The forgotten skill.* New York: Wiley.

Butler, G., & Mathews, A. (1987). Anticipatory anxiety and risk perception. *Cognitive Therapy and Research, 11*(5), 551–565.

*Butler, P. E. (1981). *Self-assertion for women* (rev. ed.). San Francisco: Harper & Row.

Camper, P. M., Jacobson, N. S., Holtzworth-Munroe, A., & Schmaling, K. B. (1988). Causal attributions for interactional behavior in married couples. *Cognitive Therapy and Research, 12*(2), 195–209.

*Carkhuff, R. R. (1983). *The art of helping* (5th ed.). Amherst, MA: Human Resource Development Press.

Chelune, G. J. (1976). Reactions to male and female disclosure at two levels. *Journal of Personality and Social Psychology, 34*(5), 1000–1003.

*Comfort, A. (1972). *The joy of sex: A gourmet guide to lovemaking.* New York: Quartet.

*Comfort, A. (1973). *More joy of sex: A lovemaker's companion.* New York: Quartet.

Cozby, P. (1973). Self disclosure: A literature review. *Psychological Bulletin, 79,* 73–91.

Cunningham, J. D., & Antill, J. K. (1981). Love in developing romantic relationships. In S. Duck & R. Gilmour (Eds.). *Personal relationships 2: Developing personal relationships* (pp. 27–51). New York: Academic Press.

Deffenbacher, J. L., Story, D. A., Brandon, A. D., Hogg, J. A., & Hazaleus, S. L. (1988). Cognitive and cognitive-relaxation treatments of anger. *Cognitive Therapy and Research, 12*(2), 167–184.

Deffenbacher, J. L., Story, D. A., Stark, R. A., Hogg, J. A., & Brandon, A. D. (1987). Cognitive-relaxation and social skills interventions in the treatment of general anger. *Journal of Counseling Psychology, 34*(2), 171–176.

*Derlega, V. J., & Chaikin, A. L. (1975). *Sharing intimacy: What we reveal to others and why.* Englewood Cliffs, NJ: Prentice-Hall.

Deutsch, M. (1973). *The resolution of conflict.* New Haven: Yale University Press.

Duck, S. (1983). *Friends for life: The psychology of close relationships.* Brighton, England: The Harvester Press.

Duck, S. (1986). *Human relationships: An introduction to social psychology.* Newbury Park, CA: Sage Publications.

Eakins, B. W., & Eakins, R. G. (1978). *Sex differences in human communication.* Boston: Houghton Mifflin.

*Egan, G. (1977). *You and me: The skills of communicating and relating to others.* Pacific Grove, CA: Brooks/Cole.

Egan, G. (1985). *Exercises in helping skills: A training manual to accompany the skilled helper* (3rd ed.). Pacific Grove, CA: Brooks/Cole.

Egan, G. (1986). *The skilled helper: A systematic approach to effective helping* (3rd ed.). Pacific Grove, CA: Brooks/Cole.

Eichler, M. (1983). *Families in Canada today: Recent changes and their policy consequences.* Toronto: Gage.

Eidelson, R. J., & Epstein, N. (1982). Cognition and relationship maladjustment: Development of a measure of dysfunctional relationship beliefs. *Journal of Consulting and Clinical Psychology, 50,* 721–726.

*Ekman, P., Freisen, W. V., & Bear, J. (1984, May). The international language of gestures. *Psychology Today,* pp. 64–69.

Ekman, P., Freisen, W. V., & Ellsworth, P. (1972). *Emotions in the human face.* New York: Pergamon Press.

Ellis, A. (1980). Overview of the clinical theory of rational-emotive therapy. In R. Greiger & J. Boyd (Eds.). *Rational-emotive therapy: A skills based approach* (pp. 1–31). New York: Van Nostrand Reinhold.

Epstein, N., Pretzer, J. L., & Fleming, B. (1987). The role of cognitive appraisal in self-reports of marital communication. *Behavior Therapy, 18,* 51–69.

Feindler, E. L., Marriott, S. A., & Iwata, M. (1984). Group anger control training for junior high school delinquents. *Cognitive Therapy and Research, 8*(3), 299–311.

Fincham, F. D. (1985). Attribution processes in distressed and nondistressed couples; 2: Responsibility for marital problems. *Journal of Abnormal Psychology, 94*(2), 183–190.

Fincham, F. D., Beach, S. R., & Baucom, D. H. (1987). Attribution processes in distressed and nondistressed couples; 4: Self–partner attribution differences. *Journal of Personality and Social Psychology, 52*(4), 739–748.

Fincham, F. D., Beach, S., & Nelson, G. (1987). Attribution processes in distressed and nondistressed couples; 3: Causal and responsibility attributions for spouse behavior. *Cognitive Therapy and Research, 11*(1), 71–86.

*Freudenberger, H. J. (1980). *Burnout: The high cost of high achievement.* London: Arrow Books.

Frisch, M. B., & Froberg, W. (1987). Social validation of assertion strategies for handling aggressive criticism: Evidence for consistency across situations. *Behavior Therapy, 2,* 181–191.

*Fromm, E. (1956). *The art of loving.* New York: Bantam Books.

Glasser, W. (1984). *Control theory.* New York: Harper & Row.

*Glick, P. C. (1984). How American families are changing. *American Demographics, 6*(1), 20–25.

Goldstein, A. P., & Keller, H. (1987). *Aggressive behavior: Assessment and intervention.* New York: Pergamon Press.

*Gordon, T. (1970). *Parent effectiveness training.* New York: Wyden.

Grebe, S. C. (1986). Mediation in separation and divorce. *Journal of Counseling and Development, 64*(2), 379–382.

Haase, R. F., & Tepper, D. (1972). Nonverbal components of empathic communication. *Journal of Counseling Psychology, 19,* 417–424.

Hall, E. T. (1966). *The hidden dimension.* New York: Doubleday.

Hazaleus, S. L., & Deffenbacher, J. L. (1986). Relaxation and cognitive treatments of anger. *Journal of Consulting and Clinical Psychology, 54*(2), 222–226.

Henley, N. M. (1977). *Body politics: Power, sex and nonverbal communication.* Englewood Cliffs, NJ: Prentice-Hall.

Hutson, T. L., Surra, C. A., Fitzgerald, N. M., & Cate, R. M. (1981). From courtship to marriage: Mate selection as an interpersonal process. In S. Duck & R. Gilmour (Eds.). *Personal relationships 2: Developing personal relationships* (pp. 53–88). New York: Academic Press.

Ivey, A. E. (1971). *Microcounseling: Innovations in interviewing training.* Springfield, IL: Charles C Thomas.

Jacobs, M. K., & Cochran, S. D. (1982). The effects of cognitive restructuring on assertive behavior. *Cognitive Therapy and Research, 6*(1), 63–76.

Jacobson, N. S., Follette, V. M., Follette, W. C., Holtzworth-Munroe, A., Katt, J. L., & Schmaling, K. B. (1985). A component analysis of behavioral marital therapy: 1-year follow-up. *Behaviour Research and Therapy, 23*(5), 549–555.

Jacobson, N. S., & Margolin, G. (1979). *Marital therapy: Strategies based on social learning and behavior exchange principles.* New York: Brunner/Mazel.

Jacobson, N. S., McDonald, D. W., Follette, W. C., & Berley, R. A. (1985). Attributional processes in distressed and nondistressed married couples. *Cognitive Therapy and Research, 9*(1), 35–50.

*James, J., & Schlesinger, I. (1987). *Are you the right one for me?: How to choose the right partner.* Reading, MA: Addison-Wesley.

James, W. A. (1983). Decline in coital rates with spouses' ages and duration of marriage. *Journal of Biosocial Science, 15,* 83–87.

*Jampolsky, G. G. (1983). *Teach only love: The seven principles of attitudinal healing.* New York: Bantam.

*Johnson, D. W. (1986). *Reaching out: Interpersonal effectiveness and self-actualization* (3rd ed.). Englewood Cliffs, NJ: Prentice-Hall.

*Jourard, S. M. (1964). *The transparent self.* New York: Van Nostrand Reinhold.

*Jourard, S. M. (1971a). *The transparent self* (rev. ed.). New York: Van Nostrand Reinhold.

Jourard, S. M. (1971b). *Self-disclosure: An experimental analysis of the transparent self.* New York: Wiley.

Kagan, N. (1984). Interpersonal process recall: Basic methods and recent research. In Larsen, D. *Teaching Psychological Skills* (pp. 261–269). Pacific Grove, CA: Brooks/Cole.

Kaplan, H. S. (1974). *The new sex therapy: Active treatment of sexual dysfunctions.* New York: Brunner/Mazel.

*Kassorla, I. C. (1980). *Nice girls do.* New York: Berkley Books.

*Kassorla, I. C. (1984). *Go for it: How to win at love, work and play.* New York: Dell.

*King, M. L. (1963). *Strength to love.* New York: Harper & Row.

Kinsey, A. C., Pomeroy, W. B., & Martin, C. E. (1948). *Sexual behavior in the human male.* Philadelphia: W. B. Saunders.

Kinsey, A. C., Pomeroy, W. B., Martin, C. E., & Gebhard, P. H. (1953). *Sexual behavior in the human female.* Philadelphia: Saunders.

*Kohn, A. (1987, February). Shattered innocence. *Psychology Today,* pp. 54–58.

*Lewinsohn, P. M., Munoz, R. F., Youngren, M. A., & Zeiss, A. M. (1986). *Control your depression* (rev. ed.). New York: Prentice Hall Press.

Lopez, F. G., & Thurman, C. W. (1986). A cognitive-behavioral investigation of anger among college students. *Cognitive Therapy and Research, 10*(2), 245–256.

Maslow, A. H. (1962). *Toward a psychology of being.* New York: Van Nostrand Reinhold.

Maslow, A. H. (1970). *Motivation and personality* (2nd ed.). New York: Harper & Row.

*Masters, W. H., & Johnson, V. C. (1975). *The pleasure bond.* New York: Bantam.

McKie, D. C., Prentice, B., & Reed, P. (1983). *Divorce: Law and the family in Canada.* Ottawa: Statistics Canada.

*Meichenbaum, D. (1983). *Coping with stress.* London: Century Publishing.

Meichenbaum, D. (1985). *Stress inoculation training.* New York: Pergamon Press.

Meichenbaum, D., & Deffenbacher, J. L. (1988). Stress inoculation training. *The Counseling Psychologist, 16,* 69–90.

Moon, J. R., & Eisler, R. R. (1983). Anger control: An experimental comparison of three behavioral treatments. *Behavior Therapy, 14,* 493–505.

MORI. (1983). *Survey.* London: Market Opinion Research International.

Nelson-Jones, R. (1984). *Personal responsibility counseling and therapy.* New York: Hemisphere.

Nelson-Jones, R. (1988). *Practical counselling and helping skills* (2nd ed.). London: Cassell.

*Nelson-Jones, R. (1990). *Thinking skills: Preventing and managing personal problems.* Pacific Grove, CA: Brooks/Cole.

Nelson-Jones, R., & Coxhead, P. (1980). Neuroticism, social desirability and anticipations and attributions affecting self-disclosure. *British Journal of Medical Psychology, 53,* 164–180.

Nelson-Jones, R., & Dryden, W. (1979). Anticipated risk and gain from negative and positive self-disclosures. *British Journal of Social and Clinical Psychology, 18,* 79–80.

Nelson-Jones, R., & Strong, S. R. (1976). Positive and negative self-disclosure, timing and personal attraction. *British Journal of Social and Clinical Psychology, 15,* 323–325.

Nelson-Jones, R., & Strong, S. R. (1977). British students' positive and negative evaluations of personal characteristics. *Journal of College Student Personnel, 18*(1), 32–37.

Novaco, R. W. (1977). Stress inoculation: A cognitive therapy for anger and its applications to a case of depression. *Journal of Consulting and Clinical Psychology, 45,* 600–608.

Oakley, A. (1972). *Sex, gender & society.* London: Temple Smith.

*Pease, A. (1981). *Body language: How to read others' thoughts by their gestures.* Sydney: Camel.

Pietromonaco, P. R., & Rook, K. S. (1987). Decision style in depression: The contribution of perceived risks versus benefits. *Journal of Personality and Social Psychology, 52*(2), 399–408.

Platt, J. J., Pout, M. F., & Metzger, D. S. (1986). Interpersonal cognitive problem-solving therapy (ICPS). In W. Dryden & W. Golden (Eds.). *Cognitive-behavioural approaches to psychotherapy* (pp. 261–269). London: Harper & Row.

*Powell, J. (1969). *Why am I afraid to love?* London: Fontana.

*Pryor, E., & Norris, D. (1983). Canada in the eighties. *American Demographics, 5*(12), 25–29, 44.

*Robey, B., & Russell, C. (1984). Trends: All Americans. *American Demographics, 6*(2), 32–35.

Rogers, C. R. (1959). A theory of therapy, personality and interpersonal relationships as developed in the client-centred framework. In S. Koch (ed.), *Psychology: A Study of Science* (Study No. 1, Vol. 3, pp. 184–256). New York: McGraw-Hill.

*Rogers, C. R. (1961). *On becoming a person.* Boston: Houghton Mifflin.

*Rogers, C. R. (1973). *Becoming partners: Marriage and its alternatives.* London: Constable.

*Rogers, C. R. (1980). *A way of being.* Boston: Houghton Mifflin.

Rubin, Z. (1970). Measurement of romantic love. *Journal of Personality and Social Psychology, 16*(2), 265–273.

*Russell, C., & Exter, T. G. (1986). America at mid-decade. *American Demographics, 8*(1), 22–29.

Rutter, M. (1972). *Maternal deprivation reassessed.* Harmondsworth, England: Penguin.

*Satir, V. (1972). *Peoplemaking.* Palo Alto, CA: Science and Behavior Books.

*Selye, H. (1974). *Stress without distress.* Sevenoaks, Kent: Hodder and Stoughton.

*Simonton, O. C., Matthews-Simonton, S., & Creighton, J. L. (1978). *Getting well again.* New York: Bantam Books.

*Solomon, M. R. (1986, April). Dress for effect. *Psychology Today,* pp. 20–28.

*Spain, D., & Bianchi, S. M. (1983). How woman have changed. *American Demographics, 5*(5), 19–25.

Steck, L., Levitan, D., McLane, D., & Kelley, H. H. (1982). Care, need, and conceptions of love. *Journal of Personality and Social Psychology, 43*(3), 481–491.

*Steiner, C. M. (1981). *The other side of power*. New York: Grove Press.

Stuart, R. B. (1980). *Helping couples change: A social learning approach to marital therapy*. New York: Guilford Press.

*Tavris, C. (1982, November). Anger defused. *Psychology Today,* pp. 25–35.

Taylor, D. A., & Altman, I. (1966). *Intimacy-scaled stimuli for use in studies of interpersonal relationships*. Bethesda, MD: Naval Medical Research Institute.

*Timnick, L. (1983, September). When women rape men. *Psychology Today,* pp. 74–75.

*Trotter, R. J. (1986, September). The three faces of love. *Psychology Today,* pp. 46–50, 54.

Warren, N., & Gilner, F. H. (1978). Measurement of positive assertive behaviors: The behavioral test of tenderness expression. *Behavior Therapy, 9,* 178–184.

Watson, O. M. (1972). *Proxemic behavior: A cross cultural study*. The Hague: Mouton.

White, K. M., Speisman, J. C., Jackson, D., Bartis, S., & Costos, D. (1986). Intimacy maturity and its correlates in young married couples. *Journal of Personality and Social Psychology, 50*(1), 157–162.

Willison, B. G., & Masson, R. L. (1986). The role of touch in therapy: An adjunct to communication. *Journal of Counseling and Development, 64*(4), 497–500.

*Wilson, B. F. (1984). Marriage's melting pot. *American Demographics, 6*(7), 34–37, 45.

*Wilson, B. F., & London, K. A. (1987). Going to the chapel. *American Demographics, 9*(12), 26–31.

Wolf, S. S., & Etzel, B. C. (1982). Reciprocity and marital counseling: A replication and analysis. *Behaviour Research and Therapy, 20,* 407–410.

*Zimbardo, P. G. (1977). *Shyness*. Reading, MA: Addison-Wesley.

Author Index

Subject Index

To the owner of this book:

I hope that you have been significantly influenced by reading *Human Relationships: A Skills Approach.* I'd like to know as much about your experiences with the book as you care to offer. Your comments can help me make it a better book for future readers.

School: _____ Instructor's name: _____

1. What I like most about this book is _____

_____

2. What I like least about this book is _____

_____

3. How much personal value did you find in the Exercises? _____

_____

4. Of how much interest and value were the Experiments? _____

_____

5. Specific topics in the book I thought were most relevant and important are:

_____

6. Specific suggestions for improving the book: _____

_____

_____

7. Some ways I used this book in class: _____

_____

8. Some ways I used this book out of class: _____

_____

9. The name of the course in which I used this book: _____

_____

10. In the space below—or in a separate letter, if you care to write one—please let us know what other coments about the book you'd like to make. We welcome your suggestions!

Optional:

Your name: _____ Date: _____

May Brooks/Cole quote you, either in promotion for *Human Relationships: A Skills Approach* or in future publishing ventures?

Yes _____   No _____

Sincerely,

Richard Nelson-Jones